MW01234788

# Prepared Not Paranoid

# Prepared Not Paranoid
## Lessons from Law Enforcement
## for Living Every Day Safely

Jana M. Kemp and Doug Graves

Westport, Connecticut
London

**Library of Congress Cataloging-in-Publication Data**

Kemp, Jana M.
   Prepared not paranoid : lessons from law enforcement for living every day safely /
Jana M. Kemp and Doug Graves.
     p. cm.
   Includes bibliographical references and index.
   ISBN 978–0–313–34719–1 (alk. paper)
1. Crime prevention. 2. Self-protective behavior. 3. Survival skills. 4. Preparedness.
5. Safety education. I. Graves, Doug, 1953– II. Title.
   HV7431.K444 2008
   613.6—dc22      2007048619

British Library Cataloguing in Publication Data is available.

Library of Congress Catalog Card Number: 2007048619
ISBN: 0–313–34719–0

First published in 2008

Praeger Publishers, 88 Post Road West, Westport, CT 06881
An imprint of Greenwood Publishing Group, Inc.
www.praeger.com

Printed in the United States of America

The paper used in this book complies with the
Permanent Paper Standard issued by the National
Information Standards Organization (Z39.48–1984).

10  9  8  7  6  5  4  3  2  1

This book is dedicated to DeeAnn Palmer, whose daily life represents courage and an unstoppable commitment to training people how to become police officers, and to all of the police officers, sheriff deputies, and elected law enforcement officials whom I know personally, because they and their work directly and indirectly contributed to this book.

—Jana M. Kemp, 2008

This book is dedicated to the Victim/Witness Coordinators, Victim Advocates, and all those other professionals and volunteers who work tirelessly to help heal those who are wounded by crime and whose stories and insight proved invaluable to this writing, as well as to the men and women of Idaho law enforcement who work tirelessly keeping their communities a safe place to live and work. It is the lessons they have taught me over the past three decades that contribute to the heart of this work.

—Doug Graves, 2008

# Contents

**Appendixes**

*Preface*

My first recollections of learning to be safe in the world are of tornado practice drills in elementary school in Fort Wayne, Indiana, during the 1970s. We'd sit in the hallway with our hands over our heads, and on two occasions it wasn't a practice drill. Tornadoes darkened the skies, passing over the school but damaging nearby homes. Separately, two kids' parents committed suicide during elementary school, and one kid was killed at an intersection while crossing the street to get to school. Then there was the school library remodel that went awry, killing a worker when the roof somehow collapsed. After these years of safety awareness at elementary school, I had my first brush with my own space being invaded—a Minnesota junior-high boy grabbed my breast when I was getting out of the swimming pool. Thankfully, no further harm or invasions of my space occurred during my remaining Minnesota and Illinois school years.

Years later, working in Boise, Idaho, as a radio show host, I was told by a colleague to "always be aware of your surroundings. Nutty things happen to radio announcers. Always lock your car doors. Always be aware." I took his suggestion seriously and to this day judiciously lock my doors upon getting into and out of the car: not out of paranoia, but out of prudence.

After being in radio for several years, in 2000 I received a strange "fan letter" that arrived with a name and return address, a stick of incense, and a cassette tape. I started listening to the tape in my car, and it was so strange that I waited until later in the day to listen to it with a friend. My friend almost immediately said, "Call one of your cop friends. This is creepy." So, I ended up filing a police report and making my telephone number unlisted. I discovered that the letter's sender had a police record and that I needed to be aware because he knew what I looked like because of my business website. However, I had no way of knowing what he looked like. Because I knew his name and had his address from his letter, for about two years I did not shop at the grocery store next door to where he lived.

During the four years of hosting my radio program, I frequently interviewed police officers for a segment called "Lessons from the Force—Police Officers Give Us Personal and Business Tips for Being Safe." One officer, Doug Schoenborn, often used the phrase "prepared not paranoid" when talking about how to keep personal and family safety at the forefront of one's thinking. His messages about plans and approaches that are manageable in a variety of environments made preparation without paranoia seem very possible. About this same time, at a literacy fundraiser I bid on and won Gavin de Becker's book *The Gift of Fear: Survival Signals That Protect Us from Violence* (New York: Dell Publishing, 1997). At the time, I wasn't quite sure why I had bid on the book. Then, after reading the book and taking in the overriding message that "everyone must listen to themselves and not talk themselves out of an instinct that is communicating danger," de Becker's book theme—"instead listen to the danger messages and take action to protect yourself," became clear. His research draws on his own life experience, on interviews with both criminals and victims, and on his security company work. Awareness is always the beginning of being safe.

The years 1999–2000 continued to be a busy span of safety awareness and learning for me. I completed the Citizen Police Academy and was urged to become a police officer. I moved my place of business, only to discover my office backed onto a park pathway near where two women had been murdered. I survived a divorce that was mostly amicable, until the night I was very nearly choked by the former Marine's hands. My father's brother was murdered at a Utah rest stop in 2000. Again and again, the reasons for reading de Becker's book became clear. I took the first of several self-defense classes that, upon reflection, I've discovered I sign up for about every three years. During the very first class, with Jeet Kune Do master Chris Kent, I learned that "no" is a complete sentence, a statement that has fed two books that I've written, including this one.

By 2002, my now coauthor, Idaho state Peace Officer Standards and Training Deputy Director Doug Graves and I had met. Doug convinced me to participate in the academy as a full-fledged student in order to give them a best-possible set of feedback on the curriculum. I kept thinking something would prevent me from attending as a student and that I'd be able to participate as an engaged observer. However, after passing the psychology test, the intelligence test, the background check, the hearing test, and the eyesight test; getting a doctor's approval; and passing a physical fitness test that showed one weakness (push-ups), I was in for a ten-week full-on student experience that has changed my life. And of course, it was an experience that contributes largely to this book. I'll share some of my academy stories in the chapters ahead.

In 2007, my understanding of what it means to be safe in the world again changed. A 4-year-old stepchild came into my life, won my heart, and continues to provide opportunities to learn what it means for a child to be safe in today's world.

All of this is just in my ordinary, fairly sheltered upbringing, and good—decision-making life. These personal experiences, along with the continued levels of fear perpetuated in the aftermath of September 11, 2001, prompted me to pursue writing this book. There are hundreds of ways to be aware and safe without becoming paranoid. *Prepared Not Paranoid* is about raising your awareness, offering you ways to change your behavior to minimize becoming a victim, and managing your fears by having action plans that keep you prepared and as safe as possible every day.

Jana Kemp
Coauthor, 2008

In 2004 the United States experienced the lowest amount of crime since 1973. Yet every day in conversations around the watercooler or having lunch with friends you hear, "It is so dangerous living in our world today," or "There are so many bad people out there who want to hurt you or take what you have" or "It isn't even safe to allow our children to walk unaccompanied to school." The fear of crime is real.

We understand that fear of crime and of becoming a victim is in the hearts and on the minds of many people today. Whether it is concern of terrorist attack or being caught in the path of a deranged gunman, *fear* seems to permeate our daily life. We live in what can arguably be the safest time in our nation's history, yet it doesn't feel that way.

Central to the American way of life is the idea that we each have the right to live in peace and tranquility. The preamble to the Constitution states that very thing: "We the People of the United States, in Order to form a more perfect Union, establish Justice, insure domestic Tranquility, provide for the common defense, promote the general Welfare, and secure the Blessings of Liberty to ourselves and our Posterity. . . ." How then do you embrace the fact that we are fairly safe in our daily living? How do I get rid of these feelings of fear? How do we regain that feeling of tranquility that is at the core of who we are as Americans? These are the questions that we work to answer in this book.

Being prepared is at the foundation of finding peace. As you read this book you will hear us saying over and over that the very best way to keep from being a victim is to be prepared for whatever situation you may find yourself in. All of what we will tell you is common sense. Most of the things presented are things that most of us already know but fail to put into action. We do not want to increase paranoia and believe that we will relieve it by helping you understand your legitimate risk and by increasing your ability to be prepared to address it.

My hope, my belief, is that by being prepared you will be safer. You will feel safer. When you feel safer, tranquility will return and fear will be lessened.

Doug Graves<br>
Coauthor, 2008

*Acknowledgments*

The following individuals were committed to this book being written: Jeff Olson and Suzanne Staszak-Silva, editors at Praeger/Greenwood, and Stan Wakefield, who has now secured publishers for four of Jana's books.

These individuals directly and indirectly contributed to the content of this book: The Honorable Gregory S. Casey, Curt Crum, Gary Compton, Jan Egge, Curt Egge, Rebecca Evans, David Graves, Gary Raney, Ron Shepherd, Doug Tangen, Jerrilea Archer, Tina Perkins, Sarah Wilson, and Lisa Bostaph.

# Introduction: This Crazy, Feels-Dangerous-Every Day World We're In

We are who and what we protect; we are what we stand up for.
—Unknown

In a post-September 11, 2001 stunned world and partially paralyzed culture, two more generations of children know more about fear than they do the joys of childhood freedoms such as running out the door to play in the neighborhood, and two generations of adults hover more than ever over their children and their mates, all the while worrying for their personal safety. "The world is not safe": certainly previous generations have lived with this feeling, those who lived through World War I, World War II, the Korean War, the Vietnam War, the cold war, and decades of Middle East conflicts; it seems there has always been a reason to feel unsafe. Yet, today's mindset appears to be one of paranoia rather than preparedness. The goal of *Prepared Not Paranoid* is to raise awareness and provide information so that you feel more personally confident moving through daily life as safely as possible. Ultimately, fear of becoming a victim of crime is reduced when people are armed with knowledge and prepared with personal plans of action for keeping and getting out of harm's way.

*Prepared Not Paranoid* includes checklists for easy-to-assemble safety plans and supplies; they serve as helpful references when outfitting a new car, when traveling, or when moving into a new home. You'll also learn how to build your own Individual Safety Plan and help children learn how to implement a safety plan: for instance—teaching kids where they live, who their parent(s) are and how to contact them, how to dial 911, and other useful information. Daily workplace safety is also addressed through a presentation of the key elements your workplace should have in place to guard your safety. Finally, you'll discover what your own Feel-Safe Quotient is and what the Feel-Safe Formula for daily living includes.

Current thinking in the personal safety field is largely focused on "take a personal safety class in self-defense and that's what will make you feel more safe." While this is certainly a part of the Feel-Safe Formula, it is just one aspect that comes into play to help a person feel safe and to live safely. *Prepared Not Paranoid* provides knowledge and resources for all aspects of staying safe. The following is an overview of the book.

**Chapter 1: Recognizing Safety, Recognizing Danger**—What do safety and danger look like and feel like? What do criminals look for in behavior? Recognizing danger is often more easy than recognizing safety. Yet, even when in danger, some people convince themselves they are still safe. This chapter details what to look for in ourselves, in others, and in the environment in order to recognize both danger and safety. The chapter also presents what criminals watch for in our behavior to determine whether they will attack or otherwise harm us.

**Chapter 2: Strategies for Staying Safe Every Day in Every Way**—This chapter offers tips and strategies, ways to not project the feeling, "I'm a victim." This chapter goes into detail regarding how to create safety when at home, when walking and exercising, and when interacting in your typical daily environments.

**Chapter 3: Travel Safety**—Whether commuting to work or traveling away from home for business, potential dangers exist. Learn to recognize the dangers and be prepared to avoid them. Learn what choices to make to keep yourself most safe at airports, in hotels, on mass transit, and in transportation hubs.

**Chapter 4: Family Safety at Home**—Discover how to keep your family safe without becoming paranoid yourself and without causing your children to live in constant fear. Build a family safety plan for a variety of dangerous situations such as fires, getting separated at an event, getting separated at school, or being approached or even attacked by anyone. Learn about community safety programs your family can participate in, such as Neighborhood Watch.

**Chapter 5: Safety at School**—Over the last two decades, school safety has taken on heightened levels of concern for communities. School shootings, drugs, child abuse, and on-site security measures including police officers seem the norm. Discover what you and your kids can do to be safer at school and going to and from school.

**Chapter 6: Safety at Work**—Keep yourself safe when parking, when interacting in your place of work, and when working early or late. Being able to get help when in danger depends on you and others having access to help. In this chapter, you'll learn to create personal safety and coworker safety plans. Discover dozens of tips for staying safe, such as never having your back to your office doorway because you can get taken by surprise too easily.

**Chapter 7: What about Weapons and Safety?**—If you've ever thought "I'll buy a gun and then we'll be safe," think again. This chapter talks about the process of deciding to buy a weapon and how a weapon can both create safety and at the same time create danger. The chapter also addresses critical considerations and steps to take before purchasing a weapon. Checklists for weapon safety are included.

**Chapter 8: What to Know about Disasters**—In this chapter you'll learn how to recognize a disaster in the making, how to listen for directions about what to do, and how to determine what actions you and your family will take to get to safety. Learn about community responses to disasters. You'll also learn to build a Personal and Family Disaster Plan. The chapter includes checklists and Personal Disaster Plan worksheets.

**Chapter 9: What You Need to Know about Bad Guys**—Learn about the people who commit crimes so that you can be scared-to-safety and so that you can let others know why it is important to take personal safety into your own hands.

**Chapter 10: Being Vigilant without Being Paranoid: Keeping Your Resolve to Stay Safe**—The closing chapter pulls everything together: the tips, the watchwords, and the actions that can be taken every day to be safe without becoming paranoid. The chapter also includes fun and inspiring ways to keep your resolve to stay safe and to inspire friends, family members, and coworkers also to stay safe without becoming paranoid.

**Appendixes**—As usual, appendixes provide extra information for immediate referencing. You'll find checklists for your car and your home that are meant for use in your ongoing personal safety planning. There are also checklists for your workplace and your travels that are meant for workplace and employee safety planning. In Appendix 3, which serves as a summary of key ideas in the book so that you have the ideas in one place and ready for action, you'll find approaches for creating your personal safe space. Finally, Appendix 4, titled Additional Resources for continued learning, is for study and ongoing research.

From the time we are children, lessons about safety are drilled into our heads: "don't touch that—it's hot; don't touch that—you'll get hurt; don't cross the street without checking for cars first; wear a bike helmet (for today's kids); wear your seatbelt; and stay in your car seat." Adults admonish children with warnings such as these nearly every day. Another way that adults impress safety lessons onto children is through fairy tales, nursery rhymes, religious stories, and fables, for instance, Aesop's story, "Boy Who Cried Wolf." It's the story of a bored shepherd boy who took pleasure in shouting "Wolf! Wolf!" just to see the town's people come running. After repeated shouting and repeated admonitions "not to cry wolf when there isn't one," a real wolf did appear one day on the shepherd boy's scene. At the end of this particular day, the town's people went up into the hills in search of their sheep and the shepherd boy, only to discover the sheep were gone. "I cried wolf and no one came," reported the shepherd boy, to which a town elder replied: "nobody believes a liar ... even when he is telling the truth." *Prepared Not Paranoid* is not a "wolf cry" in an otherwise safe world. This book is about learning to recognize how your choices and behavior can contribute to or prevent your becoming a victim, or worse yet a repeated victim, of crimes.

Today's post-9-11, violence-filled, dangerous world calls for daily personal power that overcomes paranoia and puts people back in control of their lives and their sense of safety. Drawing on 34 years of law enforcement work and training, coauthors Doug Graves and Jana Kemp have collaborated on this book to present useful information and actionable ways to keep you, your family members, and your coworkers as safe as possible every day. *Prepared Not Paranoid* presents thinking approaches, methods for recognizing challenges or threats, frames of mind for safety, and checklists with actions to take and items to have handy for everyday safety.

In a world in which children and adults alike live in daily fear for their safety, it is time to reclaim our individual ability to be as alert and as safe as possible without living in paranoia and fear.

# One

# Recognizing Safety, Recognizing Danger

Everyone has experienced a sense of danger at some point. Some people, because of the countries, territories, or cities in which they live, experience great danger on a daily basis. Other people live in fear because of a singular dangerous experience. Whether the sense of danger you experience is "oh my gosh, the car behind me is about to hit me" or a constant sense that "gunfire could strike me down at any time" or a series of dangerous-feeling moments that fall somewhere in between, danger is real. Today's challenge is that the media bombards us with deaths and crime rates, and in information overload, an overwhelming sense of not knowing what to do prevails. This not knowing what to do prompts some people to stop paying attention to the things around them. Recognizing the dangers that need a response begins with recognizing when you feel safe. Without an understanding of what feels safe, it is difficult to recognize when you feel danger.

A sense of feeling safe happens when you can go through life without a constant feeling of dread or uneasiness. Feeling safe occurs when you have done everything that is possible to be safe. It happens when you make good decisions about your life and follow through with them. Can we guarantee safety? No, nothing is for sure. We can each do all of the right things and still find ourselves the victim of a crime.

## RECOGNIZING SAFETY

Many people feel most safe at home. Yet, some people feel most safe in their secured workplaces where abusive friends or family members cannot get to them. Still others feel most safe at a friend's house. Wherever you feel most safe, there are some defining elements of that felt safety, for instance, a feeling of calm, an ability to interact with those around you in a confident healthy manner, freedom from threats and insults, a sense of wanting to stay where you are, and the feeling that the people you love are safe, too.

In addition to "feeling safe" there are visible and audible signals that communicate safety messages. Walking with confidence and your head held high says "don't mess with me" and that is a signal to others that you plan to keep yourself as safe as possible. Using a firm tone of voice communicates to others that you can't be walked over, pushed over, or taken advantage of, and that works in favor of your safety. Beyond your personal messages of safety, there are postings, directions, and sirens that provide information about safety, for example, exit signs, stairway markings, and weapons-prohibited signs communicate safety. Exit maps and use the stairs in the event of a fire and hazardous material safety placards provide directions for being safe in the event of an emergency. Marked locations for first aid kits and fire extinguishers are tools for responding to injury or danger. Flight instructions to passengers give directions for safety during an emergency. Also, safety, or a lack thereof, can be cued with audible signals such as birds singing. When the birds sing, all is well; when the birds stop singing, it is usually a signal that a dangerous animal is near or that the weather is about to change dramatically. Other audible safety signals are typically warnings that danger has occurred or is about to occur: fire engine sirens, tornado or hurricane sirens, police car sirens, ambulance sirens, marine horns, and tsunami warning horns. Seeing a uniformed person's response communicates that help and a restoration of safety is on the way. Seeing a police car on patrol can communicate safety. Just as citizens look for safety, so too do police officers and their families.

Police officers are trained to recognize safety as the absence of a threat. An officer on the street is never in the absence of threats. One would think that an officer would be able to relax while in the safety of the station or squad car or the uniform. Yet, there are numerous instances where officers have been aggressed and killed while working in their offices. Idaho State Trooper Linda Huff was attacked and killed by a gunman in the parking lot of her District Headquarters in Coeur d'Alene, Idaho. Trooper Huff did not let her guard down. She was ambushed in an area where one would expect to be relatively safe, yet she was able to wound the shooter so that he could be caught even though she herself died. Here is an example of doing all the right things and yet still becoming a victim.

Every time a police officer is on a call for service, there is at least one gun present: the officer's and any others held by those present at the scene. Law enforcers are trained to recognize that any situation can turn bad at the drop of a hat. Officers live and operate on a daily basis at a heightened state of alert. Dr. Kevin Gilmartin refers to this as "hypervigilance."[1] Every officer exercises hypervigilance; it is a necessary function of survival. It results from continually being on guard, ready to react at any moment. The problem is that officers are not able to turn it off. They are just as hypervigilant off duty as when they are on duty. At home they often exhibit the same attitudes and take the same actions as when they are working. Officers must learn to recognize when they are in safe zones and be able to let their guard down. It is an unfortunate truth that law enforcement officers suffer an unusually high level of mental and physical health problems directly attributable to hypervigilance. Every year in this country two to three times the number of officers who are killed in the line of duty take their own lives. A recent study revealed that New York City officers kill themselves at a rate of 29 per 100,000 a year. The rate of suicide in the general population is 12 per 100,000. Most of the officer victims are young males with no record of misconduct, who shoot themselves while off duty.[2]

Suicide is not the only issue plaguing officers. Substance abuse, domestic violence, heart disease, diabetes, and a host of other maladies haunt officers. If our nation's police suffer from the accumulated stress of continual hypervigilance, cannot the same be said for citizens who become consumed by the fear of crime? If you spend an inordinate amount of time being concerned about your well being you are subjecting yourself to similar mental and physical health issues. *Prepared Not Paranoid*'s goal is to help you prepare for dangerous situations without wearing yourself out, harming your health, or becoming paranoid.

## RECOGNIZING SAFETY—FIND YOUR FEEL-SAFE FACTORS

Recognizing your personal definitions of safety is the place to start. Until you can put into words and lock into your memory what feels safe, it can be difficult to recognize when danger has entered your environment. In each of the following paragraphs, you'll discover words and descriptions that reflect how you might feel and sense safety. As you read each description and set of details, create your own list of factors, situations, and experiences that demonstrated your safety and your sense of feeling safe.

What makes you feel that you are safe? As you read above, police officers sense safety in the absence of a threat. For the rest of us, feeling safe comes from knowing that you are generally liked, that no person is threatening you, and that no object or environmental condition is threatening to harm you. Friendliness conveys safety. Knowing someone for a long enough period of time to establish mutual trust is a sign of safety. Feeling safe also comes from knowing that you make good decisions about how you travel and with whom you travel and that you make good decisions about frequenting high-risk neighborhoods and nightspots by yourself.

What situations have you been in where you knew you were safe? Being safe at home is a desire that all human beings have whether or not actual safety exists in the places people live. A lack of gunfire is a situation in which safety, at least for the moment, would seem to exist. A pool with a lifeguard communicates that safety is important and will be pursued in the event that danger arises. Work, play, and shopping environments that have clear safety messages and directions communicate that they are safe places to be.

How do you feel when you "feel safe?" This is an exercise in putting into words what safety feels like and how it sounds, smells, and looks. Safety feels like a calm, fun, or fright-free interaction with friends. Safety feels like a day in the sun relaxing at a beach. Safety may also feel like the smell of chocolate chip cookies coming fresh out of the oven. For someone else, the scent of the perfume your mother wore when you were a child may feel like safety, and for yet another person, safety may smell like fresh laundry and a bleached-clean house. The taste of chicken noodle soup may tell you that you are safe, or the smell and taste of tomato soup or some other favorite food may remind you of your safety. Some people gauge safety by the texture of the materials around them or by the "thickness" of the air in a room. For instance, in high-stress environments tension can actually be felt as a presence, even though no one is speaking. The sounds of present safety include quiet, laughter, peaceful conversation, music playing, and the breathing of a child peacefully asleep. When your body feels safe, your heart beats at its resting rate, your blood pressure is lower, and your breathing is easy and slow. You are in the state of homeostasis, which is where your body likes to be. When your brain is free from warning messages, concerns, and worries, then all of you tends to feel safe.

How do you respond to safety? Just as we all feel safety in different ways and based on different signals, we all have different responses to safety. Our response to safety is largely dependent on our sense of feeling safe as both a child and as an adult. Some people respond to feeling safe by also feeling relaxed, at peace, and ready for anything to come along. People who are not used to experiencing safety on a regular basis may respond to a sense of safety with so much relief that crying is a natural reaction. Other people not familiar with a sense of safety can respond with a sense of uncertainty and hesitance because being in a safe place feels foreign. When an experience feels foreign, even though safety has been found, a potential reaction can be yelling, fighting, or moving out of the safe situation. Yet another response to safety can be to freeze: that's right, to freeze right in one's tracks, because the sense of safety either feels so good that the person wants to stay forever or because the situation feels so foreign that the person has no idea what to do, what to say, or how to react. Only you know what your response to safety is now, is likely to be, or has been each time you've genuinely felt safe.

## RECOGNIZING SAFETY FACTORS

Now that you've begun putting into words what makes you feel safe, there are some additional safety factors that are recognized as necessary for keeping yourself safe. These factors fall into three areas: What to look for in ourselves, what to look for in others, and what to look for in the environment.

What to look for in ourselves: First, make plans to ensure each aspect of your life is being managed safely (more about this in Chapter 2). As a part of planning, you can build for yourself the deep understanding that you have done all of the necessary planning to be as safe as possible. This involves making good decisions so you do not to become a victim of crime. Living a low-risk lifestyle is more conducive to safety than is living life on the edge. Also, look for your confident walk and your confident smile so that you can communicate your ability to keep yourself safe without having to say a word.

What to look for in others: picking acquaintances who make good choices about public and private behavior also helps to guarantee personal safety. When you surround yourself with people who are not in denial about personal safety, who are also vigilant and cautious, and who will help to create a safe environment whenever you are together, you are making safety-focused decisions about friends and colleagues. Associating with people who choose to have a healthy, realistic outlook on life can create a safer atmosphere than associating with those who deny that there is any danger out there at all.

What to look for in the environment in order to recognize safety: do you live in an area that would be considered "high crime?" Making the decision to either manage the risks or to mitigate them by moving to a safer neighborhood helps to reduce daily threats to your safety. For many people however moving is not an option, economically or emotionally. In these cases, knowing your risks and going about your daily life with more awareness can help to reduce the opportunities available for becoming a victim. The more you recognize and create safety for yourself, the less likely you are to fall prey to crime. The more you own your sense of confidence and safety, the less likely you are to become the victim of a predator.

## WHAT IS A PREDATOR?

In the Introduction, you read the recap of the "Boy Who Cried Wolf" story. Certainly a wolf is a predator, an animal in search of another animal to eat. In children's literature, the wolf is probably the most widely recognized predator because we hear of a wolf again in "Little Red Riding Hood" and in the story of the "Three Little Pigs," as well as in several *Aesop's Fables*. In each of the stories the wolf is the "bad guy" (more on bad guys in Chapter 9), and in each of the stories, the bad guy causes harm and even a loss of life (the sheep, the grandmother, and two pigs). These stories provide vivid introductions to safety, safety planning, and ultimately, survival. We learn from each of the three pigs' experiences the importance of being prepared in order to protect ourselves and our homes. The predator wolf in the story was outsmarted by the third pig, which had built a secure home, had good problem-solving skills, and clearly took action on the spot when his plans appeared not to be working. How well have you built your house for safety? How often do you practice your problem-solving skills? Finally, how often do you overcome the threats and fears in your life to go about "living happily ever after?" If you have not prepared your mind in advance when the predator wolf (or threat or challenge) comes knocking at the door, you are more likely to become a victim than to chase or scare the predator away.

As it relates to real life and daily safety, what is a predator? The kind of predator this book is focused on is the one that pays attention to you, to what you do, to when and how you do it, and to whether you are a target for a mugging, assault, robbery, or rape. In this discussion, the predator is one who makes a plan to get you and then follows through on the plan, whether it is an instantaneous act or a methodically created multi-month plan. Criminal predators include individuals who prey on you and your property. For predators to survive, they must have prey. In the animal kingdom, prey is the weaker, slower, sicker, or unaware animal that the predator can capture and eat. Prey in the human realm could also be described as the person who is weaker: without a plan; slower: slower of mind and body; sicker: not physically fit to run or fight; or in denial that they could become a victim. In some cases, though, the prey may just be an average person going about his business without really taking notice of his surroundings. In the chapters ahead, *Prepared Not Paranoid* provides strategies for you to not be prey to criminal behavior. Criminals, like predators, are watching for your weakness, your ability to be overcome and taken advantage of, and your likelihood of not fighting back. Your ability to plan and prepare for predatory behavior is part of "hardening your target" (discussed at length in Chapter 2).

## WHAT IS FEAR?

Predators in the animal and human kingdoms typically invoke fear on the part of their prey. Fear is that gut instinct or raw emotion that communicates to every fiber of your being that "something is wrong, there is a threat here, and you better get away from it." Fear is what keeps animals alive, but humans have worked to overcome and eliminate fear to the point that one of life's most powerful tools for staying alive has been diminished. Fear to the point of paralysis or to the end of never leaving home is not the level of fear that saves lives. In fact fear at this level can be classified as paranoia that prevents life from being lived.

Indeed, from the time of our childhood we've all been prompted with stories of being safe, making plans to be safe, and of not "crying wolf" when no danger exists. However, we forget to plan, fail to be aware, and allow fear to come into our daily lives. Fear is natural. Picture a surge protector that is used to protect electronics from electrical surges that could destroy the equipment. Everyone needs a similar surge protector for managing fear. Fear has a place in keeping us safe, but too much fear creates paranoia and can paralyze us. The key is to face your fears, to develop a plan of action for the time when your fears become reality, and to practice your plan so that your mind and muscle memory can take over when danger strikes.

## RECOGNIZING DANGER

Recognizing danger is often more easy than recognizing safety. A sense of danger has been described as a variety of things, including: "trembling at the knees," "a horrible feeling in the pit of my stomach," "the hair on the back of my neck stood up," and "I broke out in a cold sweat." Some have also described it as follows: "I heard a voice screaming 'run, run'"; or "my heart rate increased and I felt a flush, as if every nerve in my body was tingling." Bold and blatant dangers as well as subtle dangers can trigger these signals, but even when the danger signals are loud, clear, and repeated, some people convince themselves they are safe. The desire to "be nice" or to "not be judgmental" has become such a large part of culture that the very signals that indicate danger are often tuned out. However, there are ways to rekindle your sense of danger. For instance, there are things to look for in yourself, in others, and in your environment that are real indicators of your potential safety. For instance, always saying "yes" makes you an easy target and look like prey to a criminal. In her book, *NO! How One Simple Word Can Transform Your Life*,[3] Kemp tells the story of recognizing the danger that a classroom participant had moved into with her daily attitude of always saying "yes" and living to meet everyone else's needs:

> One day, I heard a depressed-sounding woman repeat the refrain, "You just don't understand, I can't say *no* at work." My self-protection alarms began to sound. I reasoned, if she can't say *no* at work, can she say *no* at home? And if she can't say *no* at home, what happens when she's taken advantage of during a shopping trip or during a walk in the park?

The resounding danger signal for Kemp is that this woman had moved herself into a mental outlook that prevented her from saying "no" even if it meant she'd be protecting herself from harm or outright danger. Most self-defense classes start with learning to say "no," because until you can say no to someone else you stay unable to establish a boundary that is healthy and safe for you. You also become an easy mark or target for a criminal when you can't stand up for yourself and say "no." In fact, internationally recognized Jeet Kune Do instructor and self-defense trainer Chris Kent says that "no is a complete sentence." So the fact that this participant had moved herself into a dangerous, always-say-yes outlook on life meant that she was more likely to become a victim of a crime, a mugging, a robbery, or rape.

So what are some of the danger signals to look for in ourselves? Finding your stomach in knots is either a sign of danger or of stress, and ongoing stress ultimately creates danger. Unexplained uneasiness or tension can be a sign of danger. A danger signal can also be a sixth sense of sorts that something is just not right. Coauthor Doug Graves recalls an experience where he was very literally the prey during a postcollege job with a road-surveying crew on the Olympic Peninsula in Washington State. His crew was designing a logging road that went several miles through old growth national forest land near the Hood Canal. At the end of each workday, there was nearly an eight-mile walk back to the truck. It was not unusual for members of the survey crew walking back to the truck to spread out on the trail and to be walking alone. One evening, just at dusk, while making the trek back to the truck, Doug had a very immediate sense of danger. He had not heard or seen anything but felt the hair on the back of his neck standing on end. He stopped, looked around, but did not see or hear anything, so he continued on his hike out. A second time the feeling overtook him. This time he stopped, turned, and looked behind him and up the hill. Approximately 30 yards behind him was a full-grown mountain lion. It appeared to Doug that the big cat had been hunting him and was sizing him up for dinner. As soon as Doug spotted him, the cat disappeared. Needless to say, Doug did not waste anytime making the remainder of the hike out. From that day on when making the hike out, he always stayed with another member of the crew. Doug's experience is common in western states and rural areas where animal predators are sometimes as prevalent as human criminals. In many cases, when an animal threat occurs in a community, law enforcement and park rangers become involved in creating safety again for the community.

When interacting with people, there are signals that hint at your safety, too. Watch for facial expressions that tell you the other person's emotions and actions are not going to match up with the person's words. Screams indicate both fear and anger. When someone is screaming at you, it may be in anger; other times you may hear a scream that you know means someone is in trouble and needs help. Quick movements may indicate aggression. Doug recalls a time when he was responding to a disturbance call at a state-run alcohol treatment unit. As he entered the residents' day area and was speaking to the treatment staff, he noticed a man about six feet tall crossing the room toward him at a very rapid rate. Judging by the man's movements, it was evident that he had a problem with a uniformed officer being on the unit. Being alert and noticing the man's aggressive attitude gave Doug the time to move to a position that put a table between him and the man. It was the right move: the man had one thing in mind, hurting a policeman. The man began yelling at Doug, threatening him, and continuing to be aggressive toward him. Fortunately several orderlies were nearby and restrained the man, who obviously was mentally impaired. The point is that the man's movements were a precursor to his actions; he gave his intentions away by the way that he approached Doug.

Then there are obvious signs of danger such as seeing a gun held in a threatening way, seeing a fight in action, seeing a lone male or pairs of males lurking in the alleys in a downtown area of a city. Drunkenness can signal poor decision making and outright danger. Erratic behavior can signal sickness, drunkenness, or drug use that can lead to a dangerous outcome. Seeing something suspicious such as masked men entering a bank can also signal that danger is ahead.

Police officers are trained to watch for the following signs of danger: furtive movements of an item into clothing or a place that the officer can't see, such as under the seat of an automobile, and aggressive or challenging behavior. People who are going to be a problem for an officer usually give a "tell" with body language. Like the man Doug described above, it will be something in their body position, a facial expression, or a demeanor that telegraphs that "I am going to be a problem to you." As citizens moving about daily life, we too can be on the alert for the following clear signs of danger: fire; aggressive behavior toward us or others; and the look that says, "I am angry or annoyed with you." A clenched fist is a sure sign of a person under stress; push this person hard enough, and he may explode.

Finally, in the environment there are indicators of potential danger to pay attention to. Complete darkness in a parking area, in a transportation terminal, around your front door, or around your office door is a danger zone. Sensing something is wrong, noting a change in the environment, or seeing something out of the ordinary in a typical place all may indicate that something is amiss.

## DEFINE YOUR DANGER

Jana one time described a workplace scenario in which a supervisor had taken her into a conference room and shut the door before turning on the light. The situation made her feel very uncomfortable and feel that she was at risk of being harmed. She learned about defining a sense of personal danger when Police Officer Mike Barker said to "put it into words, how did you know something wasn't right?" That's what this exercise is about, putting into words what you see, feel, hear, taste, and sense that tells you when you are in danger. Most law enforcement and security professionals will tell you to "trust your instinct and your intuition; don't talk yourself out of it."

Let's define what makes you feel that you are in danger. Consider that a professional football player may not feel a sense of danger if he encounters a strange man in a dark garage. However, an average citizen might think twice about walking through an empty parking garage late at night, especially if a stranger lurks in the shadows. Perhaps you're a woman, in your twenties, an athlete, but not a big person. Perhaps you work long hours at a retail store that requires you to wear heals and a suit. You are the last person to leave the store and your car is parked across the garage. Though the garage is well lighted, there is no one around. You head for your car, keys in your handbag, backpack on your back. Your heels click loudly, announcing your presence. There are no other cars in the garage, and the security guard is off duty. The garage is not known to be a threat and few incidents have occurred here. However, your safety could be compromised: you are in high heels, making it difficult to run should anyone try to chase you and a tight-fitting suit could make escape even harder. Without your keys in hand, getting into your car will be tricky. The backpack could slow you down. Alone in the garage, there is no one to help should someone overtake you. Surveillance cameras might help to identify a potential perpetrator, but this helps only after a crime has taken place. Paying attention to possible crime scenes in your own life is an important practice. The woman in the story above may smell burning tire rubber, an unusual scent for an empty garage, or perhaps there is cigarette smoke, but no one in her immediate line of vision. Perhaps there is a smell of alcohol or of cologne, indicating the presence of another individual. Being observant enables you to be prepared for an unexpected event. Think about your daily activities, perhaps just opening a door to a stranger is a danger in your particular neighborhood. Perhaps driving through your city makes you a target for carjacking. Perhaps your place of employment is known for criminal incidents. Assessing your daily routine and the opportunities a criminal might have for invading your life is an important step in preparing for events that you hope will never happen.

Now consider the situations that make you feel you personally could be in danger. Identifying your personal, potential-danger situations is half of the planning for keeping yourself safe. Once you've identified your feel-danger situations, you can take measures to avoid or to mitigate any potential dangers. Start by identifying what situations have you been in that you felt were dangerous. Think back to any situations where someone physically invaded your space or even actually attacked you. Recall any environments in which you were verbally attacked. Think, too, about any occasions in which you just knew that something wasn't right or was outright dangerous even though you had no visible proof at the moment you were in the situation.

Now think about how you feel when you sense you are in danger. Does the way your body feels change when you sense danger? Reflect on whether your heart rate speeds up or your tension rises, signaling that something isn't right. Next think back to what your brain tells you when sensing danger: the message might be clear: "danger, get away," or it might be subtle: "something's not right," or yet again, the message might be an argument of sorts, "he seems nice enough, why am I being so judgmental when he's offered to help me with my groceries?" All three of these messages from your brain are telling you that you are in some level of danger. In addition to your body and brain giving you danger signals, there are smells and sounds that can trigger your sense of danger. The odor added to natural gas is a danger warning that there is a gas leak. The smell of smoke means somewhere there is a fire and a move to safety is needed. Smells that you don't recognize may be a sign of danger or a signal that people around you are making less than good decisions about their activities. Sounds can also communicate clear and present dangers. For instance, sirens of any sort usually mean someone is in danger and you must get out of the way. Warning bells, oral announcements, and media alerts can also signal that danger is on the way or has already arrived. Even the sour taste of a food or medicine can communicate that it was not safe and that you needed to take preventive action to keep yourself from getting sick, experiencing food poisoning, or having a negative medical reaction.

Listening for and feeling danger can also come from the sense, what some people call a sixth sense, that something simply isn't right. You can't put it into words at first or perhaps ever, but you simply know because "the hair on the back of your neck" stands up or because the anxiety you feel all over your body is screaming to move to safety. Which brings us to looking at how you respond to danger: do you know what you do? Some people yell, take control of the situation, and fight back with everything they've got for staying alive. Other people yell, or conversely say nothing, and get away from the situation. Still others when faced with danger of any kind will freeze without any idea of what to do to move to safety. This is where *Prepared Not Paranoid* comes into play: helping you to recognize when you are safe and when you are in danger and helping you build a personal plan of action for keeping yourself safer every day.

## BACK TO BEING SAFE

There are a variety of things you can do to reduce your likelihood of being in danger. Start with being aware of your surroundings. Maintain a sense of who is in the area and whether you feel safe. Look for well-lit and well-traveled areas when walking, exercising, or driving. Watch for sudden movements and quickly changing situations. Identify people and activities that seem out of place. Let someone know where you are if you are doing laundry alone in an apartment laundry room. Communicate with property managers if you feel security is lax or is not being kept up to standards. Don't get into elevators with people you don't know or who make you feel uneasy, just as you wouldn't get into a car with a stranger. Secure your home (more on this in Chapter 4). Leave porch lights on. Be aware of places where people could jump out and surprise you. If you feel you are being followed on foot, get to an area where there are other people. If you feel you are being followed in a car, drive to a police or fire station to get help. Lock your car. When you return to your parked car, have your key ready so that you are not fumbling for it by the car. Park in well-lit places.

You can also adjust your outlook and attitude to project an image of "I'm not a victim" by learning to be assertive and setting clear limits about what is acceptable to you. For instance, what are your limits around sexual interactions, around drinking, around traveling with others, and around anything that causes you to feel uncomfortable or concerned. Be comfortable and confident asking people to leave or to leave you alone. You have the right to say no to someone who is making you feel uncomfortable. When you do this in a confident manner, you are letting the person know that you are not going to be a victim. You become less of a favorable target for him.

Learn to be comfortable making a scene, causing a disturbance, and making lots of noise to attract help. If someone who is bothering you does not respect your request to stop, you then need to let others know of the problem. If you are in public, do not hesitate to draw attention to yourself. You can simply say loudly and directly to passers by, "Excuse me this guy is not leaving me alone as I have asked him to, would you please call the police for me." Jana did this one time in a downtown restaurant when a panhandler she had denied giving any money to followed her and a friend into a restaurant to again ask for money. Jana immediately asked the wait staff to call the police; it took three requests, but the staff did call 911. Police came, took a report, and then later found the man. The point is that bringing attention to yourself ups the ante for and increases the risk to the perpetrator by bringing another individual into the equation, and if he persists, the police will soon be there as well. If you are alone in a deserted area (the first question is "why are you?"), use your voice to scream, "Help! Call the police" at the top of your lungs. If you carry a whistle, use it. Keep using it until you are out of danger or someone comes to your assistance. Other things you might consider carrying are discussed in Chapter 7.

## FEEL-SAFE QUOTIENT SURVEY

This survey is designed to assess your confidence in moving about your life safely and to help you identify just how much you can benefit from the rest of this book. You'll discover what your Feel-Safe Quotient is: Always At Risk; Aware but Not Feeling Safe; Oblivious/Unaware; Safe but Wanting More Confidence; or Feel Safe but Constantly Learning. As you respond to the questions, go with your first response because it is the one that will most accurately describe how you are moving about your life right now. At the end of the survey, you'll discover which of five modes of feeling safe you are living in.

Use the following scale for your responses to the survey: **rarely** means you hardly if ever feel this way, experience this, or do this; **sometimes** means you occasionally feel this way, experience this, or do this; **not sure** means you really haven't given any thought to this idea, statement, or experience; **often** means you often feel this way, experience this, or do this; and **nearly always** means you nearly always feel this way, experience this, or do this.

**The Survey/The Choices: Rarely, Sometimes, Not Sure, Often, Nearly Always**

1. People tell me I'm naïve. _____
2. People tell me to make better decisions. _____
3. I do things by the same routine every day. _____
4. I exercise or engage in most activities alone. _____
5. I constantly worry about my safety. _____
6. I consistently worry about the safety of my family. _____
7. I'm unaware of my surroundings most places I go. _____
8. I don't know any of my neighbors by name. _____
9. My house/residence is not well lit. _____
10. I am the victim of crimes. _____
11. I leave my house unlocked. _____
12. My family does not have a safety plan. _____
13. I leave my car unlocked. _____
14. When I get into my car, I just get in and go. _____
15. I carry my wallet/purse in a way that makes it easy to be stolen. _____
16. I carry my keys in such a way that I can lose them easily. _____
17. I don't have any self-defense skills. _____
18. I am not physically fit and don't think I could get away from an attacker. _____
19. I don't know where all the emergency exits are at work. _____
20. When shopping, I forget how to get to my vehicle or transportation safely. _____
21. When traveling, I never take the time to find the stairway in the hotel. ____
22. When traveling by plane, I don't read the safety card, so I wouldn't know how to get out of the plane. _____
23. When commuting by train or bus, I realize that I don't know how to stop the train or bus and how to get out. _____
24. When I meet new people, I quickly invite them to my home. _____
25. I don't spend time to meet the parents of my children's friends. (If you don't have kids, what would you do if you did?) _____
26. I don't know how to conduct checks of the sexual predators living in my neighborhood. _____
27. I don't participate in neighborhood activities. _____
28. People say that I say "yes" too often. _____
29. People tell me to "snap out of your victim mindset." _____
30. People tell me I'm too nice for my own good. _____

## Scoring

Now that you have rated the thirty feel-safe questions, you can score your results. Note that the lowest point total could be zero and the highest could be 30 (which means you selected the same response for all 30 questions).

## Count each response and enter the total count in the point totals column.

|  | POINT TOTALS |
| --- | --- |
| **Rarely** response: give yourself one point for each. | _____ |
| **Sometimes** response: give yourself one point for each. | _____ |
| **Not Sure** response: give yourself one point for each. | _____ |
| **Often** response: give yourself one point for each. | _____ |
| **Nearly Always** response: give yourself one point for each. | _____ |

Be sure your total of the five Point Totals is 30. If it is not, count again until the five items add up to 30. Next, circle the highest point total. This is the score that you will use to determine what level of safety you typically feel.

## Survey Debrief

### If your highest point total was for

| | |
| --- | --- |
| **Rarely,** then you are probably feeling | Safe, yet constantly learning new ways to protect yourself and your family. |
| **Sometimes,** then you are probably feeling | Safe, yet want greater confidence in handling a variety of situations. |
| **Not sure,** then you are probably feeling | Oblivious/unaware about your safety. |
| **Often,** then you are probably feeling | Aware but not safe. |
| **Nearly always,** then you are probably feeling | Always at risk. |

These five Feel-Safe Quotients provide you with insight as to how you feel, what your mindset is, and how you are likely to be treated by others when it comes to matters of your personal safety.

An Always at Risk quotient is characterized by making poor choices and putting yourself unnecessarily at risk. An Always at Risk quotient also means you can easily be targeted by criminals and easily become a victim. This quotient is recognized by others who see you as "an easy mark" whether or not they have any intention of taking advantage of you, and ultimately, it is not a safe place to live. The chapters ahead will provide ways for you to move out of feeling always at risk.

An Aware but Not Feeling Safe quotient is characterized by being vaguely aware of what is happening around you but not recognizing the potential danger, and if danger is recognized in this state, you don't have an understanding of what to do or any real skills to protect yourself. This quotient is recognized by others because they see you as "aware but not able to avoid or handle trouble." This is a better mindset to have than Always at Risk or Oblivious/Unaware because you are aware of your surroundings and yet still need tools, approaches, and behavioral habits that can keep you safer. You are not in denial about danger. The chapters ahead will provide ways for you to move out of "aware but still at the mercy of others" and of your environment.

An Oblivious/Unaware quotient is characterized by not taking care of protecting yourself by making good decisions and taking stay-safe actions. You usually don't pay attention to the danger signals around you, making yourself an easy target and victim. The Oblivious person is recognized by others as someone who "doesn't even pay attention to what's happening around you" or the state of being "clueless." In the oblivious/unaware mindset you are not even aware that danger is about to befall you, so this is the worst of the five quotients to fall into. Keep reading and learning so that by the end of this month you can take the survey again and move into one of the other four Feel-Safe Quotients.

A Safe, but Wanting More Confidence quotient is characterized by awareness of surroundings and of the need to be safe and by a partial lack of knowledge and skill for taking action to be safe. This Feel-Safe quotient is recognized by others who see you as fairly confident when moving about the world. This is a better mindset because your awareness is high, yet skills need to be acquired so that your confidence grows and you become a less likely target of crime than someone in Always at Risk, Aware but Not Feeling Safe, or Oblivious/Unaware.

A Feel Safe, Constantly Learning quotient is characterized by high confidence, clear decision making, stay-safe actions, and skills for self-protection. This most-safe quotient is recognized by others as having high confidence and being someone "no one is likely to mess with," and this is the best-yet mindset because awareness has been augmented by the ongoing development of stay-safe skills.

In Chapter 10, you'll discover why each of the thirty behaviors in the survey is dangerous and what you can do to not fall into their individual traps. Chapter 10 also presents a Feel-Safe Formula for moving yourself ever closer to the "Safe, Constantly Learning" quotient, which is where ultimately you want to live to be prepared and not paranoid as you move about your daily activities. Remember that children are often taught to listen to the cues, detect the dangerous ones, and plan for potentially bad situations. Even in the story of Peter Pan there are lessons about listening for danger. Consider the relationship that Peter Pan and Captain Hook have: it is a violent relationship at best, and the violent nature of their relationship leads Captain Hook to deliver a "present" to Peter Pan. Now Tinkerbell knows that there is a bomb inside the nicely wrapped package, and she works diligently to convince Peter Pan to get rid of the box. Peter Pan chooses not to listen to Tinkerbell. In the end of this scene, however, it is Tinkerbell who saves the day and gets Peter Pan out of his sleeping quarters just in time to save his life. The safety lesson in Peter Pan's story is multifold: listen to your trusted advisors (including your instinct) about whether danger lies ahead, investigate before discounting a story of impending danger, and take swift action to protect yourself.

Fear of crime is on the minds of more people than ever today. Is it justified? That depends. The key question is—are you at risk of becoming a victim? By increasing your understanding of the nature of crime and of how criminals behave and act, you can improve your chances for not becoming a victim. Coupling knowledge with common sense steps of preparing against danger, an attack, or a natural disaster will reduce your fear and increase your joy of living. *Prepared Not Paranoid* provides tips, suggestions, and resources from the field of law enforcement so that you can take your own safety into your own hands.

## A PLAN FOR RECOGNIZING SAFETY AND RECOGNIZING DANGER

1. Own your Feel-Safe Factors.
2. Know what your "danger signals" are.
3. Understand where you currently scored on the Feel-Safe Survey.
4. Learn to make good choices and decisions around staying safe.
5. Stay out of harm's way.
6. Be prepared—mentally and physically.
7. Learn to trust your personal danger signals and stop talking yourself out of danger.
8. Understand body language and other "tells" of people who may want to harm you.
9. Evaluate the high-risk behaviors you may be engaged in.
10. Keep reading to discover how you can be more prepared to protect your safety and at the same time prevent paranoia.

## NOTES

1. Kevin Gilmartin, *Emotional Survival for Law Enforcement: A Guide for Law Enforcement Officers and Their Families* (Tucson, AZ: E-S Press, 2004).

2. Claud Lewis, "Police Suicide is an Alarming Problem Rarely Discussed Publicly," *The Philadelphia Inquirer* (September 1, 2004).

3. Jana Kemp, *NO! How One Simple Word Can Transform Your Life* (New York: AMACOM, 2005).

Two

# Strategies for Staying Safe Every Day in Every Way

In today's popular culture we hear much about how terrible things are and how dangerous it is to live in this modern world. Sometimes it seems like we are hearing "crime, predator, terrorist, or shooter" at every turn and on every newscast. Sometimes we are lulled into complacency because we hear it so often that we start thinking there is no need to heed the call or everything is OK, the danger won't come to my door. This is denial, and criminals depend on denial to exploit you. We, the authors, are not being alarmists; rather we want to help you heed the warning that there are criminals moving around you every day and they may be closer than you think. Do not despair however; you can be ready. In fact you can prevent them from ever showing up at your door.

Sir Robert Peel, Home Secretary of England in 1830 wrote that "the police are the public, and the public are the police,"[1] as principles of modern policing. Peel laid down the idea that the job of policing a community rests with the members of the community itself. It is a common notion that an individual's safety is dependent on how well the police do their job. The police force as an institution cannot possibly impact every criminal act that may occur. At best they may deter, interrupt, and bring to justice the worst offenders. The responsibility for policing our communities lies as much with you and me as it does with those who make a vocation of policing.

As citizens we each have a responsibility and an obligation to take proactive measures in our own lives to ensure that we do not become victims of crime. In fact, the criminal justice profession devotes an entire study to the people who become victims of crime and investigates how and why they did. We are not suggesting that you begin actively pursuing criminals whom may be working in your neighborhood. However, there are many things that you can do that will make you less of a "target" and help to keep you and your family more safe.

It is the nature of the criminal, as will be discussed in more detail in Chapter 9, to look for targets of "opportunity," those people, places, and things that are easy pickings or leaving themselves open for being taken. The vast majority of criminals do what they do for fast, easy rewards. They are looking to make a fast buck. The majority will tell you that the reason they picked a particular house to burglarize or person to rob was because it was easy.

Your job then is to make it more difficult for the bad guys to get your stuff. We invite you to do what threat assessment professionals call "hardening" the target. There are simple, common-sense precautions that everyone can do to lesson the chance of becoming a victim of both violent physical and property crimes. Sometimes, hardening the target involves taking the time to install a more effective lock. Other times it is changing your daily routine to make yourself less predictable and more difficult to target. Often it is simply a state of mind, prepared thinking, and a presentation of yourself as something other than an easy mark.

## HARDENING YOUR PROPERTY

The Uniform Crime Reports (UCR), those statistics captured each year by the FBI, tell us that by far one of the most common crimes in the United States is burglary. According to the UCR definition burglary is the "unlawful entry into a structure to commit a felony or theft." In research conducted by Richard Wright and Scott Decker[2] the way that burglars choose their targets is predicated on these factors: high payoff, easily accessibility, and low risk of detection. Knowing this, we can develop a strategy to foil their attempts.

The first item is high payoff. A thief wants to steal items that can be easily converted to cash. He would prefer that you simply have large amounts of cash stashed around your house for easy taking. Of course that is not often the case, so most go for the next best thing: high-value items that are easy to transport and to convert to cash. This includes jewelry, coin collections, guns, and expensive electronics. Once the thief gains entry into your home, he makes a beeline to your bedroom. As humans we tend to keep that which is of highest value close to us. How can we protect our things at night if we don't sleep with them? This very predictable habit will draw the bad guys, like a moth to the flame, right to the dresser drawer that contains your valuables. The next stop is your bathroom, to search for prescription medications that can be sold for cash.

On the way out is the check of your stereo, plasma television, and computer. If they are expensive and portable enough, they go out the door, too.

Your home is your first place to harden. If you keep large amounts of cash in your home, which you shouldn't, keep it in a wall or floor safe. Take your high-value jewelry, coin collections, and other portable high-value items to a safety deposit box. At the very least, keep them out of sight to the casual visitor or service person in your home. Although most burglars do their own "casing" of a target, many will get information from associates who have access to your home.[3] The service professionals who access your home include the cable installer, housecleaner, lawn maintenance person, home-remodeler, caterer, babysitter, or other service providers who enter your house. Whether you use service people once or regularly, do not allow them to come into your house unattended. In the case of housekeepers or babysitters, insist on references that include criminal background checks.

If a potential burglar does not know what valuables you have, your odds of being a target are greatly reduced. Now that you have your most valuable items either in a safe, safety deposit box, or secure place out of sight, what about those items that you want to have on display for your guests to see? It is understandable for you to want to show a particularly nice piece of art or a collection of fine silver. Position such items so they are not on display for the whole world to see. Crime prevention experts call this "environmental design": using lighting, landscaping, and exterior/interior decorating to reduce easy views of and access to the valuables you may have in your home. For example, Doug recalls being on patrol at night and marveling how many people leave their living room curtains wide open and how easily it was to see exactly what was there. In particular he recalls the home of a wealthy businessman in the small town where he worked who had an extensive gun collection, a large part of which he displayed in his front room. From the street you could see very expensive rifles and handguns displayed in decorative cases. On one warm fall night while the businessman and his family were vacationing in Europe, burglars broke in and stole all of his guns and a very valuable coin collection that was in one of the gun cabinets. It is very likely that the crooks had spotted the loot when standing on the street and did enough casing of the house to know when the family was out of town. Ironically the living room curtains were closed on the night of the burglary. They had been closed while the family was away. If they had been open, perhaps someone would have noticed the intruders in the house. Reduce the "fishbowl" effect. You've seen it, the homes that you can see into just as well as people can see out of them. If the potential thief can see your silver tea service from the street, chances are he can figure out a way to get in and take it. Use window dressing that truly blocks views into your house at night. Put up outside lighting that not only illuminates the shadows but shines in such a way that makes it difficult for those on the outside to see in.

The second item is easy access. Seldom does a burglar pick your lock to gain access to your residence. The burglar will enter your backyard while you are away and see if he can gain access through a door or window. If you leave one unlocked, that will be the burglar's point of entry to your house. If not, he will kick the door in or use a sledgehammer to smash it in. Using an instrument such as a sledgehammer will be rare because most burglars don't plan ahead and do not see the need for carrying heavy tools with them. It is not usually necessary. If they cannot access a door or window, they will remove or break out the sliding glass door. This is a very common entry point for a thief. Lifting a sliding door from its track is relatively easy even when it is locked. Try it yourself to see just how easy it is. Use a wooden dowel or other mechanical device on sliding doors and windows to prevent sliding-door removal by lifting from its track.

If a window or door cannot be removed, the burglar's next choice will be to smash it. This often is the least attractive way to gain entrance because of the noise it makes. Shatter-resistant glass can be put into doors and windows. While this is a costly solution, it will make the break-in much more difficult. If the burglar is unable to defeat your locking systems or smash out your glass, chances are he will move on to another target that is not as well prepared.

Seldom does a burglar come at night. Sixty-five percent of burglaries are residential, and 61% occur in the daytime.[4] The majority of burglaries occur in the middle of the day while you are at work. How does the burglar know when you are away? He has been watching you. His "job" is to get your stuff without getting caught. He wants to be in and out as quickly as possible. He has time to case or watch properties that he believes will provide a high return with a low risk.

The third and final item in the burglar's list of choosing his target is low risk of detection. As mentioned earlier, environmental design comes into play here. Because we humans like privacy, we build fences, plant trees and shrubs, and generally cut ourselves off from others in an effort to keep others from seeing what we are doing in our own spaces. The same blockades we put up for our privacy create safety for a would-be thief who needs time and privacy to get in without being detected. Consider providing natural surveillance points from the street to your residence. These natural surveillance points are simply obstruction-free corridors that allow unobstructed views of your entrances. Depending on the amount of privacy you want to surrender, you may want to provide natural surveillance corridors for your neighbors to clearly view places that a thief would likely enter your home. For instance, upon moving into her home, Jana removed from around the front door and garage four shrubs that had grown more than 12 feet high, to create a surveillance line of sight to the front door. She also installed new brighter front entry light fixtures because there are no street lights in her section of the street. Some public and commercial properties have recently reduced the amount of lighting around their facilities in an effort to discourage graffiti artists from plying their trade. There is some evidence of success because lack of light makes it more difficult to artistically spray paint the side of a building; however, residential burglars who work at night prefer the darkness to make entry into a house. The more light that can be focused around residential entry points, the less likely a burglar is willing to stand in the light and be seen attempting to make entry.

At the same time, you do not want to make your home look like a fortress. Bars on the windows and security stickers on every entrance may make your house look like a jewelry store and give the impression to the outside world that you have something very valuable inside to protect. In some cities, the barred look is both a stylistic architectural approach and a security measure. In these cases, looking like other houses in the neighborhood does make sense because you want to keep your target as hardened as your neighbors' appear to be.

Residential burglar alarms are a deterrent. Depending on the sophistication of the system, burglars will often not chance the detection that an alarm system may provide. However, many thieves are well versed in defeating the average home alarm system. Do not get lulled into thinking that because you have an alarm system and the proper signage to go with it that you will be exempt from a burglary. The unfortunate truth is this 98% of alarms received by the police are false. Because of this, responses to alarms are often less than enthusiastic. Officers try to take every call seriously; however, sometimes the alarm system call may be pushed down the queue, knowing that it may very likely be false. The point here is that a home security system, on its own, will not adequately protect you from a burglary while you are away and certainly will not thwart a home invasion.

## HOME INVASION—A REAL STORY

It was a quiet evening in February 2007, and 54-year-old James Patterson and his wife Molly were watching TV in their living room. Suddenly a stranger armed with a handgun walked through the front door. The intruder pointed the gun at them and ordered them into a back bedroom of the house. The compliant couple did as they were told. Once in the bedroom the invader demanded to know where the narcotics were. James had chronic back problems and took a variety of pain medications, among them Vicodin. It became apparent to the couple that this stranger knew things about them that they assumed were private. Patterson took the attacker to the medicine cabinet and gave him several bottles of prescription drugs. The man warned them not to call police and ran from the house. Shaken, Patterson did call the police. After he gave them a description of the intruder, they inquired as to how he may have known that Patterson had a significant quantity of prescription narcotics in the residence. This puzzled the Pattersons because they did not live a public life. The few close friends they had knew of James' back problems but did not know what medications he took for pain. Then a thought occurred to James; his 26-year-old daughter had a drug problem of her own. She had lived with them off and on, but because of her drug use the Pattersons insisted that she stay away from the house. There was a good chance that their own daughter had either purposely or inadvertently given information to one of her street friends concerning James' condition and the quantity of narcotics he usually had on hand. This in fact turned out to be the case. The Patterson's daughter had revealed information to an associate, who in turn told another who was not beyond simply walking into the house and forcibly taking what he wanted.

It is hard to say just how many home invasions occur each year in our country. This is due to the way the FBI keeps track of these types of events. UCRs are how law enforcement agencies report criminal activity in their jurisdiction. There are only seven categories of crime for which data is sought, and home invasion is not one of the seven. Generally jurisdictions will list home invasion as a burglary or a robbery because the crime of entering someone's house usually has elements of both.

However it is recorded and catalogued, a home invasion can be a terrifying attack on your person and property. The invader will use one of several strategies to gain entrance to your home. Most common is a ruse to get the homeowner to open the door. When the door is opened, explosive force is used to push the way in. Another common method is to wait until the garage door is up, entering right behind a vehicle and surprising the homeowner in the garage, then closing the garage door to get out of sight, and subduing her. Once the invader has control over the occupant(s), he is now free to move about the residence.

## HARDENING AGAINST A HOME INVASION

How do you stop someone from forcing their way into your house? There are a few easy approaches that will dramatically reduce the already slim chance of this happening to you. First, never open your door to someone you do not know. If someone knocks on your front door, identify them, either through a peep hole or side window. If you cannot identify the person, don't open the door. Second, keep the door locked at all times. If you have a screen or storm door, keep it locked too. Remember, the home invader depends on surprise to accomplish his crime. If you aren't surprised, his plan fails. You should have at a minimum of two locks: a dead bolt in a solid wood door and a solid intrusion lock similar to those used in hotels. This way if you do open the door, you have a barrier that an invader will have to work through. Forget about a safety chain-type lock; these are so easily defeated that they present no deterrence. For a little more money, various locks designed to prevent home invasion can be purchased. These are known as "surprise doorstops" and, simply put, are metal posts in your floor that allow the door to come open only about four inches. If you decide that it is safe to admit the person on the outside, you can remove the metal pin and the door opens normally.

It is human nature to open the door when someone is knocking. What do you do if the bad guy has gained entry? The best offense is a good defense. Have a plan worked out in the chance that this happens. Remember that the home invader is counting on surprise and compliance with his threats. If you move outside of his script, chances are you will defeat him. Your plan need not be complicated or take much if any rehearsing. It may be as simple as designating one room in the house as the safe room. In an emergency such as a home invasion all family members who are able to should retreat to this room. Equip this room with some kind of lock. Even if this is a hollow core or foam core door that can easily be broken down, you have bought yourself some time. If you own a weapon, this should be in your safe room. There should be a cell phone in this room. One person Doug knows told him that her family keeps their cell phone chargers in different bedrooms of the house. This way they have more options in case of an emergency.

Equip your safe room with an emergency exit. This may be as simple as being able to open a window and jump to the ground. In the case of a second-story safe room, it may involve having a stow-away ladder that can be attached to a window and that family members can climb down. If you have made it to your safe room and you have the time, get out! Don't worry about what is left behind; you are most valuable if you are free from the house and can call 911 to get help. Most important to a successful safe room strategy is having a plan. As mentioned earlier, it does not have to be complicated or fancy. What is important, however, is that everyone in the household is aware of it. It is helpful to rehearse your plan, even if only verbal run-through is what you do to practice your plan. In the safety plan conversation, talk about the what-if's of a home invasion and also things such as a fire, earthquake, or other natural disaster that may occur where your home is.

By taking these few simple steps you have prepared your mind to react if the unimaginable should happen: The invader breaches your outer defenses and is on the inside, and he expects you to comply with his use of force. You force him off balance by immediately retreating to your safe room. Most likely he will flee at this time because his plan is falling apart. If not and he follows you, he meets another barrier, a locked door. You have gained time and placed a 911 call or better yet, escaped from the house to make the 911 call. When the risk associated with staying in your house becomes too great, the thief is likely to flee.

## HARDENING YOUR VEHICLE

Every 27 seconds a car is stolen in this country. The odds of a vehicle being stolen were 1 in 190 in 2003.[5] Your car is at its most vulnerable when parked in the mall parking lot. The next places where your vehicle is most at risk are the street in front of your house and your driveway. If you park your vehicle in your garage, there is very little risk of its being stolen. Very few cars and trucks are stolen for the purpose of keeping the vehicle. The vast majority are for what the police call "joyriding." This joyriding occurs when the perpetrator (or more often perpetrators) find a vehicle in front of a house left unlocked, with keys in the ignition or with the motor running, or if they can find keys concealed inside an unlocked passenger compartment. It is a plum waiting to be picked. For the perpetrator, most often a juvenile, this is a crime of opportunity: an unattended vehicle left running invites "let's go for a ride." Often after the fun is over, the vehicle will be ransacked and abandoned. Anything of value is removed, and commonly the vehicle is vandalized and left along side the roadway or in a parking lot.

Garden-variety joy riders can be prevented by some very simple preparation. First and foremost, do not leave your keys in the vehicle or the vehicle unattended while it is running, even if only for a minute to run back into the house to get something. Do not hide a key on your vehicle; hidden keys are easy to locate. Use an antitheft device in the vehicle itself, such as a visible steering wheel lock or armored collar around the steering column.

If your car is stolen by a professional thief, chances are that it is going to be broken into parts, or "chopped," and possibly even sent directly out of the country to either get chopped or sold outright. Professional car thieves, just like any other crook, are in the business for just one thing: Money! Trying to sell a stolen vehicle in the United States is now fairly difficult. All vehicles have a vehicle identification number (VIN), which can be tracked by law enforcement through one of many available criminal information databases available to law enforcement, such as the National Criminal Information Center (NCIC) or National Law Enforcement Telecommunications System (NLETS). The VIN appears in several places throughout your vehicle: on the dashboard, doors, frame, and other fixed parts. This is why most vehicles stolen in this country are chopped up for parts in a chop shop or taken out of the country. Many vehicles stolen in the United States are transported across the boarder into Mexico or Canada. From there they are shipped to various locations around the world. Programs such as HEAT (Help End Auto Theft) in Texas are an attempt to stem this trend. Those involved in HEAT attach a sticker to the car giving the police and border crossing guards permission to stop and search their vehicle if it is on the road between 1:00 A.M. and 5:00 A.M.[6]

Preventing a professional thief from getting your vehicle may be more of a challenge. Parking your car in your garage or, when you are out, in an attended lot is your best defense. Towing a vehicle is a fairly common way of stealing a vehicle. Seldom do we question a tow truck who is hooking up or towing a vehicle; we assume that they are doing so on request of the owner or because of improper parking. In order to prevent theft-by-towing, here are some parking tips. If you park on the street or driveway, turn your wheels into the curve. If you own a car with rear-wheel drive, back it into the driveway with the rear of the vehicle close to the house, garage, or other structure. If you own a front-wheel drive vehicle, pull into your driveway with the front of the vehicle as close to another structure as possible. By doing this you are preventing access to the drive wheels of your car so that they can not easily be lifted off of the ground, making your car easy to tow away. For many, an automobile is a most prized possession, whereas for others it is merely a tool of necessity. Whichever it may be for you, preparedness can reduce the fear attached with losing your vehicle and can prevent damage to and theft of your vehicle.

## HARDENING YOUR WORKOUT

Thirty-six-year-old Nancy Grey was running in the foothills on the edge of her town. As she ran down the gravel grade, enjoying the view of the city beneath her and the clear spring air, an older model sedan drove slowly past her going in the opposite direction. She looked away from the car as it passed; however, she did notice that it was a man behind the wheel. Nancy thought little of the encounter: this was a fairly popular outdoor recreational area; it was probably just a hiker out to enjoy one of the many trails on the front.

About five minutes later, Nancy heard a vehicle behind her, and she moved closer to the left hand side of the road. It was him again, in the same car that had passed her earlier. Slowly as before, the car crept past her, the driver staring at her intently. Nancy felt a chill run through her as he passed. The car went around the corner ahead of her. She relaxed. As she rounded the curve, she caught her breath: there was the same car parked directly in her path. Her mind raced, wondering what she should do.

The man who appeared to be in his late twenties stepped from the vehicle, moved to the middle of the road, and waited. Nancy slowed and looked away, seemingly distracted. "Excuse me" he said, "can you help me? I am apparently lost." Nancy stopped, turned toward the man, and smiled, "I might be able to help" she replied. Instantly he was on her, knocking her to the ground; she fought back and screamed "No." She felt a sharp pain in her right chest; he had stabbed her. "My God, this guy is going to kill me," she thought. He stabbed her a second time in the chest. Nancy was getting weak now, and she could not keep up the fight. He dragged her to his car and raped her. When he was finished, he rolled her into the ditch and left her for dead. Fortunately for Nancy, she was in excellent shape and had the will to survive; it was not long until a passerby found her and summoned an ambulance for her. Nancy survived. Her attacker was never found.

More than ever, people are taking to the streets running, biking, and walking in an effort to stay in shape or just for the sheer joy of exercise. Sometimes we think because we are doing something positive, no one is going to bother us. While generally this is true, there is a risk inherent with using public streets for our exercise room. The greatest risk is also the most obvious one: getting struck by a vehicle. Over the past 20 years or so, Doug, who is an avid runner, has been struck three times by cars. Fortunately he was always in the right position and was able to see them before being struck and to take evasive action to minimize the damage. The worst injury was a badly bruised thigh. Most recently he was in a crosswalk with the light in his favor. He ended up on the hood of a car making a right turn, whose driver never saw him until he was lying on the hood looking in through the windshield.

You can lessen your odds of being hit by a vehicle by wearing reflective clothing. If you run at night, carry a flashlight; this will not only make you more visible to drivers, but will also reveal any hidden hazards along the shoulder of the road. Over the years Doug has been more severely injured by stepping in holes or tripping over obstacles while running in the dark than by being struck by vehicles. Runners and walkers are to use the left shoulder of the roadway facing traffic. Bikers are to use the right side of the roadway, riding with the flow of traffic.

Tell friends or family the route that you will be using while exercising. Don't always use the same route. Vary your exercise routine by day, time, and place. This will not only help keep your workout fresh, but will also not let a potential attacker target you as easily. Run with confidence and purpose. Look those you pass directly in the eye. Show your strength. The more confidence you exude, the less attractive target you make.

These days personal audio devices such as iPods and portable music systems are perceived as required equipment for the outdoor exerciser. Although music may be very helpful to your workout and these devices are becoming smaller and easier to carry, don't use them. Listening to music is distracting, and you can't hear or don't pay attention to your surroundings. If you must use a music device, keep the volume low so you can hear what is going on around you. Exercisers tend to get into a "zone" when working out intensely. In the zone they tend to tune out everything around them. Resist this temptation in order to stay safe from a would-be assailant, not to mention hazardous traffic. To stay safe, you must be aware of your environment. Not only that, but there have been many recent cases in which the iPod was the target of the attack: those white ear phones are a dead giveaway.

In Nancy's case above what might she have done differently to prevent becoming a victim? For the most part she did everything right: she was running where she should have been, she was aware of her surroundings, and she was suspicious of the man. Nancy was alone: you should find an exercise partner; not only does it make working out more fun, but it will keep you considerably safer. If one becomes sick or injured, the other can go for help. The adage that there is strength in numbers certainly applies here.

By not looking at the man when he passed, Nancy gave a message of weakness. Most of us would not think twice about it, but to a predator it is an indicator that he has found a possible victim. Had Nancy looked her attacker straight in the eye, he might have given a second thought to attacking someone of this mental strength. She stopped when asked a question. This is what we are taught to do; it is only polite to stop and reply. Not in this case. Nancy was a woman alone in a fairly remote area. She needed to have a survival mindset and to listen to that voice telling her: something is not right here. Gavin de Becker calls it the "fear instinct" in his book *The Gift of Fear.*[7] As the perpetrator moved to the middle of the road, that was when she needed to turn her long run into a speed workout and get as far away from this guy as quickly as possible. He might actually have been lost, but if he had found his way there, he could find his way back. Chances are good, that if she would have simply sped up instead of stopping, that this man would have seen her as a victim who would be too much trouble and would not have pursued her on foot.

## HARDENING YOUR PERSONAL TARGET

Most of what has been covered in this chapter has to do with preparing your things in such a way as not to become a victim. You also must prepare your mind. At the police academy young officers are told to never give up, to fight on no matter what the odds or situation that they find themselves in. Is this some positive self-talk technique designed to put them in a place of overcoming an assailant? Not really. It is simply training their minds to keep going even when their body says quit. We know that when officers are well trained and a situation gets critical, they automatically fall back onto how they were trained. It is second nature. This also applies to their thinking: if they are taught "to survive at all costs," when the time comes, they become survivors.

You can prepare your mind to survive. When you have thought through and mentally rehearsed how you will respond when someone crashes through your front door or grabs you from behind and drags you toward the bushes, you are hardening your mind. You now are a more difficult target because you will not just passively allow yourself to be a victim.

Dr. Kevin Gilmartin, author of *Emotional Survival for Law Enforcement,*[8] speaks of two types of thinking. One is probability thinking: "what are the chances, what might happen, and what are the odds of this happening to me." This is how most people think. This is also where denial lives: "it probably won't happen to me, so why should I even think about it." The second is possibility thinking: "this could happen; therefore, I should prepare myself for it." This is how officers are taught: "When I approach this car what might happen, what can I expect, what could go wrong?" To be truly prepared you must prepare your mind the same way. Think of it as a rehearsal, if you will, of how you will respond if you are faced with a dangerous situation. Imagine you are walking alone across a dark parking lot. Suddenly you hear footsteps approaching from behind. What action will you take? What will you say? Will you run? Will you confront the stranger? If attacked, will you stand and fight? Do you carry personal weapons? If so, will you use them? Are they readily available? Consider this scenario: There is a knock at the door. You open it to see who is there, but before you know it, an armed gunman has forced his way into your living room. What do you say to him? What is your first action? Do you yell for help? Do you run to your phone? Do you turn and run to your safe room?

Jana says that one of her most clear mental rehearsals happened before she attended the police academy. "I was working in radio and had received a letter with a cassette tape and a stick of incense. It was weird, but curiosity drew me in and I listened to the tape with a friend. It was the friend who said, 'Call one of your cop friends; this guy is crazy.' Well, I listened to my friend and ended up filing a police report only to learn that the guy had been arrested for a variety of things including assault on a police officer. So, because I knew this guy knew my voice, knew what I looked like, and could figure out where I lived, I mentally rehearsed what I would do if he accosted or assaulted me. At home, I focused on how I'd get to a phone, and how I could get out of the house. I was alert when out shopping and of course when going to and from the radio station. I stayed aware of whether other people were around who could call for help or whether I was in a situation alone. All of my mental planning helped me to feel prepared. Thankfully, nothing came of it: I was never attacked and never contacted beyond that first letter."

Jana also recalls a more recent, post-academy experience of mental rehearsing that kept her awake until midnight one night. "Early in the day, I attended a family picnic at which a former member of the military expressed great frustration with some of my comments about protecting children and the need to protect children. In fact, his frustration was so great and so personally vindictive that I lay in bed that night rehearsing the following. 'If someone comes in the front door, I can get out the back door. If someone comes in the back door, I can get out the side door. If someone comes in shooting (which was a reasonable thing to prepare for because the guy had bragged once about how many people he had legally killed while in the service), a safe place would be the bathroom behind a locked door and in the bathtub, or leaving the house and getting over the backyard fence and into the neighbor's yard'." And again Jana was protected because thankfully she did not have to implement her rehearsed plans and scripts for action.

These rehearsals are the last step in preparation for safety. They do not take a lot of time, nor do they have to be intricate or perfect in scope. What you have done is to lay down a map in your brain for action. This becomes important, because when the time comes and you are in an intense confrontation, much of the thought process that you normally have access to will be gone; your actions are now running on the rehearsals. If you have not prepared your mind in advance, when the wolf comes knocking on the door, there will be no one ready to act to protect you when you answer. Training your mind or hardening your mental target is as important a step in personal safety as making sure you have good locks on your doors. Probably you will never have to run one of your scripts in an actual situation. However if you do find yourself in a situation that demands your fast action, you can find confidence in knowing that you have a plan and that you can respond according to what you have prepared to do. You have given yourself an advantage that you did not have before. As a result of hardening potential targets of crime and having a personal script or plan for action, you can now move through your world more relaxed than before.

## OPT TO AVOID RISKY BEHAVIOR

Along with mental preparation for staying safe is making good choices. Time after time people in law enforcement see the victims of crime become so because of making poor choices. This is not "victim blaming" but is just common sense. If you live a risky lifestyle, you put yourself at risk of becoming a victim. Consider the following scenario:

Julie Young, an attractive, single, 22-year-old female decides to go to a downtown club to relax after a particularly hard week at work. She calls several of her friends, but they are all busy with other plans. So not wanting to be denied a night out, she decides to go on her own. Once at the local "hot spot" for people her age, she consumes several alcoholic beverages in short order. With her inhibitions lowered from consumption of alcohol, she accepts drinks from a nice looking male who may be a few years older than she is. She is having fun with this guy and drinks more than she knows that she should. Julie thinks she will be safe. The next day she wakes up alone in a cheap motel. She does not remember leaving the club. Julie does not know how she got to this room or what happened while she was there. She fears that she was raped. She calls a friend to come and pick her up, and she goes to the police to report what happened. The police take her to the hospital where a rape exam is conducted. The doctor confirms that Julie has had sexual intercourse in the last 12 hours. The police suspect that she was given some kind of "date rape" drug that caused her to blackout. The police will follow up with the evidence that they have, which is not much: a partial description of a male who is similar to 60% of the people in the club that night and the results from the rape exam, which if they are lucky will give them DNA. However, DNA alone, without a suspect to compare it to, is not of much use in tracking down the perpetrator.

When talking to the victim/witness coordinator for the police, Julie made the following statement: "I should have the right to go into town and have a couple drinks and not have to worry about being raped." She is right; she has the absolute right to go to a club alone and drink. However, what does she give up for that kind of behavior? Is this risky behavior? Many would say yes; some would say no. We are familiar with the children's story, "Little Red Riding Hood" by Charles Perrault. Little Red Riding Hood was naive in thinking that she could go into the woods alone and have an innocent conversation with the harmless-appearing wolf. It was risky behavior on her part, but she did not know any better. Single and married women like Julie need to understand the risk they take when going into the "woods" alone. You are not hardening your personal target when you participate in this kind of behavior: moving around town alone at night and drinking more than you know you should.

Julie tried to do the safe thing when she started out for the night. She tried to get friends to go with her. More than likely this one thing would have prevented her from becoming a victim. Young people like going to where the action is. After all, it is the social thing to do. Go in a group with people whom you trust. Make an agreement before the partying begins to watch out for one another. Take responsibility for yourself and your friends, and be sure that they have made the same commitment to you. Do not let one of your group go off with someone whom you do not know. Even if she says it will be fine, she will thank you later for watching out for her.

If you do go out by yourself, drink responsibly: for most people this is about one drink an hour. Buy your own drinks and never leave a drink unattended. Do not accept a drink from anyone you do not know and trust personally.

It is okay to strike up a conversation with someone;. just be sure that you remain in a very public place. Do not go with him to his car or into the alley for some "fresh air" or to "his place" or to a hotel room. Like everything else in staying safe, personal safety is common sense. Take a moment to stop and think. Ask yourself, "what can happen in this situation?" If you follow a few simple rules, you minimize the risk in risky behavior. Don't give the wolf the opportunity to show you his teeth and take advantage of you.

## HARDENING YOUR PHYSICAL PRESENCE

Now that you are thinking like a survivor, do you have the necessary conditioning and skill to stay safe personally? At the police academy we teach officers the importance of staying physically fit. We know that an officer who is in good physical condition has the upper hand. She not only has the endurance and strength to handle any situation that she is confronted with, but the mere fact that she looks like she is in shape will cause the bad guy to think twice about challenging her. We know that if an officer can fight at 100% for two minutes, the odds of winning the battle are very good. Most people, even those tough guys who like to victimize those smaller than them, cannot last in an all-out brawl for more than a couple of minutes.

The same applies to you. Staying in shape is an investment in your own personal protection. We are not saying that you must be an Olympic athlete, but having good cardiovascular endurance and a modicum of physical strength will assist in your own physical protection. We are not necessarily advocating physical resistance if confronted by a threat; this is up to you and the circumstances in which you find yourself. However, if you can outrun an attacker, you have frustrated his attempt to make you a victim, not to mention the fact that if you look like you are in shape and can defend yourself against a threat, the chances are an attacker won't try. Remember, the wolf or criminal is looking for an easy target; don't give him one.

This brings us to the skills required for personal protection. How much do you need to know? How proficient do you need to be? This is the main drawback we see to learning any of the self-defense arts; they take a large amount of personal dedication. Doug Tangen, a master self-defense and arrest techniques instructor in Washington State and Idaho and master instructor for the Idaho Peace Officer Standards and Training (POST) Academy who holds a second-degree black belt in Tae Kwon Do, a first-degree black belt in Modern Arnis, and a first-degree black belt in Ho Ju Tsu (the integrated art of shooting and fighting), tells us this about personal defense training: "A lot of the training that is out there today is like 'fast food' to a well-balanced diet. It isn't worth much. To become proficient in any of the marshal arts or self-defense systems, it takes an enormous amount of time and money." Tangen tells us that reputable instructors of the marshal arts have a great concern that many people out there who pass themselves off as being credible are merely selling black belts and certifications.

Tangen points out the danger, not only are people not getting their money's worth from the instruction, but they are getting a false sense of security that they have made themselves safer, less at risk of being victimized, when just the opposite may be true. They may have become emboldened to go into a situation where in the past their fear reaction warned them of danger. With the fear reaction lessened, they are now more at risk than they were before.

The bottom line in this discussion is this: if you are going to take a self-defense or street survival class of any kind, consider these things. First, find a reputable instructor, one who is blatantly honest about how much effort becoming proficient will take. As Doug Tangen tells it, "It wasn't until I had spent a couple years studying martial arts that I realized that I had finally learned enough to learn something useful. It's a matter of years not days to be good enough to actually use the things that you are taught." Second, make the commitment to spend the time practicing the techniques. Next, don't be fooled into thinking that you are now impervious to street crime. There is always someone out there who is bigger, better, and tougher than you. Finally, the most important thing you can learn from a self-defense class is how to avoid a conflict. Physical force is the absolute last tool in your belt that you resort to. Walking away is always the better answer, and when walking away turns out not to be an option, have an alternative plan of action and hope that community policing is alive and working on your behalf.

## COMMUNITY POLICING

Community policing became popular in 1982 when "Broken Windows" by James Q. Wilson and George Kelling was published in the *Atlantic Monthly.* The theory holds that aggressive enforcement of small problems keeps them from turning into larger ones. If police work directly with the community in problem solving small things like a broken window, they do not turn into larger issues of urban blight and crime-ridden neighborhoods. The premise is that by the police officer's knowing the people in the community, less crime will be likely to be committed. In the process of hardening your personal target, you too can take the attitude of community policing, which for non-law enforcement people means knowing your neighbors, knowing who owns which cats and dogs, knowing your neighbors' kids' names, and calling the police when a problem that needs police attention arises. Do call the police when you know something is not right. The corresponding phrase that comes to mind is "better to be safe than sorry." As police Captain Gary Compton says, "When you think something is wrong, trust yourself because it probably is."

So whether it is making your property safer by increasing the number or type of locks on your doors or reducing your profile as a target by not flashing large amounts of cash or expensive jewelry when you are out, all of these strategies begin in the same place: being prepared. You are going to read it over and over again in this book, "the very best way to keep from becoming a victim is planning." Whether it is planning a safe room in your house or planning a safe room in your mind, it all starts with planning.

## STAY-SAFE STRATEGIES FOR YOUR "HARDEN THE TARGET PLAN"

1. Harden the target of your home.
2. Harden your personal target by increasing your stay-safe knowledge and mindset.
3. Harden your personal target by becoming more physically fit.
4. Have a plan for getting out of your house in an emergency.
5. Have a plan for exercising safely.
6. Harden the target of your vehicle.
7. Get to know your neighbors.
8. If you truly want to learn self-defense, choose wisely who you want to learn it from and then commit to the effort needed to be proficient.
9. Learn more about community policing and what your neighborhood can do (more in Chapter 4).
10. Avoid high-risk behaviors: don't let the wolf have a chance to show you his teeth. In other words, don't be an easy target for criminals.

## NOTES

1. Police Department Crime Prevention Office, New Westminster Police Service, "Sir Robert Peel, the Founder of Modern Policing: Sir Robert Peel's Nine Principles," New Westminster, BC, Canada, www.nwpolice.org/peel.htm.

2. Richard T. Wright and Scott H. Decker, *Burglars on the Job: Streetlife and Residential Break-ins* (Boston: Northeastern University Press, 1994).

3. Ibid.

4. Paul B. Weston and Charles A. Lushbaugh, *Criminal Investigation: Basic Perspectives,* 10th ed. (Upper Saddle River, NJ: Prentice Hall, 2006).

5. Available at: http://www.Auto-theft.info/ (2004); (accessed August 18, 2007).

6. Texas Department of Transportation, "Help End Auto Theft, H.E.A.T.," June 26, 2007.

7. Gavin de Becker, *The Gift of Fear: Survival Signals That Protect Us from Violence* (New York: Dell Publishing, 1997).

8. Kevin Gilmartin, *Emotional Survival for Law Enforcement: A Guide for Law Enforcement Officers and Their Families* (Tucson, AZ: E-S Press, 2002).

# Three

# Travel Safety

When you leave your home, you leave behind your defendable place and your comfort zone. You leave the safety and security that you have carefully created; you are in an unpredictable space. Can you mitigate the risk? Traveling presents unique challenges in staying safe, and just as with home safety, with a minimum amount of thought and planning you can travel safely and enjoy the adventure without fear or worry of becoming a victim. The sections ahead speak to a variety of travel modes and vehicles.

## AUTOMOBILE TRAVEL

For many people their most common purpose for travel is going to and from their place of work. This is possibly the most dangerous thing that you will do during your day. More people are killed traveling our nation's highways each year than are murdered. The odds of being injured in a motor vehicle accident this year are more than one in 1,000,[1] and yet many of us mindlessly get into our cars and drive to work without giving much thought to our personal safety while on the roadways. For years Doug had a note taped to the dashboard of his patrol car that read, "this is the most dangerous thing you will do today: STAY ALERT," as a reminder of the risk that he was taking getting into his car. Herein is the first step to travel safety: acknowledge the risk. Once you are aware, you approach the challenge and any potential problems differently.

Let's start with the basic automobile travel rule: Fasten Your Seat Belt. It is amazing that even today, with irrefutable evidence, nearly one-half of all drivers (and passengers) do not wear seat belts while driving or riding in a motor vehicle. The excuses are as many and variable as there are deaths due to failing to buckle up: "it is uncomfortable;" "it is too restraining" (that's why they are called passenger restraints!); "it wrinkles my clothes;" "my car is equipped with airbags;" and Doug's favorite, "I don't want to get trapped inside my vehicle if I should happen to crash." In Doug's experience the most common cause of death in a car crash is being ejected from the vehicle. In 28 years of law enforcement experience he has never unbuckled a deceased person. Chances of serious injury or death increase dramatically when you travel in a motor vehicle without the use of a seat belt. Not only should you be concerned about securing yourself in the vehicle, if you are the driver you are also responsible for everyone in the car. This includes small children and infants who must sit in car or booster seats. All 50 states have child safety restraint laws, which are all slightly different and have different child restraint requirements. All states require that a child under 4 years old and 40 pounds be in certified safety restraints. Some states' requirements go as high as 8 years old and 80 pounds. If you travel often by car and cover several states your best choice is to find the most stringent state law and follow it. Remember that you are subject to the laws of the state who controls the road that you are traveling on. If you live in a state that has minimal child restraint laws, you may be out of compliance when traveling to another state. Regardless of the state standard you can never be wrong if you use the higher standard of safety, and your child might be safer because you did. Seat belts and car seats save lives. The statistics are compelling. ProChild safety seats reduce the risk of death in passenger cars by 71% for infants and by 54% for toddlers aged 1 to 4 years.[2] Properly installed car seats can save children's lives. The key words are "properly installed." Hospitals as well as fire stations in your community have programs available to check for proper installation and use of car seats.

Buckle up so that your kids see that safety is important to you, and get your kids to buckle into their car seats or buckle up in the vehicle's seat belt. At Jana's house, the car rule is "the car doesn't move until all seat belts are buckled." Jana reports that some days, when the child battle-factor is high, the parked car, running with the air conditioning working to cool down the car for the drive, has been turned off to wait for a child to "buckle-in." On this front, Ada County Sheriff Gary Raney says: "Wear a seat belt. You're far more apt to get hurt or killed in a car crash than you ever are by being assaulted." We won't belabor this one; you've likely heard, seen, and read the details on why wearing a seat belt is a good idea. Buckle up.

Most states require that you place children of child restraint age in the backseat of your car. The backseat is generally thought to be the safest place for a child under 12 years of age to sit. When putting young children in the backseat of your car, remember to get them out, because you can easily forget that they are back there. Leaving a child in your car can turn deadly. In the summer, temperatures inside an enclosed vehicle can reach easily reach 130°F to 180°F, and surprisingly, the outside temperature does not have to be much above 70°F for a child to be a risk of severe hyperthermia. Hyperthermia is the heating of the body's core temperature to 104°F or more, and a core temperature of 107°F is said to be lethal because irreparable damage is done to internal cells and organs. A small child's ability to cool down on his own is not as efficient as that of an adult, and their bodies warm at a rate three to five times faster. On a 90° day, temperatures in an enclosed car reach 115°F in less than 10 minutes and after an hour temperatures are above 135°F.

In the mid-1990s child restraint advocates began recommending putting children into the backseats of vehicles because of the problem that airbags posed to very young children. It is widely accepted that kids riding in the backseat of cars in approved child-restraint devices are safer when in an accident than when riding in the front seat. An unintended consequence of shifting children to the backseat has occurred. What has been noticed is that children's deaths due to hyperthermia from being left in cars have risen dramatically since 1998. Prior to this there were on average eleven hyperthermia deaths of children left in vehicles or who crawled back into an unattended vehicle. Since 1998 an average of thirty-six children dies every year in hot cars. The dramatic increase is attributed to the fact that when children are in the backseat, they are more likely to be forgotten by the caretaker. It is hard to believe that someone can forget the child that they are caring for, but according to research reported by the San Francisco State University, Department of Geosciences, 49% of the deaths of children who were left in vehicles was because they were forgotten in the backseat.[3] In today's society, everyone is in a hurry, overworked, and stressed out. The demand on our time is greater than ever before. Have you ever been so busy thinking while driving, about the many things that are demanding your time, that you missed a turn or drove someplace you never intended? Have you gone to the grocery store only to forget that you were just there, and upon arriving home left the groceries in the trunk or backseat of the car? No real damage occurs in these cases, if you don't count the ice cream that melted all over the backseat. The common denominator for people who accidentally leave kids in cars seems to be that they are very busy, stressed out professionals who were exhausted themselves, running on too little sleep, and something interrupted their routine on the day that tragedy struck. They are not malicious or even bad parents most of the time. On this day, the life they chose to live simply caught up with them, and tragedy followed.

Only eleven states have laws that directly address children left unattended in a vehicle. Most of the rest of the states are able to use child endangerment statutes to deal with those who leave a child in the vehicle. Either way these are very difficult cases to deal with. Some suggest that anyone who would leave a child unattended in a car should be charged with a felony, and if the child dies, life in prison is too good for them. Others argue that the unintentional act of leaving a child unattended in a vehicle and the child's either dying or being severely injured is enough punishment for the parent or caretaker. Although this may be true for those whose children are killed or injured, what about those who just leave the child for a minute to run into a store? The eleven states that have statutes that make this illegal are able to easily prosecute this offender. The jurisdiction that is depending on a child endangerment statute to fulfill the need may find proving that the child was in immediate danger by the action somewhat difficult. Twenty-seven percent of the children dying in hot cars are those who got into the car themselves and were unable to get back out.[4] Parents have to be proactive here; it is a simple matter to lock your vehicle when it is unattended. Not only will you eliminate the possibility of one of your children or a neighbor's child crawling into a hot car and dying, but you will also protect your vehicle from theft. The problem of children dying in hot cars is one that is increasing, and it will take a systemic response of increased education and legislation to impact the issue and reduce the problem. One child dying needlessly is one too many.

## AGGRESSIVE DRIVING OR ROAD RAGE

Aggressive driving and road rage are not the same thing. Aggressive driving can be defined as driving recklessly with disregard for traffic laws and other motorists. Aggressive driving incidents are normally relatively minor. However, they are a particular problem when they precipitate road rage. Road rage occurs when a driver becomes so infuriated with another driver that he commits serious criminal acts, often in a rage. Road rage may or may not start from an aggressive-driving incident. It does seem to be the case that many of the incidents begin when one party commits an aggressive-driving violation that is rude and thoughtless to those around him and violates the right-of-way of another. Road rage is a common occurrence on the nation's highways. The story below is becoming all too common. Although this event happened recently in a small town in Idaho, it is repeated hundreds of times across the nation. It apparently started in an argument over a parking space, and it ended with two people dead for no good reason. Here's the story.[5]

> Caldwell, Idaho. Thirty-year-old Jose Ramirez-Salas and his 13-year-old son Kevin had just gone to Wal-Mart to pick up a pizza and movie. As they were leaving the parking lot, two pedestrians blocked the roadway. Ramierz-Salas asked them several times to move out of the roadway and allow him to pass. The man, 23-year-old Jimmy Duncan, refused and stood his ground. Ramierz-Salas exited his vehicle and an argument that had started earlier continued. Duncan drew a handgun and shot Ramierz-Salas twice in the chest, killing him. Duncan was later confronted by police; he again produced the handgun and was killed by the officers. At the time of this writing there is no clear explanation as to what precipitated the event; it appears to have started over a parking space. What is clear is that if either one of the men involved in the dispute would have chosen not to engage the other, they probably would both be alive today.

Driving can be a very frustrating experience: you are late, you have an important appointment, and traffic is at a standstill. Someone cuts you off, there is an insulting hand gesture, and the next thing you know you are looking down the barrel of a .45. People become irrational when faced with the pressures of driving. The best thing you can do while behind the wheel of your vehicle is keep your cool. It is amazing how people choose to put themselves at risk by allowing their emotions to get away from them, becoming belligerent and aggressive behind the wheel of a car. When you allow this to happen, you place yourself at risk in several ways. First, when you lose control emotionally, you can expect to lose physical control, too. Second, you are inviting others to react to your out-of-control behavior. You may have just cut off and then flipped-off a person who in a worst-case scenario may be carrying a firearm and may decide that you are a likely target, or at best you run the risk of being punched out at the next stoplight.

Across the country the outcomes of the incidents are the same, although the event that started them may differ from place to place; for example, in Tampa, Florida, a 35-year-old woman was chased for miles down the freeway because her political bumper sticker infuriated a 31-year-old male, who chased her yelling and holding up his own political statement sign. In Alabama, a woman stood trial on murder charges after chasing another woman down the freeway after being cut off in rush hour traffic. She caught up to the woman and shot her. In Tennessee, a man was shot six times, twice at close range, when he pulled off the road after a road rage incident that began when he failed to signal a turn. In Wrightwood, California, state highway officials were forced to shut down a section of state highway 138, which they were trying to keep open during repairs, because of numerous incidents of angry, frustrated motorists injuring the highway construction workers who were trying to do their jobs. Other California communities are not exempt; in the San Francisco Bay area three occurrences of road rage occurred in the same week. First, according to police, a man was shot in the back after he tailgated the shooter and engaged in other unsafe driving practices. Next a motorcyclist was run down, severely beaten, and thrown into a ditch after a road rage incident, and finally, a motorist was clubbed and stabbed after a traffic disagreement.

Protecting yourself against aggressive drivers is simple; don't become one yourself, and be courteous. If you are polite and drive using common sense, you will not have to worry about being involved in a road rage incident. Here are a couple more tips that may help you avoid an incident. Don't use your horn in anger. Use your turn signal when making lane changes. Pass only on the left. Don't tailgate, and don't use your brakes as a message to drivers who may be tailgating you. Don't make obscene hand gestures. If you are following the safety rules of the road and are doing the most important things to stay safe while traveling to work, what else should you be doing?

Depending on who you are, you may want to consider changing your route to work occasionally. Being less predictable makes you less vulnerable. If you are a public or high-profile figure, this particularly applies because of the attention drawn to you because of your status. There are thieves who believe that, if they kidnap a public figure, they can demand a ransom or will simply drive them to a bank or ATM and empty their account. This kind of thief will do her homework. She will put you under surveillance and will depend on your predictability. Her plan will involve snatching you or a family member at a predetermined location. Vary your routes to your office. Not only will it make you less of a target, but you will get to know your community better. Doug knows many officers who vary their commute to work each day just as they vary their patrol pattern while on the beat. The whole purpose is to not become predictable and to keep the bad guy guessing. If they can't predict what your next move will be, you have given them just one more reason why they should select another target, one who will increase their odds of being successful in their criminal endeavor. Knowing alternate routes well will also help you in times of emergency if you should have to evacuate at a moment's notice or simply to get around a traffic problem on a particular day. These incidents are extremely rare, yet you can reduce your risk of being a target by taking these very simple precautions.

Doug has been asked about riding alone after dark and suddenly discovering what appears to be a police officer behind you who is trying to pull you over, but something just does not feel right. It may be a remote area or the light-bar configuration on the car does not seem right or it is an unmarked car. It is important to know that there are offenders out there who will impersonate an officer to get you to pull over and will try to either rob or assault you. There is a simple solution to this dilemma. Simply keep driving. Don't speed up or try to elude him. Continue driving, and head for the nearest populated, well-lit area that you can find. If this really is an officer, soon there will be many more of her friends joining her to find out why you haven't stopped. Then you will know that you are safe to pull over. When asked why you failed to yield, simply explain to the officers what your fear was, and they will understand. If no other officers show up shortly, your feelings were correct: the guy behind you is probably not an officer. Continue driving until he breaks off his pursuit. Once in a populated area he will not be likely to continue following you with lights on because the risks of being discovered are too great. Drive to the nearest police station, and report the incident immediately.

Be sure to stay current on all of the laws governing driving in your state. Some states have begun outlawing the use of cell phones while driving. States also have regulations about where you can pull over to change a flat tire. Still other states have laws about where cars can be parked until they can be towed. There also are laws against hitchhiking, which has real dangers: in short, don't do it and don't pick up hitchhikers. For more information about car travel safety equipment, see the appendixes.

## COMMERCIAL FLIGHT SAFETY

Today, flying is the most common way of moving from place to place over a distance. Because there are so many people flying on commercial flights these days, there are several things you should be aware of. First, since September 11, 2001, restrictions on what you can take onto an airplane has changed dramatically. Security is paramount to the aviation industry and to our national well-being. The Transportation Security Administration (TSA), a branch of Homeland Security, is responsible for aviation security in the United States. TSA regulations are dynamic and vary with the national threat level and in response to incidents worldwide. The best way to keep informed on the current rules at airports in this country is to visit the www.TSA.gov website prior to travel. This way you will always be current on what to expect when you arrive at the airport.

There are some things that you can do to make your air travel experience less stressful. If you have an electronic ticket, which virtually all domestic flights use, check in on the Internet prior to arriving at the airport. If you are checking luggage, you will still have to check in prior to going to the gate, but having checked in early takes away much of the pressure of getting a seat on the aircraft. Arrive early. Most airlines recommend two hours for international and an hour and a half for domestic flights. Some people who seem to pride themselves on cutting the time down to check in and get aboard their flight say: "I am too busy to spend my time sitting in airports." There is no rule that says you have to be there early; it is a recommendation. Other people have missed flights because they have not allowed adequate time to get through security. Giving yourself ample time to check in and get through security will help minimize the stress that is inherent with traveling by air. There are a few tricks to help you get smoothly through that security line. Number one, stay calm and relaxed; realize that you will be asked to do things that you may not like and that do not make a lot of sense to you. In order to get on your flight, you must pass through a security checkpoint. Regardless of how ridiculous or inept you may think it is, you must comply with their rules or you will not be allowed to pass. TSA takes this process very seriously; it is best to relax and do as you are asked.

Start before you approach the security check point by empting your pockets into your carry-on bag. Place anything with metal into your carry-on bag, for example, cell phone, wallet, etc. Have your government-issued identification ready for inspection. You will have to remove your shoes because they have to be x-rayed. Computers need to be out of the case for inspection as well. As you are being put through this exercise that seems to be endless, remember this is being done to make your travel safer. Keeping this in mind will make the experience a little easier to tolerate.

## HOTEL SAFETY

Hotels stake their reputation on the quality of your experience while on their property. They work diligently to be safe. They know that if their clients have a bad experience while with them, it can have a severe negative impact on their business. For safety's sake always request a room on an upper floor. The lower floor rooms are more vulnerable to street crimes. Once you have a room, make sure that you remain aware of what is happening around you and stay in tune with your surroundings. Doug recalls an incident while in Hawaii with his wife on a delayed honeymoon. They had just checked into their room, and with the excitement of finally being in a place to relax after traveling most of the night, they had not closed their room door securely. Doug's wife was out on the balcony overlooking a turquoise ocean, and Doug was marveling at the sound of the breakers hitting the beach; they were in paradise. He turned around to find a man standing in the room. He was dressed like an islander in a casual Hawaiian shirt and white slacks. Doug caught his breath and assessed the situation. Doug wasn't a lot bigger than the man, and he figured he could probably knock the man down and make it to the hallway to yell for help, but that would leave his wife in the room with this stranger. Doug hesitated as the stranger reached into his pocket and wondered how he could have been so stupid as to leave the door ajar; now he was going to be robbed. The man brought out a wallet containing a badge. "Hotel security," he said. "I noticed your door ajar as I was walking down the hallway so I came in. Easy wasn't it? Please make sure that the door securely closes behind you and then be sure to lock both locks. We don't often have problems here with thieves or muggers, but when we do it is because someone just didn't check their door behind them. I hope you enjoy your stay with us, *mahalo*." With that he turned and left, and Doug started breathing again.

Doug learned a valuable lesson that day, one that he thinks of every time he enters a hotel room. Close and lock the door! The rules of being safe don't change on the road. It is just as important to make yourself less of a target, to make it more difficult for the bad guy to get to you. When you do this you are lowering the odds that you will be a victim of crime. Stay alert to what is happening around you. Traveling can be a very disorienting affair: you are in a strange place; you are tired, two or more time zones away from home, and it is easy to let your guard down. Resist this temptation. This is what a thief is counting on. Blurry-eyed travelers who are not paying attention to what is happening around them are easy targets. Once in your room, take stock of your surroundings. It is important to know how to get in and out of your room in case of emergency. After you have settled into your room, take the time to familiarize yourself with your surroundings. Start by looking at the hotel's information book. Look at the floor plan for the floor you are staying on if it is available. Locate the nearest exits. Next, take a walk out of your room. Can you see the nearest exit? If so, is it on the same side of the hallway as your room or the opposite? In either case count the number of doorways between your room and the exit, and make note of this number. This exit will be a stairwell. This becomes important if there is a fire in the hotel and the hallway fills with smoke.

If you are asleep and hear the fire alarms sound and smell smoke, you know how to get out. Check your door. Is it hot? If not, you can open it. If you open your door and find the hallway filled with smoke, drop to your hands and knees; the air will be clearer there. Go to the side of hallway the exit is on and begin crawling toward it. Count the doors as you go by each room. Because you have counted previously, you know when you are at the stairway exit, even if the smoke is so thick that you cannot see the exit sign. Go through the stairway exit door and proceed out of the hotel to safety. On a recent trip to Salt Lake City, Jana found herself in an older hotel that had outdoor hallways, a slow elevator, no escape route maps in the room, and unmarked stairwells. She spent time locating the stairwells in the three-story building and found them only after talking to a couple also staying on the second floor.

Hotels also have a system of locks on doors that you need to make yourself familiar with. Whether your entry is with a key or a computerized keycard, the first lock is the one built into the door and doorknob. The second lock is often a deadbolt that you are responsible for turning, and a third lock (sometimes only the second) is typically the chain or flip bar that you slide or swing into place to prevent the door from opening easily if the first two locks are defeated. Be sure to use all the locks on your door. Also, be sure you can undo them quickly in the event of a fire.

Contrary to what you have seen on television or in the movies, fire is not likely to chase you down and burn you to death. It is normally the byproducts of fire that will kill you: super-heated fire gases (smoke) and panic will almost always be the cause of death in a fire. This is very important: you must know how to avoid smoke and panic to survive a hotel fire, because the fire may not reach your location. When exiting down a stairway, beware of the phenomenon of stacked smoke.[6] This occurs in escape stairwells, because as the smoke cools, it seeks this level. The smoke from the fire will stack up at a particular level in the stairwell. If you run into stacked smoke, you know two things: that someone left a stairway door open and that you now have to turn around and go up. Do not go through the stacked smoke; the smoke may be so thick that it will overcome you and you will not be able to make it completely through it before being overcome. Continue up the stairs to the roof; when exiting onto the roof, be sure to block the roof door open in case you should have to retreat back down the stairs; proceed to the windward side of the roof top, sit down, and wait for firemen to arrive.

Hotel safety includes being prepared for the event of a fire, room safety, and personal safety. For instance, travelers are easy targets for pickpockets. In larger cities with high volumes of pedestrian traffic pick-pocketing is a very common form of street crime. It is particularly prevalent in large international cities. Pickpockets often work in teams and are very practiced at their craft. Take great care to carry your values securely on your person. Do not carry large amounts of cash on you if you can avoid it. Place what you will not need for your immediate excursion in your room or hotel safe. This way if you are targeted, your entire trip will not be ruined.

A cruder form of pick-pocketing is purse snatching. In these cases the assailant merely grabs a woman's purse or other items that may be carried on the outside of clothing and with the use of force takes it and runs off with it. These thieves often work in groups as well, passing the purse from one to another like part of a shell game to create confusion on where the valuables went, making it more difficult for those pursuing to catch them with the goods. Purse snatching is best prevented by carrying your purse or any other item very securely close to your body. Keep both of your hands tightly on your purse. If it is obviously secure, you are less likely to become a target.

## CABS AND PUBLIC TRANSPORTATION

Metropolitan cities around the world have established transportation rules that are often posted in airports. Pay attention to these rules because they are meant to protect travelers. Especially watch for signs saying, "Only use cabs that are in the queue and that have a city license posted." This is a huge warning to "be careful of all others." So, be careful what pathways you are on and which vehicle you get into. Use only designated waiting areas for transportation. Make sure that other people are around. Beware of the individual who confronts you while you are making your way to the cab stands and offers to take you to your destination at a reduced rate. Chances are very good that they are not a licensed vendor, and you may get a ride that you had not anticipated. You will find that many of these are van shuttles and will be quite full; you may get a tour of the city that you didn't want while en route to your stop.

When Doug travels, he likes to use public transportation where possible. He wants to experience the community to which he has traveled and has found that using public transportation allows him to experience the community in a way that driving a rental car does not. In some of the major cities of the world public transportation is an interesting adventure. If you chose to use public transportation, be sure you are prepared. Be ready to walk. Some places are better than others, but you generally have to walk several blocks regardless of where you are. Control your belongings; make sure you are not carrying so much that you can't keep track of them, which screams, "I'm a tourist and I'm a target." Be confident in what you are doing; if you become lost or confused, find an employee of the system that you are using, and they will help you out. Be on your guard; in many of the systems around the country you will find many helpful people. While many are just that, this is a ploy some would-be thieves use to test the waters for an easy mark. If you appear lost, confused, or disoriented, they may move in on you. If a stranger asks you if you need help, tell them confidently "no, thank you" and act as if this is an everyday excursion for you, even if you have never been there in your life.

Protect your property while riding on subways, trains, or buses by keeping a hand on anything you are carrying. Leaving a bag unattended is an invitation for a thief to make it their own. Doug routinely carries his wallet in his front pocket. It is much more difficult for a pickpocket to remove it from a front pocket, although one might still try. Doug recalls walking on a crowed street in a major city when he was bumped hard on his left side. Something flashed in his mind: "bump and grab," an approach he had learned about in a street crimes class sometime during his career. This is when two pickpockets work in tandem: one bumps you to distract you from one side and the pick gets you from the other side. On trained instinct, Doug reached for his wallet on his right side and found a man's hand going into his pocket. Doug grabbed the man's hand and, without thinking, put him into a wrist lock. The now partially trapped man pulled a knife. Doug came to his senses, released the would-be thief, and pushed him away. The good citizens of the city intervened at this time and stepped between Doug and the armed man. The thief turned and ran. Doug's wallet was still in *his* pocket. He never felt the pick. He was lucky; they are very good at their craft. Doug is particularly grateful to the everyday people of the city who came to his aid. We so often hear of people not getting involved when they see a street crime happening. Doug's experience has been just the opposite; there are good people everywhere who will not tolerate bad behavior in their community. Times like this certainly restore our faith in the human condition.

Always know your route and destination before pursuing and using public transportation. You want to know that you are headed safely in the right direction. And as you select various modes of public transportation, know what the safety rules are for each, such as not standing too close to train tracks, standing clear of dangerous intersections, doorways, and openings, and so on.

## WILDERNESS TRAVEL AND RECREATION

Both Jana and Doug enjoy camping, hiking, and backpacking in the outdoors. These activities have become increasingly popular since the 1980s. They are fun, relaxing, adventurous, and also inherently dangerous. Wilderness dangers include injury, wild animal attacks, weather changes, terrain changes, and running into less-than-friendly people on the way. The majority of people like to enjoy these opportunities with others. Although Doug usually finds someone to join him on his wilderness treks, occasionally he has gone solo. Here is what Doug says about solo backpacking.

One thing I realize when I am out on my own is that I cannot afford to take any chances. I am very conservative when hiking alone. I stop and consider the risk of every action. A simple stream crossing is now coupled with, what happens if I go down and end up in the water; can I get myself out? I find myself double checking every maneuver. When lighting the backpacking stove, I ask myself whether it is going to blow up in my face. When hiking on exposed ridges, I consider whether rocks are loose and whether I could get pinned. What is the weather like, and is there lightening in the area? If you have a partner with you, caution is still important, but not nearly as critical as when you are by yourself.

Whether you are solo camping or are with a group, be sure to leave your planned route and itinerary with someone who will be willing to notify authorities if you are not back on time. Know the trail system that you will be visiting. What condition is it in? Learn whether it is well used and well marked. Discover whether it is passable or whether there will be snow in the higher elevations and on the north-facing slopes. Be sure to have detailed maps of the area you are traveling in. Carry a compass or GPS. The new GPS systems available today make locating yourself on a map very easy and will ensure that you do not get onto a trail or into an area that you did not intend to visit. Also carry a well-stocked first aid kit with you. At very least this should contain Band-Aids, gauze pads, tape, first aide cream for burns, tough skin or new skin for blisters, sunscreen, and bug repellant. Emergency waterproof matches are a must to have in case you experience wet weather and need to get a fire started to dry out.

When traveling in the wilderness it is important to have a good water source for drinking and cooking. Even though the streams and lakes look clear and clean, you take a big chance drinking unfiltered water, even in wilderness areas. Bacteria and parasites can be found in the most remote pristine waters. Backpacking water filters are available to ensure that you have a potable water source. You should be carrying one.

When leaving vehicles at the trailheads, be sure to park them properly out of the way. It is not uncommon for trailhead parking to be quite limited; leave as much room as possible for others to park as well. Do not leave items that will attract attention of thieves in plain view. Lock your valuables in the trunk of your car. Lock your passenger compartment. Make sure others in your party know where you are carrying the key in case you should become injured or lost so they will know where to find the key and be able to go for help. While vehicle burglaries and vandalism are rare at these locations, they do happen on occasion. Taking the above precautions will reduce the likelihood of becoming a trailhead target.

Planning and packing correctly for your trip contributes to the safety of your adventure. Jana recalls a winter adventure with a friend who had just been given doctor's approval to go backpacking after a recent illness. Her concern was about whether an injury would incapacitate the friend and whether she'd have to get both of them out on her own. So, Jana's plan and packing included a small sled that could be used to carry gear into the snow camp and that could be used to get her friend out in the event of a medical emergency. Fortunately, good health prevailed during the two-night adventure, and no emergency plans had to be put into action.

## INTERNATIONAL TRAVEL

Traveling internationally whether for pleasure or business is an adventure for most people. There are those who spend so much time traveling out of the country that it becomes quite tedious. However for most of us it is still an adventure. When traveling internationally it is critical to prepare carefully. Begin by researching where you are going. What is the culture like, what will the weather likely be like, and what is the current state of affairs for the country you are going to visit? Is there political turmoil that you need to be aware of? What is the system of currency, and what is the exchange rate? Becoming very familiar with where you going will make the experience much more enjoyable. A little time preparing will make the streets and your trip a lot more even.

Be sure you have all of the proper travel documents. You will need a current passport. When traveling into Canada and Mexico a passport is now required. Do you have proper travel and work visas? It is important to check on visas well before you plan on traveling. Depending on the country, they can take quite some time to secure. Make copies of all of your travel documents and credit cards and store them in a bag that is separate from the originals. The copies will be helpful to you if the originals are lost or stolen.

Once in the country be prepared for life to be different from what you are accustomed to. The authors have visited countries where a change in culture and perceived safety concerns were hardly noticeable; other than language or accents differences, it was not apparent that they were in foreign countries. Other times it was like stepping onto the moon, and things were very different. Be prepared to watch and learn; after all, this is why you came, isn't it?

Depending on where in the world you are going, you may want to purchase some kind of emergency travel medical and extraction policy. This is useful if you should become injured or sick and need to get to reliable medical facilities rapidly. It is also helpful should some kind of political event occur that would make the country unsafe and conventional travel options are reduced. There are several companies that provide this service (see Appendix 4, www.worldtravelcenter.com) for reasonable rates. If you find yourself in need of emergency evacuation, they will come and get you. This was recently the case when a group of foreign students was studying in Lebanon as fighting broke out with Israel. Those students with evacuation insurance were able to get out much sooner than those who did not have it.

Whether you are traveling across the state or around the world there are basic common sense rules that you should follow. If you do, you will be rewarded with all the adventure and wonder of seeing new sights and having new experiences that you have dreamed of. If you don't, you may be in for a nightmare (such as loss of property or even jail time) that you never planned. Traveling involves careful planning. Careful planning means you will be prepared. Being prepared will ensure your travel experience will be a good one. Your safety whether in a car, bus, or airplane depends on deciding to take your destiny into your own hands and reducing your risks. Follow the "Plan for Travel Safety" below.

## PLAN FOR TRAVEL SAFETY

1. Learn multiple routes for your daily commute.
2. For every trip you make, know how and where you can stop to get help.
3. Check the www.TSA.gov website for alerts and updates before traveling.
4. Travel with your identification and money in a safe place.
5. Always find the stairways and exits when staying in a hotel.
6. Use only licensed and clearly registered cabs and public transit systems.
7. Use car seats and passenger restraints every time you ride in a vehicle, no matter how far you are going.
8. When traveling in the wilderness, be prepared for injuries, animal attacks, and bad weather that can force you to change your route to safety.

9. When traveling internationally obtain Emergency Evacuation Insurance.
10. No matter where you go or how you get there, let someone know your plan.

## NOTES

1. The Disaster Center's Motor Vehicle Accident Death and Injury Data Index; http//www.disastercenter.com/traffic (accessed August 20, 2007).

2. U.S. Department of Transportation, National Highway Traffic Safety Administration (NHTSA), Traffic Safety Facts 2005: Children. Washington, DC: NHTSA; 2006. http://www-nrd.nhtsa.dot.gov/pdf/nrd-30/NCSA/TSF2005/Children TSF05.pdf (accessed December 7, 2006).

3. Jan Null, "Heat Stress from Enclosed Vehicles: Moderate Ambient Temperatures Cause Significant Temperature Rise in Enclosed Vehicles," *Pediatrics* 116 (2005): 109–12.

4. Ibid.

5. Kristin Rodine, "Minor Dispute Leads to Two Deaths," *The Idaho Statesman*, July 21, 2007.

6. Chris E. McGoey, Hotel Motel Security: Safety Advice for Travelers, http//www.crimedoctor.com/hotel.htm/ (accessed May 9, 2007).

# Four

# Family Safety at Home

Whether you are a single person living alone, a single parent with kids living at home, a parent with no more kids at home or a part of a couple with or without kids living at home, family safety is important to you because at the very least you have yourself to take care of, because your "family at large" wants you to be safe. A family at large includes your blood relatives, your friends, your coworkers, and the people in your social circles. And whether you live in a gated subdivision, a secured high-rise condominium, an apartment complex, or an unsecured neighborhood, there are still things you need to do to be as safe as possible at home. If you will, your home is the place you sleep. It may or may not be the place you spend the most amount of your time. In fact, you may spend so little time there that others don't even know you live there. The point is that the building in which you sleep, eat some meals, and possibly interact with family and friends is your residence or home.

When it comes to being safe at home, there is building safety as well as family member and visitor safety. Starting with building safety and preventing crime there are fairly obvious improvements, such as better lighting around your doorways, and less obvious ones, such as improving the locking mechanisms on sliding glass doors and on windows that you may leave open overnight. Family member and visitor safety includes the adaptations you make to the physical structure of your home as well as the rules you have in place for protecting people whether they are at your home or someone else's or at a school function. For instance, teaching your children not to answer the door or the phone when you are not home is a family safety rule. Another is "no sleepovers unless the parents are home." Yet another is "no drinking until you are of legal age." Without clear rules for safety, danger is more likely to strike you or your children.

## SAD BUT TRUE—REAL STATISTICS AND STORIES

There are adults who will abuse, exploit, and neglect children in their own homes. Children are most at risk in their own home. Their likelihood of being injured neglected or abused at the hand of a caretaker is 12.1 per 1,000 nationally.[1] Before we can even think about keeping children safe from the hand of a stranger, first we must find ways to protect them from the very ones whose job it is to ensure their safety. The drug epidemic in this country has always taken its toll on children. In the 1980s and 1990s it was crack babies; in the 21st century it is children being born addicted to methamphetamine. The nightmare only starts there.

Children living in the home of parents addicted to methamphetamine have little or no chance of experiencing the safety that a home should bring them. The drug becomes the major focus of the user. Any children on the scene now take a backseat to its use. Very young children are left to fend for themselves in homes that are in complete disarray. Filthy is a gentle way of describing the conditions that so many children are forced to live in. As an example of how many people are affected by a single crime, here is a story from a detective who works child neglect cases and has found living conditions so deplorable that action has to be taken on behalf of the children. This is not a rare case and this is not a third world country story. It is a story from here in the United States of America and it is happening, over and over throughout the country every day. The names and details have been adjusted to protect the real people involved.

Upon arrival at the address we had to drive quite a distance off of Anderson Road, down a long driveway to access a number of buildings and at the end of the lane there was an electric wire fence blocking any further entrance. We had to walk into the property by stepping over the electric wire. The first thing I noticed when leaving my car was the overwhelming stench of garbage and decay. I had smelled farms in the past, but this smell was not just from animals or farming. It smelled like a landfill or garbage dump.

I could see an abundance of trash, garbage, household items, numerous "junk yard" items scattered throughout the property. It took us approximately 3–5 minutes to determine which building was actually the house and then because of the appearance of the house, I was not sure anyone would really be living in it. There were two goats and a dog in separate cages in the front yard of what we determined to be the house. The front porches of the house were littered with mattresses, discarded household items, a refrigerator and garbage. I went around to the back of the house and noticed through an open downstairs window, a female sitting on a bed. I identified myself and asked her if she was "Jackie Oldham." She affirmed she was Jackie. I identified myself as a detective with the County Sheriff's Office and that Health and Welfare's Child Protective Services was with me, and we needed to speak to her about her children. Jackie requested we wait outside while she got dressed. A dog jumped out of the open window to the outside where we were. Soon Jackie and another large dog came out the back door.

Jackie then took us into the house. The house was littered with garbage, discarded items, clothing, and dog and cat feces. There was so much trash and garbage that the obnoxious and nausea smell was overwhelming. I could not catch my breath and could not decide if the outside or the inside of the house smelled worse. The smell was a combination of rotting garbage, animal feces and urine, and everything else imaginable discarded throughout the house. The floors appeared to not have ever been swept or cleaned. There was some carpet in areas of the house, but it was stained and worn and difficult to distinguish that it was carpet.

The two bedrooms on the main level where the two older girls slept were littered with discarded items, clothing, food, animal feces and urine. There were a number of new puppies in the bedrooms and a cat came outside of one of the bedrooms when the door was opened. (Jackie thought there were about four puppies, three adult dogs, and all but one dog was allowed to wander freely in and out of the house) There were ants crawling around all over the floor of one of the bedrooms. You could not walk inside of the bedrooms without walking on top of all the items or the animal feces that was fresh and old. The bathroom was in similar condition. There was mold growing up the walls. The plumbing was exposed in the bathtub area. The toilet and sink appeared to not have been cleaned in a quite a long time, though the bathtub was relatively clean inside and free of objects.

The main living area was cluttered with garbage, household items that had just been discarded any and everywhere. There were chickens inside a dog cage in the living area. There were two aquariums containing lizards, frog, and a mouse all that had been caught inside of the house. Jackie said the lizards and frog came in through the open window and the mouse was one of the three to four they would catch on a daily basis inside of the house. Jackie stressed that they catch the "critters" in humane traps so they do not get hurt and that was why they were able to keep the one mouse. The ceiling had a large leak from the roof and was hanging down and falling open. The corners of the floor were covered with large amounts of mice droppings.

The kitchen was filthy, and the counters, sink, stove, and cupboards were all dirty and caked with built up grease and dirt. Jackie said that there was no use in cleaning the counters because the mice just continually were on it and it never would stay clean. Jackie stated they kept the majority of their dry foods in the microwave because it was the only area where the mice could not get to the food. There were gallons of sour milk on the floor near the kitchen/hall area. Jackie stated the milk was for the farm animals. There were two small refrigerators, compact size, one for the family and one for the farm animal items. The refrigerator for the family had rotting food in it and when it was opened I started to "gag" because of the terrible smell. Jackie stated there was rotting lettuce in the refrigerator but she had not thrown it out because Mike would never take the garbage out and the dogs would just get into it.

When Health and Welfare asked about going to the downstairs area, Jackie said, "I wouldn't recommend it, but you can go down there." She continued to explain that they had had a huge water problem after buying the house and the bathroom downstairs had "bottomed out" which caused a lot of damage to the basement. Jackie described the basement as "horrible down there; musky." She said that was one of the reasons for moving the laundry room to the out building.

Downstairs were where Jackie and Mike had their own two rooms. Jackie's room had a very small path leading to her bed. There were food, clothing, household items and garbage everywhere. Jackie pointed to a hanging area behind a pile of furniture and items and said that was where the children's clothes were kept. I was hardly able to see the hanging area to photograph it. The main source of heat was a wood stove in the bedroom, but it was totally covered with items.

I was not able to get to Mike's room, but Health and Welfare went into it and they described it as in the same condition as the rest of the house. They said there was a gun lying against the wall, unsecured, but Jackie had told them it was not loaded. The room was filled with cobwebs and was very dirty, musky and smelly. Mike also had chickens in a cage in his room.

Jackie stated the "house was a disaster area" but there were reasons. Jackie defended the odor of the house as "living on a dairy farm" and that it was natural. Later in our conversation, Jackie said she did understand about the health concerns for the children as well as them because of the deplorable living conditions.

The absolute squalor that so many children are forced to live in is becoming epidemic. Filthy living conditions are only the beginning. Drug-addicted parents are unable to provide any of the necessities of life for their children. Food is often scarce or nonexistent, and clothing is dirty and limited. Saddest of all, love and nurturing does not take place. Who takes on the task of protecting these children when the parents are no longer willing? A three-year-old living with meth-addicted parents cannot be expected to be responsible for her own safety. So the responsibility falls onto the community to step forward and protect the vulnerable.

The stopgap for these children are individuals who are willing to open up their homes and give them some stability if only temporarily. The foster care system in our country is in need of quality people to step up and give shelter to abused and neglected children. If you are interested in becoming a foster parent you can contact the Child Protection Services (CPS) in your state. In some states this will be the Department of Health and Welfare or perhaps Health and Human Services. At the state agency contact the coordinator for foster care services. This person will tell you the requirements and training required to be a foster parent. By providing a safe, stable home environment you can directly impact the life of a child. CPS and law enforcement will continue to provide emergency protection for neglected and abused kids. Child abuse and neglect laws need to continue to be strengthened. Mandatory reporting needs to be just that, mandatory. Too many loopholes exist, leaving children at risk. The rights of individuals have to be balanced with serving the best interests of children.

## HARDENING YOUR HOUSE AND YOUR FAMILY

For most people, their house is their largest asset. For others it is a car or these days a television or video-game/media system. The point is that everyone has property that is an investment to be protected. In order to keep your property safe, there are a variety of approaches from which to choose. For instance, you can put a locked fence around your property, bar your windows and doors, put a security system in, and have guard dogs in the yard. However, this is not a typical neighborhood-friendly approach to securing your property.

Ada County Sheriff Gary Raney has 25 years of law enforcement experience and makes these suggestions for keeping yourself and your family safe: "Be aware of your surroundings; avoid giving criminals opportunity. Victims become victims because there is an opportunity to take advantage of them or because they are targeted. However, when someone is targeted, it is because they're perceived as an opportunity, just one that the criminal has to wait for. Therefore, the key to safety is not to be a person of opportunity to a criminal. Isolation is opportunity; witnesses can prevent crime. Weakness is opportunity: self-confidence is not. Poor security is opportunity: locked doors and adequate lights are deterrents. Freely sharing information is opportunity: be protective of your personal information and affairs whether it is on the Internet, the telephone, or at the grocery store." Raney, a parent himself, goes on to say that one of the best ways to keep your children safe is "to teach and empower them to tell a stranger 'no.' As a parent, be wary of adults who seem to socialize better with children than they do with other adults or who seem to draw children into settings where they are alone." As sheriff, Raney's duties include a variety of statutory obligations, including law enforcement patrols, waterways patrols, sex offender monitoring, issuing drivers' licenses, and operating the Ada County Jail that holds well over one thousand inmates. In addition, by cooperative agreement he runs a consolidated emergency dispatch center that serves twelve different public safety agencies, the main information storage and sharing system in the county, the Metro SWAT Team, and Metro Narcotics Team as well as a number of other criminal justice services.

## KEEPING YOURSELF SAFE AT HOME

Here, too, there are a variety of approaches from which to choose. Know your neighbors, and pursue disaster training in your building, complex, or neighborhood to be as prepared as possible for earthquakes, tornadoes, hurricanes, floods, disasters, and emergencies. Participate in annual block parties. When traveling, be sure it still looks like you are home. Have the grass and plants watered, the lawn mowed, and the papers and mail picked up daily. Even newspaper headlines include discussions of home security and suggestions to use more than alarm systems to baffle burglars. Start by using your common sense: lock your windows and doors, and don't leave ladders outside where they can be used to access your house. In addition to keeping your property safe, you of course want to keep yourself, family members, and visitors safe. Install solid doors and good deadbolt locks. Exterior storm doors provide an additional layer of defense as they can be locked as well, and more importantly you can stand on the inside of a locked door and talk to individuals outside without giving them access to you. As discussed in Chapter 2, adding good locks to your residence reduces your profile as a target.

Install and use bright lights by your entry doors. Although the majority of burglaries occur during the day, nighttime residential burglars prefer the dark, where they can break in unnoticed by neighbors or other passersby. Lights can be light sensitive, motion detector, or traditional-type fixtures. Also, use a series of timers on lights in your house so that it always looks like someone is home. The next time you come home for the night and you start to put your keys away, think of this: It's a security alarm system that you probably already have and requires no installation. Test it. It will go off from most everywhere inside your house and will keep honking until your battery runs down or until you reset it with the button on the key fob chain. It works if you park in your driveway or garage. Put your car keys beside your bed at night. If you hear a noise outside your home or someone trying to get in your house, just press the panic button for your car. The alarm will be set off, and the horn will continue to sound until either you turn it off or the car battery dies. This tip came from a neighborhood watch coordinator. If your car alarm goes off when someone is trying to break in your house, odds are the burglar or rapist won't stick around. After a few seconds all the neighbors will be looking out their windows to see who is out there, and sure enough the criminal won't want that. Remember to carry your keys while walking to your car in a parking lot. The alarm can work the same way there. Having the alarm go off could save a life, prevent a robbery, or prevent a sexual abuse crime.

Based on the variety of a colleague's work, military, and business experiences, Jana Kemp interviewed Rebecca Evans, who is a decorated Gulf War veteran, author, empowerment coach, speaker, and fitness expert. She resides in Idaho with her husband, three sons, and a Newfoundland. Evans provides the following personal and family safety tips and insights, in her own words. "Based on my military experience as a Gulf War veteran and extensive world traveler, I have learned the skill of survival in many countries and many circumstances. First, be aware of your surroundings. In the military, we use the phrase, 'check your six o'clock,' which means to know what is going on behind you at all times. You need to know the scene and the players so you can respond quickly and appropriately. You can't do this if you waltz through life with blinders on looking only straight ahead."

Evans is also a mother and says: "As a mother with three children, all with special medical needs, my first obligation has been to keep them alive, through surgeries and daily life. You simply cannot be too safe. Add all the safety features in your house for prevention—plug-ins, removing stove knobs, bed rails, locks, etc. You can prevent many injuries by simply walking through your house. Fire departments offer safety checks of your home and car seat checks as well. Buckle your kids into their car seats or into the car. Always. This is not an option. If your child needs to be in a car seat, make sure the seat is properly installed—again a free service offered through most fire departments. If your child is under the age of ten or the seat belt pulls directly under his/her chin, use a booster. Many parents feel that if their child is old enough, they don't need a booster. The fact is, if you have to stop suddenly, you could break your child's neck because of the ill-fitting seat belt designed for an adult.

## IDENTIFICATION KITS—KIDS AND PROPERTY

Have current photographs and descriptions of your children on hand, in the event that you need to describe a child to law enforcement for any reason. Have a video or a photo collection of your valuables and the contents of your home, in the event that your house is broken into. Work with your local law enforcement agencies to discover what property protection programs are in place. Programs range from Neighborhood Watch to marking property to safety surveys and are well worth the time invested in learning and hardening your family and home targets. Here are a series of tips from the Boise Police Department Crime Prevention team and Officer Curt Crum.

Take time to teach your children safety rules in a way that they can understand. For example, "Look both ways for cars before you cross the street. Only cross when no cars are coming and you are safe." Build a family safety plan. Be observant about what your family members look like and what they are wearing on any given day. Some parents recommend dressing children in similar outfits or matching colors so that if one child goes missing, they can look to the other child to remember what the missing child was wearing. Use check-in procedures so that all family members know where other family members are at all times. Learn what a Block Home (a house designated as having safe adults who are willing to help children in the event of an emergency) is and how to establish one in your neighborhood. Take a safety walk with your children so that they know how to get out of your house and how to find help in the neighborhood. Teach your children their full name, address, and telephone number. Teach your children how, why, and when to call 911. Make sure your child knows the difference between a stranger and a friend and knows what to do when approached by a stranger (get away and go to a known adult or to a known safe house). Teach your children that just because someone knows his or her name, that doesn't mean the person knows you or is safe. Make sure you know all of the routes your children take to get to and from school and with whom they go. Meet your neighbors. Make a list of your children's friends' names and parents' names and telephone numbers. Monitor the amount of time your children spend on the Internet and with whom they are communicating.

## NEIGHBORHOOD WATCH

One way to keep your home safe is to participate, along with your neighbors, in a program such as Neighborhood Watch. The national program began in 1972 to organize citizens to work with law enforcement in order to keep an eye on their communities and to prevent neighborhood crime and make communities safer. Sponsored by the National Sheriffs' Association, Neighborhood Watch reduces opportunities for crime to occur. The main ideas of Neighborhood Watch are to know your neighbors and watch for suspicious activity or circumstances. Jana has helped form two block watch programs. In Minnesota, a neighborhood without an association was experiencing an increase of speeding along school routes, so Jana worked with the local police department to find out what could be done. A police officer met with about fifteen neighbors at the local school and talked about Neighborhood Watch and how it could help. Among the things learned were how to better secure houses, how to watch for suspicious activities, and how to slow traffic on the school route. Then, in Idaho, Jana worked within an association environment to create block captains in her thirty-home portion of the larger subdivision. Contact and phone lists were created that included whether neighbors had children and pets. Annual neighborhood picnics are held to be sure that people know who lives in the area, and the "no burglar" Neighborhood Watch signs are erected on the main streets of the nearly 200-home neighborhood.

## AMBER ALERT PROGRAM

Don't give away information about your kids and your family. For instance, both Doug and Jana have noticed how much information people give away on their vehicles. Custom license plates such as "My6Boys" or "4MyGrls" or "8GrtKds" provide information to a stalker, a kidnapper, or a child molester.

And the in-fashion stickers of family members and pets, allow a criminal to approach both adults and children with messages such as "I think I found your dog; do you want to come with me to get it?" or "Your little brother has been in an accident and your mom asked me to come pick you up and meet them at the hospital." These visuals definitely provide information a would-be criminal can use to lure you away from your kids or your kids away from you. Other ways that your family may be unwittingly giving away information is via your teenagers who are online in chat rooms and on social-networking sites. Every piece of information the teen gives about himself or her cheerleading squad, debate team, or band trip, and your family provides a would-be thief or a would-be child molester with information about whether your child and your family are a good target.

Nationally recognized, the Amber Alert program is helpful before and once a crime that takes a child away from you has occurred. For instance, the Project Safe Childhood program is focused on preventing online and technology-based crimes against children. For more information visit their website, www.ambera lert.gov, and gather information about how the program works and which arms of law enforcement are involved.

## MONITOR MEDIA

During the 1970s, concern began to rise about the media's effect on behavior. Study after study suggests that what people watch affects their behaviors, their attitudes, and their health. Shortly after the advent of "cable television" came the introduction of "parental controls" over what channels the kids could view. For instance, Teenage Mutant Ninja Turtles during the 1980s appeared in comic book, television series, and movie formats and is said to have changed preschool behavior into a more fight-oriented set of behaviors. Teachers could trend the more violent behavioral change and track it back to these fighting characters. Then came computers and the Internet, posing even greater threats to child safety and to effective parental monitoring. Of course there are now also a host of tools for monitoring what your kids do on the computer and on the Internet.

As a parent the most effective tool for keeping your child safe from a computer predator is to know what your child is doing on the computer. Observe them when they are using the computer, what sites do they visit, who are they chatting with, and what kind of information are they exchanging. The easiest way to do this is to put the computer they use in a common area that they can easily observe. Your child may protest on rights of privacy issues; however, things done on the computer do not need to be private. Your goal is keeping them safe.

## INTERNET SAFETY AT HOME

A June 14, 2007, headline in the *Wall Street Journal* reads, "You Have Weapons in Your Computer to Monitor Your Kids." As early as 2005 and 2006, when the popularity of social-networking sites was at the beginning of its rise, law enforcement and attorney generals' offices began training and warning programs about the dangers of the sites. Kids give away so much information that a criminal predator or an ordinary teenage stalker can find your child, you, your house, and your child's school and extracurricular activities. This is *not* okay. In fact, Internet crimes have become so prevalent that many police and sheriff departments now have detectives who specialize in solving computer-related crimes. Places like MySpace and other online meeting places have become a haven for pedophiles and other child abusers to meet and stalk children. Children unwittingly put themselves at risk by putting seemingly innocent information, including pictures and demographic data, on these sites, which invite criminals into their home.

## GPS TRACKING OF YOUR KIDS

Some adults like the idea of being able to keep tabs on their kids via technology; other adults still aren't too sure. The point is to know that you have this option. GPS units can be installed in cars that you and your kids drive so that you can track their whereabouts in the car via your computer. Some cell phones now offer GPS tracking capabilities (if you pay for the right phone and the service) that you also tap into via your computer. When you give a phone to a kid, the chances of finding the kid without the phone in hand are slim, which means the chance of finding your child is improved.

## CRIMES AGAINST CHILDREN

Over the last two decades, most reports indicate that crimes against children have declined. For instance, according to the U.S. Justice Department statistics, juvenile homicide (murder) rates have dropped by 50% since 1993, and according to the National Child Abuse and Neglect Data System, substantiated cases of childhood sexual abuse have declined by 49%. According to the National Crime Victimization Survey, sexual assaults against adolescents have dropped by 67%, aggravated assaults by 74%, and robbery by 72%. Additionally reported is that fewer children are living in poverty today and that the rates of teen pregnancy and suicide have declined as well.

In some states bullying has been established in law, meaning that children bullying children can be prosecuted as a crime. Typically when law enforcement agencies speak of crimes against children, they are referring to kidnappings. Rather than focusing on all of the alarming and horrible statistics, let's focus on what you can do to prevent crimes against your children.

## KIDS HOME ALONE

In today's world children home alone are a fact of life. Educating your children on whom they can talk to and whom they shouldn't is key to their safety while alone. When someone calls, instead of saying "they are not home," teach them to say, "My dad can't come to the phone right now." The same holds true if someone comes to the door. Make sure the child knows not to unlock the door for anyone. If someone wants to see a parent, tell them, "they are busy and can't come to the door." If the person remains, the child should know to dial 911 and tell the dispatcher that they are afraid of the person at the door who will not leave. Let the police make the determination if the person is a threat or not. Make sure above all else that the child never opens the door to a stranger.

Here are some simple House Rules that every child staying home alone should know. No one can come in or out while parents are gone. Know the neighbors who can and will help, and make sure your kids know who they are. Post contact and emergency phone numbers on the fridge or by the phone. Keep the doors locked all the time. Dozens of great tips, suggestions, and guidelines are available from the National Center for Missing and Exploited Children and their website, www.missingkids.com. For instance, they have rules for safety for kids that include, check first with your parents before going anywhere with anyone; use the buddy system because it is more safe to go with one or more people; and it is never too late to ask for help because I can keep asking for help until I get what I need to be safe.

## STRANGERS AND FRIENDS

Strangers are people that you or your kids don't know. Strangers can become friends over time, through interaction in a variety of settings and through the discovery that you can trust them. However, strangers can also harm you and your children. For instance, strangers who are criminals use kid-friendly appeals to lure your child away with them. "Help me find my puppy," or "Would you like some candy?" are common lures. Children need to know that going anywhere with a stranger or with anyone you have not given permission to go with is dangerous. Again, it is dangerous to let children go anywhere with someone you don't know, haven't checked out, or whom you already don't have a good feeling about. Chapter 9 speaks to criminal behaviors in more detail. Be sure to read it. In the meantime, be sure to teach your children to ask your permission before going anywhere, even if it is next door to a neighbor's house to play.

Friends are people you know and trust. You know their names and you like them. Friends are people to whom you've been introduced and with whom you've had several conversations, playdates, or meetings. Teach kids to recognize the difference between friends and strangers. (The difficult part for kids and adults alike is that most crimes are committed by people known to the victim: 76% of child abductions are by families or friends[2]; recall the June 2002 Elizabeth Smart case.) "Police officers are our friends." Help your children understand that police officers are in uniform to offer help, prevent crime, and stand in the way of danger. At one point, Jana cared for a preschool-aged child who was in foster care. To her surprise, one day while walking to the park with this child, Jana heard, "We have to keep walking and talking or the police will come and take us." This child must have heard this from an adult who likely was having "trouble with the law" and who then planted the idea that police officers are bad, which of course is not their role in society. Police officers are available to help when there is trouble or concern and that is what children benefit from understanding.

Police officers can come up to us on foot, in a patrol car, in an unmarked car (there is more on this in Chapter 3), patrol motorcycles, SUVs, trucks, golf carts, police horses, and helicopters, and can arrive with a police dog. The point is we can see them (or not see them) in just about every place the public gathers for business or pleasure. Let your children know that police officers can always be approached if they are in trouble or feel threatened in any way.

What happens to you is largely affected by who you hang out with and around. Adults and children alike benefit from remembering this. The phrase that comes to mind is "guilt by association," and this is often what happens when you or your children hang out "with the wrong crowd." So "choose your friends carefully" is definitely the wise pearl to remind yourself of and to teach your children.

## WHEN YOU ARE TOGETHER, WHEN YOU ARE APART

When you are together, know where your kids are and what they are doing. When you are apart from your kids, the same rules apply: Know where your kids are and know what they are doing; additionally, know who your kids are with at the mall, at school, or when just hanging out. Any place your family members are is also an extension of your home. A law enforcement couple for 16 of their 30 years of marriage, Sheriff Deputy Curt Egge and his author wife Jan Egge[3] share these family safety tips.

KEMP: Based on your years in law enforcement, what are the top three things that you see as the causes of people ending up the victims of crime?

CURT EGGE: It seems too many people become victims of crime through no fault of their own. However, many people set themselves up for victimization by (a) not making active mental or physical preparation to prevent victimization, i.e., taking self-defense courses, "hardening" the perimeter of their resources (proper home and asset security measures), or learning to effectively and safely use self-defense weapons; (b) engaging in risky behavior (becoming impaired with alcohol or drugs) or putting themselves in high-risk environments (areas where controlled substances are commonly abused, dark alleyways, parks at night, isolated areas, etc.); and (c) being oblivious (situationally unaware) to real, everyday threats and danger cues.

KEMP: What can people do every day to not become victims of crime and also not to become paranoid about crime?

CURT EGGE: In a short phrase: Accept the reality of human behavior and make practical adjustments to it. Do what it takes to become confident in self-defense skills. Learn to move through your world with confident awareness. Make every reasonable effort to protect your assets with locks and lights. Don't put yourself in risky situations. Enjoy the clean and simple life. Make every reasonable effort to be *prepared* at all times. Rational, reasonable preparation actually reduces what you refer to as paranoia. It builds confidence. Confident situational awareness is an antidote to paranoia.

KEMP: What do you do to keep your family safe?

CURT EGGE: For Jan and me it is a team effort. She has chosen to embrace all of the reality of police family life. She has learned to use most modern self-defense weapons including firearms. I share the hand-to-hand techniques I've learned. She shares the techniques she learns with me. We *talk* about these issues all the time, and we discuss possible scenarios on a regular basis. We continually and actively observe and discuss human behavior. Whenever possible we avoid unnecessarily high-risk areas (bars, taverns, etc.). We avoid all high-risk behaviors: we never become impaired with alcohol, and we don't use drugs. Together we have "hardened our perimeter" as much as we practically can. We always lock our doors and we almost always have lethal and less-than-lethal force options close at hand. In public we watch each other's backs. We enjoy being aware of our environment.

JAN EGGE: I try to be aware of who is around me/us at all times. Curt has arrested many people in our city. Some have returned to thank him, while others have threatened his life. We have silent hand signals that we use in public to make each other aware of potential threats. We also have plans as to what we would do "if." You have to be able to think clearly and make appropriate decisions in stressful situations. For most of us, this skill needs to be developed. Thinking ahead helps. We have always used "what if" scenarios. Keeping our personal information private is also something I am aware of. There is always the potential for someone to be looking over your shoulder in the checkout line or watching you fill out a sign-up sheet in a public place. Being aware of who is around you and how you share private information publicly can prevent you from leaving a trail back to you and your home. Saying your phone number out loud in the checkout line is not a really good idea. Always be aware of who is around you. Have fun, but keep your head up and your eyes open. Make sure your family is in sight. Have cell phones *on* and a special place to meet if you get separated. Don't be afraid to alter your course, contact someone, or leave an area if you feel the least bit uncomfortable.

## DOMESTIC VIOLENCE

During the 1980s, domestic violence began to be discussed openly. In prior decades, domestic violence was treated as "something that a husband and wife needed to work out on their own." The problem with this became that more children and women were being abused, battered, and harmed than could get themselves out of their bad situations and into safety. Domestic violence affects at least 996,000 women in the United States every year and in 50% of these households if children are present, they are also abused.[4]

Today the police response to domestic violence is more aggressive than ever; it is considered a very serious violent crime that needs immediate attention. Doug has invested much of his law enforcement career in gaining expertise in this area. He teaches child abuse and domestic violence to officers throughout the country. He is on the guiding executive board of Men Today Men Tomorrow (MT2), an organization that seeks to educate the public that men's violence against women is not okay. MT2 has a focus on young men of school and college age. The message that their hands are not for hurting is central, along with dispelling the myth that it is macho to hurt, intimidate, or any other way dominate a woman or anyone for that matter. In your community, there are groups like MT2 that are providing resources and education in preventing domestic and child abuse. For more information contact your local YWCA or other Domestic Violence advocacy organizations and women's shelters.

Domestic violence is a crime that is gaining more and more attention in communities across the country. How do you know if you are in a domestic violence relationship? Obviously if you are being physically abused or battered in any way you have the right not to be. Beyond physical battering is the psychological abuse that occurs. This happens when a man takes control over a woman by isolating her from other support networks including family and friends and withholding access to bank accounts and other financial resources. This kind of abuse may be so subtle that a woman may not really realize what is happening. When friends point out what they see, the women involved most often deny that any problems exist.

What do you do if you find yourself being battered or abused? It is very well known that women who are in domestic violence relationships often feel powerless to get themselves out. This is why community support is so important. It is up to us when we see this happening to someone we know to intervene. For instance, when you hear the neighbors screaming at each other in the middle of the night, it is up to you to call 911 and notify the police. Take the time to offer help to the woman you often see with bruises on her. Talk to her about going to a shelter or talking to a counselor. As noted above, nearly every community today has resources for women who are being abused or battered. Your actions to reach out to them may prevent a tragedy. Part of being prepared in your community is stepping up to assist someone who is not capable at the time of assisting herself.

## SAFETY FOR THE ELDERLY

If you are over 65 years old, you are most likely eligible for Social Security, which is a good thing. However, a not-so-good thing is that you also may be a target of criminals because of your age. You may be seen as an easy target. Older adults tend to be more trusting of strangers, which puts them at risk from everything from phone and Internet scams to identity theft. The elderly become more vulnerable the older they get because they have to depend on more people to do things for them. If they do not have a good social network to help them with everyday activities, then they may be forced to turn to strangers for assistance.

By 2018 there will be an estimated 6.3 million elderly adults in our country. Elder abuse is severely underreported: it is estimated that only one in fourteen cases is actually reported.[5] Dementia, Parkinson's, and Alzheimer's have made the problem even worse. This very vulnerable population is easily exploited by unscrupulous care providers and con men. In 2003, 565,747 cases of abuse and neglect were reported to adult protective services throughout the United States. This represents a 19.7% increase from the 2000 survey, and 89.3% of reported elder abuse occurs in domestic settings. With 3.6 million elderly persons or 9.8% living below the poverty level in 2004 and another 2.2 million or 6.4% classified as "near poor,"[6] all of the above make the elderly even more vulnerable. Again, low income, being victim to mind-destroying diseases, and inability to care for themselves and therefore being dependent on others make the elderly a more easy target for criminals. Those aged 65 years and older must be aware of the vulnerable situation that they are in. If unable to care for themselves, they must have a trustworthy person who can: someone trustworthy, most likely a family member who will look out for the interests of a vulnerable adult. If you have an older family member in a nursing home or other care facility or have a home-care provider, it is up to you to check the reliability of the facility or provider. Visit often, ask questions about care, and if you see something you don't understand or that doesn't look right to you, be diligent and get the details. When you still aren't comfortable with what is happening, report the problems you are having to law enforcement, who can help direct you to the right resources for action. Watch the elder person's finances; find out where the money is going. Again, if you suspect abuse or exploitation, call the authorities.

## SEASONAL SAFETY

During December holiday shopping rushes, robberies and burglaries increase. Many of these robberies occur in store or shopping mall parking lots. So, to keep yourself, your vehicle, and your purchases safe, follow the suggestions we have been making throughout this book. Be aware of your surroundings.

It is easy in the hustle and bustle of the season to forget that there are still those who make a living stealing from festive holiday shoppers. When shopping, lock all your purchases in the trunk of your car out of sight. Park in well-lit lots, and shop with a friend or family member.

At Halloween, the stories continue to arise that candy has been tainted, apples have razor blades in them, or a dark-costumed child gets hit by a car. An adult should accompany children out trick-or-treating. Carry a flashlight. Wear light-colored clothing and reflective clothing so you and the kids can be seen. Use sidewalks, and cross streets together and at corners. Never go into a stranger's house.

Wedding events are times of celebration. However, be wary of announcing to the world what is happening and when you will be on a wedding weekend or event schedule. Being overly public about details creates an opportunity for criminals to steal wedding presents from the wedding party or steal those being stored in a specified location. Don't announce your honeymoon plans widely either because this, too, creates an opportunity for your home to be burglarized.

## FROM THE FIRE SIDE

Firemen and women are a part of the uniformed community team that children and adults may also interact with during an emergency. The obvious time of interaction is a fire. The less obvious times that a fire truck and team will arrive on a scene are when an ambulance is called out or when a car accident has occurred. Firemen also respond to earthquakes, gas leaks, tornadoes, and floods to help get people to safety. One of the most important things the firemen do is educate the community on fire safety. They spend considerable time doing safety inspections as well as planning and training for fighting fires. When the alarm sounds, you can be assured that the fire crew responding is prepared for what they are about to encounter.

Smoke alarms mean there is a fire. Teach your kids: smoke means fire, and get out of the house (or building) that you are in. Tell an adult. Call 911. Cover your nose and mouth so you don't breathe the smoke. Get out of the house/building. If the building has stairs, be sure to use the stairs *only* to leave; otherwise use the windows. In order for the "Get out of the house" lesson to work, your family needs to have a fire exit plan and to practice it.

Another form of fire comes in the July and December seasonal celebratory form of fireworks. Fireworks are loud and depend on fire for their explosions or results to occur. Many children and adults have lost some or all of their hearing by being too close to fireworks. Also, many children and adults have been badly burned because of fireworks fires and malfunctions. An adult should always light fireworks. Only use fireworks outside. Check to see what fireworks are legal in your state and city and in what places they are legal to use. Always follow the instructions, and always have a water bucket or a running garden hose on hand to put fireworks or fires out. Also, soak used fireworks in water to be sure no embers are left that could start a fire. Never try to relight fireworks that appear not to have worked.

## ON THE WATER SIDE

Kids tend to love water. Adults seem to fall into the camps of take it or leave it. Either way, water safety is a part of personal and family safety. In the western part of the United States, where canal, ditch, and irrigation systems are largely uncovered flows of water, annual spring and summer appeals in western states are heard: "Stay out of the water and away from irrigation canals. Never swim in a canal. Canals can kill you." Water safety is not just about learning to swim in a swimming pool. Water safety includes boating safety, knowing what bodies of water never to enter, and understanding that natural bodies of water are more complicated to swim in than a swimming pool. Children should always have a life jacket on when boating or on the water. It is wise for adults to do the same, but we understand that many will not use them. At the very least there should be a floatation device for every person onboard a watercraft. About 3,300 deaths a year occur in water-related accidents.[7]

Every year we read of young children drowning in backyard pools. A common scenario is that younger children are playing with and around older children who are not watching the little ones. The younger child gets lost in all the excitement and ends up in the pool drowned. Another and more tragic scenario is when a toddler is left unattended and wanders into a pool area, falls in, and drowns. Both of these scenarios can be prevented. It is the responsibility of the adults present to know where the little children are. Know that water attracts children; they are drawn to it. Make sure your children know that pools are absolutely off limits without a responsible adult present. If you own a backyard pool, consider a fall-in alarm: a device that will sound if someone, either a child or a pet, gets into an unattended pool. There are several varieties that are easily installed. Most states have codes concerning fencing around backyard pools. You should also alarm the gates and doors entering into the pool area.

Ocean beaches are another popular water spot during warm weather. Extreme caution must be exercised when in and near ocean surf. "Sneaker Waves," waves that are larger and more powerful than the others, can occur on the calmest of days and are not weather related. When playing in or near the surf, do not turn your back; constantly be aware of these rogue waves. Also be aware of what might be in the surf, because logs and other debris can be hidden in the waves and can severely injure or kill someone they hit.

Tides and currents on ocean beaches can be very unpredictable. Even playing in surf no more than waist deep can very quickly turn deadly if you get caught in a rip current that pulls you out into deeper water. Be constantly aware of smaller children playing in the surf because in seconds they can be pulled out of your reach and can be in trouble. Ocean beaches are wondrous places to recreate and relax, but always be aware of the dangers. As you have read over and over, being aware is the most important step in personal safety, whether it is on a boat, at the backyard pool, or the ocean beach; understand the risks, have a plan in the event of an emergency, and enjoy yourself.

## GANGS—WHAT ARE THEY REALLY?

Gangs are often a way for youth to create family. At the police academy, there was an exercise to define a gang-differentiated activity as being in only one way different from other youth organizations such as scouting, guide-groups, and youth education organizations: gang members commit crimes, often violent crimes. Whether the crime is vandalism, robbery, armed robbery, assault, or murder, gang members engage in crime. What should you watch for in your kids? A changed attitude or behavior, a drop in grades, long periods away from you and home, and a change in the people your child is associating with. To prevent gang problems, encourage positive self-esteem in your child, be a good role model for problem solving and decision making, talk about the dangers of gangs, and stay involved in your child's life. Every child (and adult for that matter) wants to feel and know that they are important to the people around them. You'll find more on gangs in Chapter 9.

## DRUGS AND KIDS

Kids struggling in school, kids without friends, a promise of having more energy and getting thin, or a promise that money will be made can all be reasons that kids and adults try and use drugs. Kids learn to use drugs from friends, from parents (yes, it is true), and from relatives (including grandparents). More details about drug addict behaviors are found in Chapter 9. Some families have found that randomly testing their kids with home drug-test kits works to keep kids off of drugs. Most importantly if your child is using drugs, you will notice dramatic mood swings (more than the normal teenage angst). Behavior will go from lethargic to bizarre mania in a matter of minutes. Over his career Doug has interviewed several dozen parents of drug-addicted children, and without exception they all knew when their child starting using. They knew because of the dramatic behavior changes that they observed. Unfortunately, the parents often chose to ignore the behavior and discounted it as some other teen affliction. Most often the parents regretted their lack of vigilance. They felt they had missed the opportunity of early intervention with their child. They told Doug that if they had confronted the behavior when they first knew that it was not right, they might have prevented months or years of heartache for both the child and family.

## FINDING HELP: BOOKS, PROGRAMS, AND EDUCATION

Most police departments, sheriff agencies, emergency medical/ambulance teams, and fire departments provide tours and educational programs for kids. Topics range from touring a facility to learning how to dial 911 to education programs about how to be safe in emergency situations. Also widely available now are children's books about interacting with police and fire people, handling emergencies, and how to be safe at home. Look for books that are age appropriate and that focus on preventing crime. Police, school counselors, mental health practitioners, and family doctors are all a part of the team that you can tap to help yourself and your family members. City and county law enforcement professionals as well as hospitals and kid-oriented organizations team up to present community "Kid Safety Day" events at which you can introduce kids to the professionals who can help them, tour fire trucks and ambulances, learn about boating safety, and even get child identification cards. The four appendixes in *Prepared Not Paranoid* also provide further guidance and resources.

## HAVE A FAMILY SAFETY PLAN

1. Have and practice all aspects of your family safety plan at home. There is more in Appendix 1.
2. Post all emergency contact numbers on the refrigerator in a location that everyone in the family can easily find.
3. Be sure every family member knows how to behave and survive in, on, and around water.
4. Know what your kids are doing, searching, and playing on the computer.

5. Ensure that your teens know how to make good decisions, when they are driving, working, playing, and hanging out with friends.
6. Check the first aid supplies, and restock them if necessary. Make sure every family member knows where to find them.
7. Learn to recognize the signs of domestic violence and whom to call for help.
8. Learn to recognize the signs of elder care abuse and child abuse and whom to call for help.
9. Work with law enforcement and fire professionals to conduct education events with your neighbors and for your kids.
10. Learn to recognize the signs of drug abuse and addiction, and act on your instinct rather than moving into denial about a problem existing.

## NOTES

1. U.S. Department of Health and Human Services, Child Maltreatment 2005, http://www.acf.dhhs.gov/programs/cb/pubs/cm05/index.html/ (accessed August 21, 2007).

2. David Finklehor and Richard Omrod, "Kidnapping of Juveniles: Patterns from NIBRS," Office of Juvenile Justice and Delinquency Prevention, *Juvenile Justice Bulletin* (2000), http://www.ncjrs.gov/html/ojjdp/2000_6_2/intro.html/ (accessed August 28, 2007).

3. Jan Egge, *Bullets in My Bed* (Fareham, UK: Legendary Publishing, 2006).

4. Health Concerns across a Woman's Lifespan: 1998 Survey of Women's Health, Karen Scott Collins, Cathy Schoen, Susan Joseph, et al. (New York, NY: The Commonwealth Fund, May 1999).

5. P. Greenwood, Elder Abuse Investigation (Idaho Peace Officer Standards and Training [POST] Academy Training, 2006).

6. National Clearinghouse on Abuse in Later Life (NCALL), http://www.ncall. us/resources.html/ (accessed December 24, 2007).

7. Nation Center for Health Statistics, National Vital Statistics System, Fatal and Non-Fatal Drowning (2001).

# Five

# Safety at School

Virginia Tech, Columbine, Jonesboro, Red Lake, Edinboro, Springfield, Fayetteville: all of these names conjure up images of death, suffering, and heartache in our nations' school. Over the past 10 years there were 51 school shooting incidents worldwide, 38 of which occurred in the United States. Worldwide 261 children and 203 adults have been killed in school shootings. An additional 868 children and adults have been injured in these shootings.[1] When we look at the figures, it is easy to say that the sky is falling and danger is at every turn. However, what the statistics tell us is not the whole story. Said another way, "Is the panic and concern over violence in schools merited?" Because the real questions are "Are our schools safe? Can I send my child to school in the morning and not worry that she won't come home in the afternoon?"

Certainly, media reports and a life-preserving drive to keep our children safe cause concern about how violent our nation's schools are. Clearly, whether you are continuing your education or supporting your children's education, safety at school is a concern. Because once the safety of a school has been violated, it is easy to feel that the sky is falling and that reconstructing a sense of safety, well-being, and sound education becomes challenging at best. Whether it is the 1999 Columbine shootings, the 2006 Amish School shootings, or the 2007 Virginia Tech shootings, annual major media stories suggest that children and students are not safe at school anymore. Schools with airport-style security at entrances and police officers permanently on assignment on-site also suggest that kids have not been safe at school. Yet, statistics show that overall kids are safer today than in decades past. While this seems difficult to believe because of the frequent school shootings covered in the media over the last decade, crime statistics indicate that crimes against children are on the decline.

Consider that during the 2004–2005 school year, the chances of your student being killed in school were less than one in one million, it was closer to one in two million.[2] In 2004, students ages 12 to 18 were victims of about 1.4 million nonfatal crimes at school, including about 863,000 thefts and 583,000 violent crimes, 107,000 of which were serious violent crimes (rape, sexual assault, robbery, and aggravated assault).[3] This means that your child's chances of being a victim of violent crime are about fifty-five crimes per one thousand students. This number continues to drop each year: in 2003 the numbers were seventy-three per one thousand students.[4] Although these signs are encouraging, school is still a place in which a child needs to be prepared to deal with any eventuality that may come her way. Violence, theft, drugs, and weapons continue to pose problems in schools. For instance, in 2005, 25% of students in grades 9 to 12 reported that drugs were made available to them on school property, and 8% of students were threatened or injured with a weapon on school property in the previous 12 months.[5]

## SAFETY THROUGH THE SCHOOL YEARS

Each era of school experience brings with it slightly different safety concerns. Whether you are the student to be kept safe or your children are, there are school safety considerations that you, your immediate family, and extended family members will want to discuss. For several decades, inner city schools have had secured entries and security guards or police officers on-site. Some schools have airport-type security at every entrance and police officers permanently assigned to the building. Now, even rural area schools are looking into camera-driven security systems as well as law enforcement partnerships for keeping schools, students, faculty, and staff safe. Other schools have no obvious security systems or measures in place, and in the middle are schools that have some security officers, some cameras for monitoring behavior, and a well-used principal's office. Find out what level of security your child's school has.

Check with your school district and individual schools to see what security measures are in place every day. You may also want to have a detailed discussion with the staff, owners, and administrators of your child's school to ensure that children are safe. Whatever discussions you choose to pursue at home and with your schools, know that parental involvement helps kids do better in and make better decisions at school. Beginning with daycare and preschool years, then moving to elementary, middle, and high school years, and concluding with college settings, what follows is a discussion of what to look for in various settings and age-servicing facilities.

## DAYCARE AND PRESCHOOL

Who can pick your children up from school? Your daycare or preschool providers should have a list of approved people along with their photograph to know who really is allowed to pick up your child. Jana knows of one daycare that requested a copy of court orders regarding a child-custody situation so that the daycare had protection in the event of having to deny the parent without custody from picking up the child. Picking up a child is just one aspect of safety for this age child. In addition, knowing what the care facility's inside and outside space is like is important. Are dangerous tools, play equipment, or water features such as canals or ponds accessible to children?

The staff at a daycare can also pose a threat to your child. Does the school have a background check for each staff person? If so, is each staff member really okay to be working with children? For instance, find out what training each staff member has had in working with children of this age.

Also, make sure the site itself is secure. For instance, observe whether there is a front desk check-in area. Find out how people can access the children. When looking at indoor and outdoor play areas, determine whether the toys and equipment are age-appropriate and safe. And for field trips, find out whether the transportation used meets safety standards for your state.

What are the ratios of kids to adults? The following are typical breakdowns based on U.S. Department of Health and Human Services national child care standards for a daycare setting: (1) children birth to 2 years of age, one adult to three kids; (2) children 2 to 3 years of age, one adult to five kids; (3) children 4 years of age, one adult to seven kids; and (4) children 4 to 5 years of age, one adult to eight kids. States and local jurisdictions can set different standards, which are sometimes a higher child-to-adult ratio. Find out what your state allows and be sure the setting you select is in compliance. Directly ask: Is the center licensed according to state, county, and city laws? Are the owners and workers free of criminal backgrounds? Are all employees trained in first aid and CPR? Are activities age-appropriate? Is the ratio of adults to children correct? (These ratios vary by state.) Is the environment of the facility safe—inside and out? Are there any sexual predators or child molesters living in the area? These are among the questions you want to ask and to research in order to discover whether you are selecting, or have selected, the right care situation for your child. In some communities, hospitals now offer workshops on how to select a daycare provider. Research what daycare education is available in your community.

Preschool age children are learning about right and wrong, about how the world works, and how to make decisions. Teach children at this age how to make decisions, how to solve problems, and then recognize them for making good choices and decisions.

## ELEMENTARY SCHOOL

In this millennia, children are faced with decision making about friends, play activities, school studies, musical pursuits, and sports play. Now, as early as elementary school, children are also faced with making decisions about drug use, alcohol, smoking, and having sex. In fact, the Safe and Drug-Free Schools programs sponsored by the federal government's Office of Safe and Drug-Free Schools start in the third grade. Drug Abuse Resistance Education (DARE) classes are offered to sixth-grade students, with many DARE officers giving lectures on safety and "stranger danger" all the way down to kindergarten.

Children face more difficult decisions at a younger age than previous generations have faced. Some girls start their periods as early as the fifth grade. Sexual and alcohol experimentation can start in elementary school, too. As a parent you can continue to model good decision making for your children so that they learn to make good choices and safe decisions.

## MIDDLE/JUNIOR HIGH SCHOOL

By sixth through ninth grades, children are dealing with raging hormones and the potential sexual and violent-leaning behaviors that come along with puberty. Parties with alcohol become more prevalent at this age and in high school. School safety includes school property and activities as well as non-school student events. More than 60% of teens report using alcohol and about 25% of teens say they drank before they were 13 years old.

The most common problem police see with this age group is after-school problems such as daylight burglaries and vandalism. This is the age where kids are trying out their independence for the first time and are apt to make poor decisions.

## HIGH SCHOOL

In high school, above and beyond all of the issues facing children you can now add the dimension of driving and all of the decisions associated with driving, drinking, preparing for college, getting jobs, and social interactions hinting at marriage. After-school hours continue to be a challenge for high school students because statistics show that the most dangerous time for teens to drive on a weekday is from 3:00 to 5:00 P.M., which is also when kids get into the most trouble. Most children today are unsupervised after school and until their parent(s) get home from work. As a result, the freedom to "run wild" is high, and kids either run into or create trouble. Typical problems during these hours are gang involvement, teen pregnancy, and motor vehicle violations. Typical youth crimes committed during these hours are vandalism, burglary, and drug crimes.

Many states have recently passed legislation in an attempt to curtail teen driving accidents. Examples of these laws are requiring more practice behind the wheel before being allowed to drive unsupervised, curtailed after dark driving, and limiting the number of people who can be with a new driver. These laws are an attempt to make young drivers safer, because statistically they are the ones most likely to be involved in vehicle crashes. Parents can also help keep their children safe by making sure that their children are as well-trained as possible. This is best accomplished by spending many, many hours in the car with the child. Second, limit the number of passengers your child may have with her when she is driving unsupervised. When there are too many people in the vehicle, young inexperienced drivers are easily distracted.

Take an inexperienced driver, add alcohol to the mix, and you have a recipe for disaster. According to the National Clearinghouse for Alcohol and Drug Information (NCADI), the leading cause of death among 15–24 year olds are automobile crashes, homicides, and suicides, and alcohol is a leading factor in all three. NCADI also reports that over three million teens are out-and-out alcoholics, with several million more with serious alcohol problems.[6] It is no secret, teenagers and even preteens drink. When they do, bad things often happen. Parents need to monitor their children's activity, and limit the time that they are unsupervised. If you suspect your child has an alcohol problem, check with the school counselor; most schools have a drug and alcohol referral program that can provide resources to both you and your child. Look at your own alcohol use, what are you modeling for your child? Is the message that you are sending consistent with the message you are speaking?

School events, football games, plays, debates, and tournaments all pose a variety of safety challenges. Teen dating violence is so much on the rise that many student organizations in states across the country are now in full education mode to let teens know that dating violence is not okay.

In fact, Jana, while judging a statewide high school academic competition in the spring of 2007 heard two teen girls give speeches on dating violence and how they had individually been treated by their boyfriends. Both girls said they were able to break away from the boys and that they are each focused on protecting themselves and their personal worth. For more information, visit www.nomeansknow.com or call the National Teen Dating Abuse Hotline at 866-331-9474.

The solution is to supervise your kids or make sure that they are supervised during after-school hours. Supervision can include hiring a babysitter or enrolling kids in after-school programs, sports, and clubs. The most common problem police see with this age is gang activity and drug and alcohol use.

Campus safety tips that apply to high school students and college students of all ages are often produced by police or sheriff departments and on some college and university campuses, the community safety department of the school. As a starting place, here are some campus safety tips from the Boise Police Department's Crime Prevention Unit. Keep your purse, wallet, keys, iPods, cell phones, and other valuables with you at all times or locked away. Avoid using stairwells in remote sections of the building and dimly lit parking lots. If attending classes or working late, let someone know, and secure the doors leading to the area you are in. Better yet, team up with someone else so that no one is moving around campus alone. Especially, use a buddy system when walking to your car late at night. Always have your keys in your hand.

Don't leave laptop computers or backpacks unattended, even for a moment, and don't keep financial information on your laptop. Then, delete personal information from your laptop when you dispose of it. Record the serial numbers of all computer and electronic equipment that you are issued or own. When rooms are not occupied, lock office and classroom doors. Always lock your bicycle. Always lock your vehicle, and keep valuables out of view. Know the evacuation plans for the buildings and offices you frequent, and finally, report suspicious persons and activities immediately. Dial 911 when you feel threatened or that something isn't right.

## COLLEGE AND UNIVERSITY SETTINGS—YOUNG ADULTS

The April 2007 shootings on the Virginia Tech campus and even the May 1970 Kent State protests that resulted in four deaths demonstrate that violence can occur in centers of higher education and learning. Nearly annually, a publicized lawsuit over a "rape on campus" has been occurring for the last two decades. By this age, it is critical to know what your personal values and limits are so that you can avoid risky situations, and if your young-adult children are off to school, help them to clearly establish what their personal limits and tolerances are for behaviors, requests to try new things, and demands on their actions when joining an organization. For instance, many sororities and fraternities include activities that are potentially criminal in nature. For on-the-spot safety, discover whether the campus has call boxes that can be used to immediately reach campus security for help. Learn who to contact on campus when a safety violation has occurred. Know who the school counselors or advisors are, and alert them to any safety problems on campus.

College and high school parties are more likely to involve law enforcement for a variety of drug, sexual assault, and other violent reasons. For your own safety and for the safety of your children, you need to know what pharming parties, RAVES, rainbow parties, unsupervised events, school parties, church parties, public parties, and private parties are likely to have in store. Popular after the turn of the millennia, pharming parties began to occur regularly among teen and college crowds. A pharming party is one in which everyone brings their own or someone else's prescription drugs and trades for other drugs or handles the drugs as candy to be tried for its flavor—or in this case the aftereffects. The obvious danger is that taking and mixing drugs that are not for the person taking them can cause medical problems up to and including death.

RAVES on the other hand are often seen as adult-supervised dance parties in which teens can stay out all night long, dance, and socialize with their friends. Parents feel safe allowing their children to attend because they are advertised events and some responsible person will be in attendance. Not true. RAVES are often an outlet for drugs like ecstasy and other hallucinogens, which give the user a sense of well being. Many users of ecstasy will tell you that it is such a mild drug that it just makes you want to hug everybody, hence the name the "hug drug." As with any drug, ecstasy is known to be dangerous and overdoses are common.

Then there are the rainbow parties, which are not parties for hippies or the Rainbow People who travel around in caravans and camp in national and state parks. In the teen and college crowd, rainbow parties include boys wearing condoms (or not) and girls wearing various shades of lipstick and then installing, if you will, a ring of color onto the boys' penises. After the turn of the millennia, media reports on pharming and rainbow parties drew national attention to problem party situations not heard about on the whole in the media during the twentieth century.

Unsupervised events for kids and teens put young people at risk because their ability to make good decisions is not yet formed. Regardless of the size of jurisdiction, law enforcement officers have concerns for children and young adults who participate in the above activities. Although there may be a minority who seriously understand the behavior they are participating in, the majority are merely attempting to fit in and do not understand the dangers they are exposing themselves to. Officers tire of seeing innocent children fall victim to activities they go into thinking that it will all be fun and then finding themselves in a nightmare. This is why you will see many officers aggressively acting to counter the potential damage that can happen at these events.

Then there are the publicly advertised drinking parties. By the time students leave junior high school, more than half report having tried alcohol. Although the legal drinking age is 21 years, during high school and college years, a drinking and partying culture is well established. In fact, in nearly every college and in some high schools, a sorority and fraternity system exists seemingly to support partying. National news stories have recounted the debauched behavior of drunken co-eds in both property destruction events and in gang-rape occurrences happening right in fraternity houses. Teach your children how to say "no" and how to walk away from danger with their heads held high. The best decision making is that which protects you in both the short term and in the long term.

School- and church-sponsored parties tend to carry an element of "it must be okay" just because of who has sponsored the event. While this may be true, it is still on your shoulders to find out what the activities will be and how much supervision will occur. Plenty of parents have been created as a result of school parties and church camps: in other words, sex, alcohol consumption, and drug taking can happen anywhere, no matter who the sponsor of the event is.

Public parties include concerts, theater shows, sporting events, and events where three or more students gather. Many of these events now include a certain level of security, such as entry checkpoints, unarmed security guards, armed police officers, and even plain-clothed security officers whom you can't detect at the event. The security provided by an event is not a substitute for making good decisions, avoiding risky behavior, or establishing universal safety. You want to teach your children that they must still be responsible for the choices they make and for the activities they pursue.

Speaking of high school and college age parties, one of Jana's neighbors had teenage sons who over a period of three years would once a year have a party at the house and be noisy until midnight or even three in the morning, well past curfew for teenagers. The first two years the late night parties happened Jana got up, got dressed, and went over to ask the kids to quiet down. By the third year, however, after hours of Saturday night noise and then being awakened at three in the morning, Jana concluded, "I'm not dealing with now-college-age students, and not at this hour." So Jana called 911 and reported the noise. By the time the police arrived, the party had broken up, and no one remained at the neighbor's house. A disturbance report was filed. On Sunday morning, Jana first visited the noisy neighbor's house only to find no one at home. Then, she called another neighbor who usually knows who is traveling and who isn't in the neighborhood. The second neighbor said "Oh, he's out of the country with the oldest son." Surprised, Jana said, "Then I wonder who was partying at the house last night. Maybe I should call their mom and see if it was the youngest son." Of course, in the spirit of community policing and with a strong desire to protect her own property, that is what Jana did, only to discover that the youngest son had been home all Saturday night with his mom, who on Sunday came over to check the house (which was left in a post-party mess of beer bottles and pizza boxes, and a ping-pong table no one knew the owner of) and locked it up. On Sunday night, Jana was out and saw a vehicle pull up to the house, but because it was dark, she was unable to get a license plate number before the vehicle driver and passengers noticed her watching them, backed up, and pulled away. It appeared that another party was planned—and who knows if there was ever an intention to clean up the mess.

A few days later, when the traveling neighbor returned, he came to visit Jana to find out what had happened. As it turns out, neither of his kids were present, but some of the kids at the party knew his kids. One of the pizza-ordering kids had even left the order form on the pizza box, and it included his cell number. The traveling neighbor filed a police report and took several of the kids to court for trespassing. The unraveling of the crime and the finding of the perpetrators happened because neighborhood community policing happened. Again, the point is that whether a party is public or private, supervised or unsupervised, both adults and teens have decision-making responsibilities for keeping themselves and others safe.

## COLLEGE AND UNIVERSITY SETTINGS—ADULTS AND WORKING ADULTS

As an adult or nontraditional college student, you are less likely to be enticed by the party scene. You are typically juggling jobs, relationships, and even kids, as well as getting an education. Your safety challenges are often managing traffic while getting to class, leaving class in the dark, and being distracted because of the constant hurriedness of your life. The tips and plans throughout this book are critical to your daily safety.

## SCHOOL-SPECIFIC SAFETY CONCERNS

When talking about sexual predators, criminals, and schools, arm yourself with as much information as possible so that you can work effectively with your schools about safety concerns. Many states have passed laws about how close to schools convicted sexual predators can live. In some states these laws are being challenged. Regardless, you can check the proximity of convicted sexual offenders to your child's school at such sites as www.familywatchdog.com. Many states have also passed drug and gun laws related to school grounds and protecting students. For instance, Safe and Drug Free schools programs have been created that make it a criminal offense to be intoxicated on school grounds. This allows the police to become involved with a child who may have a drug problem and continually comes to school under the influence. The point is not creating a criminal history for drugs or alcohol for the child; rather, the point is getting the child into needed rehabilitation. The criminal charges and court involvement often become the catalyst that the student needs to get clean. Most often the statutes are written in such a way as to allow the student to enter rehab in lieu of going to court, and once a program is successfully completed, the criminal history is expunged.

Computer use at school includes Internet use and safety policies. Just as families need to protect children from the dangers of the Internet, so too do schools. Learn what your child's school policies, programs, and protections are for Internet use. School Internet policies include blocking access to all non-child-appropriate sites, limiting computer access, and allowing Internet use only for school assignments. If the school doesn't have clear policies and protections in place, work with them to ensure the safety of all children.

Another policy to learn about in your child's school is "zero tolerance." During the 1990s, the concept of "zero tolerance" arose in schools and became a part of school policy. Zero tolerance is typically defined as a school policy that tolerates no transgressions or infractions of any laws, ordinances, regulations, rules or policies, regardless of whether they were willfully broken or ignorantly broken. Even extenuating circumstances that in other situations might be taken into consideration are not accepted in zero tolerance environments and the rule breaker is fully punished. Zero tolerance policies in schools range from addressing truancy to alcohol, drug, and weapons possession and use on school property and at school events. For instance, in Mississippi, the zero tolerance punishment for violence, weapons, and drug offenses is a one-year expulsion from school. By 2004, schools began experiencing controversy over the policies and the inflexibility of their implementation, and by 2007, several states began consideration of dropping zero tolerance rules in schools altogether.

## SHOOTINGS AT SCHOOL

A law enforcement response to a threat at your child's school is fairly predictable. After the Columbine shootings, law enforcement has trained on ways to contain what has become known as the "active shooter." An active shooter is an individual or individuals who enter a location, generally heavily populated, such as a school, mall, theater, or office building, with the intent of committing mass murder. The shooter(s) will be heavily armed and suicidal and may be ready to actively confront the police. Sometimes they have specific targets in mind, but will usually shoot anyone who happens to be in their path. Often their whole goal is to injure or kill as many as possible before taking their own life. Law enforcement officers know that these individuals must be engaged quickly to reduce the number of victims. Officers have been trained that when they receive an "active shooter" call, they will as quickly as possible engage the threat and either neutralize it or detain it until additional officers can arrive on scene.

Here is what your child needs to know about what will be happening around him or her if an active shooter enters the school. Their teachers should have drilled with them what the school response will be, most often a lock-down of individual classrooms. When the police arrive (anywhere from one to four officers), they will be heavily armed and moving quickly toward the threat. They are taught what are called the Four C's: Contain the suspect, Control the perimeter, Communicate with responding units, and Call for assistance. They will walk right past wounded and injured people, knowing that someone is coming along behind to address the injured. The officers will be yelling at all the children to stay down and not to approach them. Often scared children will run to the officer for protection, the officer is trained to disregard them and keep focused on the threat at hand. A SWAT team will be called. However, often these incidents are over before SWAT can arrive on scene. If SWAT does arrive, your child will see a minimum of four and as many as twelve officers dressed in military garb, again moving rapidly through the school. They may hear what sounds like bombs going off: these are "flash bangs," an explosive device meant to distract and disorient the shooter. Let your kids know that these will not hurt them. Kids may hear gunfire and may be in what seems like a very chaotic environment. Ensure your child that the police have planned, trained, and prepared for these kinds of incidents and everything they are doing makes sense.

When the police are satisfied that they have stopped the shooter, they will come back through and evacuate the building. Students will be asked to line up and quickly vacate the premises. Students may be told to put their hands up on their heads. This is done in case a shooter is trying to make an escape with the rest of the students the police will be able to detect any weapons. Students will be taken to a safe place for interviews and then reunited with parents.

Hearing of a school shooting at a child's school is a parent's worst nightmare. If you find yourself in this situation, this is what you should know. First, you most likely will not be allowed very close to the scene. As soon as they have the necessary resources, law enforcement will set up a rally point for parents to go. Follow instructions from officers at the scene. Remember this is a chaotic time, and many things are happening at once. Officers are doing everything they can to keep your children safe. The added burden of an unruly parent does not help the children inside the school. Once the children are out of the school, they may not be released immediately back to the parents. The investigative stage of the incident is now underway, and at the very least names, addresses, and locations of all involved will be obtained prior to being released to parents.

Active school shootings are rare. When they occur, they get national media attention, which makes us think that the sky is falling. Schools and law enforcement are trained to deal with these kinds of incidents if these should occur. Because of their planning, policies, and preparation you can be assured that your children are as safe as possible while at school.

## RESOURCES FOR SCHOOL SAFETY

America's Safe Schools Week is an annual event sponsored by the National School Safety Center for the purpose of "motivating key education and law enforcement policymakers, as well as students, parents, and community residents, to vigorously advocate school safety. School safety includes keeping campuses free of crime and violence, improving discipline, and increasing student attendance. Schools that are safe and free of violence, weapons, and drugs are necessary to ensure the well-being of all children and the quality of their education." Visit their website: www.schoolsafety.us, for more information. Additional school safety resources can be found at the National Education Association's website: www.nea.org/schoolsafety. The U.S. Department of Education also offers extensive recommendations and guides at their site: www.ed.gov, which includes a search function that takes you to safety or security information based on your search. Also at the department's site is the ninety-five-page white paper, "Threat Assessment in Schools: A Guide to Managing Threatening Situations and to Creating Safe School Climate," which is available for printing. The key is that there are local, state, and national resources in both education and law enforcement circles that you can work with to keep your kids safe at school.

Know what your children live with at school every day as it relates to law enforcement. Many schools have a School Resource Officer (SRO). The SRO's beat is that school. She is responsible for investigating any criminal activity that occurs at the school, as well as any crimes committed in the community by students from her school. She is also responsible for crimes committed against students attending her school. The SRO program is community policing in practice. This officer knows the students and the students know her. They learn that she is a safe person and that they can take concerns they have about health and safety to her. The SRO will deliver safety lectures to every grade and is a resource to the school's faculty in talking about health and safety issues. The SRO understands the challenges the children in her school face everyday and can help them successfully navigate this tricky landscape.

Know what the emergency procedures are for evacuating your children's school(s) in the event of fire, tornado, earthquake, attack, or school shooting.

Ask your children's school administrator or principal what the policies and punishments for various behaviors are. Find out whether police officers are stationed in the school. Discover what security installations are in each school. Meet the school counselors to discuss the resources available for helping your children and you through positive and negative school situations.

Clarence Wieting, a seventeen-year security industry specialist with expertise in working with schools says, "Children today seem to be more aggressive and I would say bored, or not driven by the idea of getting an education or the consciousness of not having an education, which leads to the behaviors that make taxpayers and schools have to put in security cameras and security systems. Vandalism, drugs, sexual acts, violence and guns are among the driving forces for installing and utilizing security systems." Whether or not your child's school has a security technology system installed, it should have a security and safety policy and plan in place that you can request in writing. Next, focus on learning about your child's daily school experience.

Know where your kids are going to school. Yes, know the physical location, the address, and telephone numbers. In addition to this know what routes your kids take to school and with whom they go to and from school so that you can locate your children and retrace their steps if you ever need to. Walking paths, streets, bus routes, transit routes and numbers, and the neighborhoods your kids pass through all hold different dangers and potential threats. Unless you've walked or ridden the same routes your kids travel, you really have no idea what they are faced with every day. Over and above knowing the routes and neighborhoods, you also need to know what atmosphere or attitude of thought and behavior is prevalent on the way to and from school and during the school day. For instance, as portrayed in the 2007 family movie *Bridge to Terabithia*, are older girls charging younger girls a dollar to get into the girl's bathroom? Do you really know what your kids' school day is like? Learn how they get treated, and learn how they treat others. As Clarence Wieting suggests, "Teach your kids to know their surroundings, including knowing where the exit doors are located and what other buildings are near the school or on the routes between home and school. Also teach kids to be kind to everyone and know who's who at school. For instance, encourage your kids to learn who can help and who is likely to pick on them rather than helping. As a parent, you can ask the school for their exit plans, meeting areas, emergency plans, and safety manuals."

Are your kids picking on other kids and even harassing teachers? How do you know? You can find out by keeping your kids talking to you, by talking with faculty and staff members, and by listening to other parents. Conversely, are your kids getting picked on by other kids or by faculty or staff? You can find out by listening to your kids' words, behaviors, behavioral changes, and body language as well as randomly checking in at school (of course, follow school rules about checking in at the office for visitor badges).

The bottom line on school safety is that kids, parents, faculty, and staff need to be aware of what threats are real in their community and how to plan to confront the hazards if they occur. Everyone needs to know what to do when things go bad. When a school shooting happens, what is the response expected of students, teachers, administrators, and parents? When a tornado or an earthquake strikes, everyone again needs to know what to do, where to meet, and whom to contact with questions.

Teach good decision-making and problem-solving skills to your children. Be willing to serve as their "no" when an unsafe request is being made or when safety can not be ensured. Work with teachers, administrators, and the whole school district to be sure your kids' schools are safe. Rather than living in the fear that the "sky is falling," get involved with your children's educational experience and the issues of safety tied to each school day. One of the best public service announcements Jana says she's ever heard about parenting carried the message, "Keep your kids talking to you. When they stop talking, you stop knowing what they are doing, and who they are."

## SCHOOL SAFETY PLAN

1. Talk to school administrators, principals, and school board members about school safety plans.

2. Request and understand the safety plans that are in place for each of your children's schools.
3. Communicate the plans with each child so they understand the safety rules and emergency procedures.
4. Teach your kids to make good decisions starting in preschool and continuing through their school career.
5. Reinforce good decision making with yourself and your kids every day.
6. Determine whether your family will use cell phones as a part of your family's school safety plan.
7. Have a contact and phone number list for emergencies registered with the school and in your child's backpack.
8. Meet with the law enforcement officer assigned to your kids' schools to learn what the current challenges are for kids in each age group.
9. Explain to your children what to expect should a school lockdown occur or when there is an active shooter on campus.
10. Listen to your children, talk to them about what their fears about being on campus are, and take steps to relieve those concerns.

## NOTES

1. International Action Network on Small Arms (IANSA), "Number of children and adults killed and wounded in school shootings around the world since 1996," http://www.iansa.org/ (accessed December 24, 2007).

2. Jill F. DeVoe, Katherine Peter, Margaret Noonan, Thomas D. Snyder, and Katrina Baum, Indicators of School Crime and Safety: 2005 (National Center for Education Statistics [NCES] 2006-001/NCJ 210697), (Washington, DC: U.S. Departments of Education and Justice, 2005).

3. Rachel Dinkes, Emily Forrest Cataldi, Grace Kena, and Katrina Baum, Indicators of School Crime and Safety, 2006 (National Center for Educational Statistics [NCES] 2007-003/NCJ214262), (Washington, DC: U.S. Departments of Education and Justice, 2006).

4. Ibid.

5. Ibid.

6. Substance Abuse and Mental Health Services Administration, National Clearing House for Alcohol and Drug Information (NCADI), http://ncadi.samhsa.gov/research/studies.aspx/ (accessed September 30, 2007).

# Six

# Safety at Work

Workplace dangers can arise from simple miscommunications, from misunderstood directions, and from equipment and chemical hazards. Workplace safety concerns have existed since the times of hunting for food, when many hunts resulted in the loss of one tribe member because of the dangers of the hunt. Monumental as well as single, house-building construction sites over the millennia have also been workplace safety concerns. Agricultural-related workplaces include such safety concerns as getting caught in equipment or in silos or grain elevators or getting attacked or accidentally injured by an animal. Manufacturing workplaces carry the risk of being physically injured or even killed. Compared to these large-scale life-threatening safety concerns, office work may seem to be risk-free. In fact, office work has danger, too, in the form of repeated-stress disorders, easy access by outsiders with an ax-to-grind with someone at the company, and medical emergencies such as heart attacks, which can happen in any work environment. While this book doesn't cover the different details of every possible workplace, it does speak to the core-plan considerations of every workplace. Workplace safety runs the gamut from obvious "must-pass-through" security measures to knowing where the first aid kit and staircases are located.

An entire security industry exists around keeping workplaces, properties, people, inventory, and equipment safe and secure. Bodyguards, information technology security analysts, security guards on-site, security checkpoints entering a site, security screening entering the building, camera systems, surveillance systems, plant safety rules and regulations, and biohazard management systems are all a part of the today's workplace safety considerations. An entire specialty called risk management exists for the purpose of projecting potential business risks and then mitigating the risks in various forms. Are you familiar with the rules of safety for your workplace? Do you know what risks need to be managed each day?

In her book, *Building Community in Buildings*,[1] Jana and coauthor Ken Baker present six variables for being more productive at work. The following are the Productivity Variables: (1) healthy buildings and healthy people, (2) safety and security, (3) comfort and control, (4) community, (5) rewards, and (6) creativity and morale. The opening discussion of Variable 2: Safety and Security closes with "The key for organizations when addressing this productivity variable is to create a sense of safety and security without creating paranoia and without creating a sense of danger, both of which contribute to low employee productivity." This of course is the point of the workplace chapter in the whole *Prepared Not Paranoid* discussion of being safe. We spend most of our waking hours in the workplace, so focusing on being safe at work is critical to staying safe.

During 2005–2006, Jana served as an elected member of the Idaho House of Representatives. During her time working in Idaho's capitol building, the following experiences reminded her of the need to have safety plans—both personally and as an entire workplace. In Idaho, there are no security devices for entering the capitol building. Just five blocks away, the county courthouse has airport-style security gates to pass through before entering the building. This seems a bit odd, to leave 105 elected officials, a governor, and four other statewide elected officials, plus all of the support staff in the building in harm's way because of no stopgap security screenings. Because of this, Jana found herself actively scanning the House Gallery for suspicious behaviors that might put people at risk. Jana also found herself mentally rehearsing exit strategies. One day, a fire alarm caused by a basement electrical problem that created smoke prompted the use of an exit plan. All legislators ended up in a small park across from the capitol building. Jana managed to grab her briefcase and cell phone on the way out. As she assessed the situation, she noticed that cars were still driving by in between the building and the elected officials, that the officials were all easy targets for potential snipers on top of nearby buildings, and that no one was protecting the people outside. Jana opted to sit on a concrete wall, with cell phone in hand and with a strategy of ducking behind the concrete wall, between the wall and the bushes, if the need arose. Thankfully, everyone was safe, and after about an hour, all were allowed to return to the building. These kinds of real workplace occurrences lead right into the discussion of workplace violence.

## WORKPLACE VIOLENCE

Workplace violence comes in many forms. Examples include an angry raised voice that leads to someone being hit, sexual advances that constitute sexual harassment, a machine or equipment accident that causes an injury or even death, an outsider coming in to hurt an employee, an employee coming in to shoot someone, and an armed robbery. The U.S. Department of Labor, Bureau of Labor Statistics, tracks workplace data including fatal occupational homicides (murders). The majority of deaths occur in the act of a robbery or other crime, where the person committing the crime doesn't have a relationship per se with the company. The next category of workplace murders is coworkers (about 10% of the murders), followed by relatives and significant others (see the domestic violence discussion later in this chapter), and murders committed by customers or clients. Thankfully, the number of people murdered while at work is low, but it does happen. As a result, having a plan may save your life. Thankfully too, not all workplace violence ends in death; less-than-lethal forms of violence can also come from within the workplace, when coworkers have disagreements that turn physical. Workplace violence also can occur when someone enters the workplace to file a complaint and then becomes verbally or physically aggressive. Still further examples of workplace violence include retail theft, which can result in a violent confrontation with the offender, or a bank robbery, which often includes a gun or the threat of a gun.

## PERSONAL SAFETY AND WORKPLACE PARKING

Parking as far away as possible from your office building in order to get exercise may not be your wisest safety option. Although it may be a good get-fit strategy, the reason it can be dangerous is this: If you arrive at and or leave from your office in the dark, the greater the distance you are walking through dark, semi-lit, or even well-lit parking lots, the easier it is for someone to target you, pursue you, and harm you. Consider your parking circumstances: What time do you arrive and leave? What are the lighting conditions in your parking areas, both natural and electrical? Are the parking areas monitored by security personnel and/or by cameras? Are other people coming and going at the same time? Do you walk in and out with other people? Do you have your car keys ready to get right into the car when you reach it? Do you visualize the backseat before getting into the car?

If you're thinking, "I don't drive to work," then think about the places you do drive and park, and if you're thinking "I don't even have a car," that's okay, too, because whether you walk to work or use public transportation, the route you take when walking is an important consideration in maintaining your safety. Do you use well-traveled routes? Do you move about during well-lit times of day and night? Do you pay attention to what others are doing around you?

## PERSONAL SAFETY AT WORK

Whether you work in an office, on a manufacturing floor, or outdoors, there are safety considerations. Ranging from paper cuts to hazardous materials and from carpal tunnel to limb injuries that lead to amputation, workplace safety is a concern. The federal government sets myriads of workplace safety standards, and OSHA guidelines abound. In the *Prepared Not Paranoid* discussion, the focus is on the safety issues that might include law enforcement. For instance, a disgruntled employee shows up intoxicated at the office and threatens to harm someone.

No matter what dangers or threats may arise, there are things you can do every day to protect your safety at work. For instance, be alert to your surroundings, hear if something is not right, see whether something is amiss, smell whether something is unusual, and recognize whether equipment and systems are functioning properly and report any problems. To better protect workplace buildings and property, invite someone from the crime prevention division of your local law enforcement entity to come and do a risk assessment with you. In 1999, Jana first learned of the Construction Identification Numbering system that law enforcement worked out with the business community to mark equipment and tools that businesses wanted to recover if they were stolen.

## SEXUAL HARASSMENT

Understanding what sexual harassment is and what laws as well as agency policies govern behavior is important in any work setting. Most companies have information available and policies in place. Whether or not any policies regarding sexual harassment are in place, the following behaviors qualify for a call to the police to file a complaint: unwanted sexual touching or assault. Other actions may not rise to the level of a call to police, but should most certainly be reported to your human resources supervisor as well as your immediate supervisor; these may include sexual suggestion, lewd jokes, or any activity that you are not comfortable with.

Plenty of books and training programs have been produced about what sexual harassment is, how to avoid it, how to establish policies around it, and what to do if it happens to you. Here, we recommend knowing what your organization's policy is and reporting when you feel that a crime has been or is being committed.

## ELEVATORS VERSUS STAIRS

Every day millions of people ride elevators. Simple safety rules should be observed when using an elevator. When entering and exiting an elevator, watch your step; sometimes the floor of the building and floor of the elevator may not align perfectly. Most elevators are equipped with sensors that will stop a door if someone or something is in the way. Sensors can malfunction; do not try and stop a closing door with your arm or briefcase; wait for the next car. If your elevator becomes stuck between floors or you experience a power outage and the elevator stops, don't panic. Emergency lighting will come on; use the emergency help button or the intercom or phone that is in the elevator to call for help. Follow the instructions given to you by the help line. If the elevator is not equipped with an intercom or if it malfunctions, try your cell phone. It may work in the elevator; call 911 and tell them the building that you are in. Help will be sent to you. Never try exiting a stuck elevator, because it may start up unexpectedly, putting you in danger. You don't need to worry about running out of oxygen in the elevator because the elevator shaft also serves as an airshaft for the building.

When an elevator arrives and the door opens, if you are uncomfortable getting on with those already on, don't. Simply state, "I will take the next car." If something is telling you this is not a safe situation, listen to that inner voice; you have trained yourself to stay safe. Safety starts by not putting yourself in a bad position. If you are on an elevator and you are attacked, yell for help, and push the floor buttons if you can reach them. Many buildings today have video surveillance in elevators; making noise may draw a security guard's attention to the monitor. If uncomfortable or assaulted, exit immediately when the doors open; don't allow them to close. This would be a time when it is okay to put a body part in the door to keep it from closing.

Elevators are so common in many workplaces that people no longer know where the stairs are in their office buildings. The danger in this is that in the event of a fire or electricity outage, the stairs are the only option. In emergency situations, people do find the energy to get down the stairs even when dozens of flights must be descended. As recommended in another chapter, find the stairs in your building. Then, once a month, take the stairs down to the ground or parking level floor. Doing this will condition your body to know what it needs to do in the event of an emergency evacuation. Another thing to find is the fire-alarm pull box. Locate the one nearest to your workspace. Study how to use it because several styles of alarm box pulls are in use. Police and fire training both require physical fitness levels that allow people in uniform to get up and down stairs as well as to be able to carry someone else down the stairs.

## WORKPLACE SAFETY INTERVIEW 1: AMERICA'S CAPITOL

The Honorable Gregory S. Casey, the 34th U.S. Senate Sergeant-at-Arms and Doorkeeper (1996-1998), was first interviewed by Jana Kemp in January 1999 when he was a guest on her business radio program *Momentum*. As the U.S. Senate Sergeant-at-Arms, Casey was responsible for the safety and security of the members of the Senate. Had President Clinton been impeached, it would have been the Sergeant-at-Arms' duty to arrest the president, thereby placing the position among the highest law enforcement powers in the country. Because of his experiences in managing and overseeing workplace safety, Jana requested another interview for *Prepared Not Paranoid*.

KEMP: When you were the U.S. Senate Sergeant-at-Arms, what workplace safety coordination efforts were required?

CASEY: Washington, D.C., is a patchwork quilt of police jurisdictions. The mall is actually a U.S. Park Police Jurisdiction as well as the Metro D.C. Police. We overlapped with both all the time because, for example, from our point of view, keeping demonstrations contained was important. The Capitol being as it is, we did not want demonstrations too close, as they became impossible to contain as the building has so many points of entry. Ergo—we would create zones to keep demonstrations from engulfing the access points. It always required close cooperation with the other departments and jurisdictions.

KEMP: When the July 24, 1998, shooting in the Capitol complex occurred, what changes were made to improve workplace safety?

CASEY: Frankly, I had testified not six months before to a congressional committee that we feared the current Capitol complex security was not sufficient because our ability to detect intruders who meant harm actually did not occur until they were already inside the existing security perimeter. The shooter in 1998 came into the office building with his pistol drawn. Secondarily, the first officer shot was giving some advice to tourists in the building and was caught blind-sided. Ergo—the entire complex was sort of an incident waiting to happen. We were aware of that possibility. We had suggested many times that we needed to create a stand-off security parameter so that we could better see, screen, and anticipate intruders who had harm in mind. That was part of our case to build an integrated, now famous and separate, visitor's center. The Hill is like an ant hill with people and entrances all over. After the shooting, all officers were more vigilant. We changed how we provided security at the doors by placing officers outside as well as inside, implemented further restrictions on who could use what entrances, and tried to create more extensive security parameters. We had *already* begun to create a new vehicle security perimeter after the Oklahoma bombing incident and had installed concrete planters to prevent vehicular traffic from accessing buildings. That was a stop-gap measure on the way to more secure iron ballards. We also had to reinforce windows and make structural safety feature changes. There was less actual change after the shooting in terms of the proposed plans but rather an acceleration of those changes we had already been seeking. This is one of those times when events forced action that was already being sought.

KEMP: As someone who worked to protect the highest elected officials of the United States, what stay-safe tips would you offer to the rest of us?

CASEY: First, just to mention some things that those providing security for potentially high profile targets should keep in mind. First, take every threat seriously until you know otherwise. Second, review number one again. Third, plan every aspect of the potential exposure scenarios, increasingly restricting the exposure as the situation warrants and resources allow. Where possible, have a trained professional run through the scenario or event. Their eye may catch vulnerabilities others simply do not see. Fourth, when developing security, do your due diligence. Don't get complacent and create or allow soft targets when not necessary. Fifth, train, rehearse the plans, and train again. Sixth, we informed security personnel that "your job is to protect while being flexible with political leaders. For elected officials, almost all security is too much." Number six for everyone else—remain alert and aware of your surroundings. Have situational awareness.

KEMP: What are the elements you would incorporate into a workplace safety program/plan?

CASEY: From a security standpoint, restrict or retard access to those not otherwise supposed to be on-site. Have an evacuation and/or emergency plan.

KEMP: What other ideas would you like to share about workplace or personal safety?

CASEY: Just to make an observation or two. People who look and act alert generally are less attractive targets than those that seem preoccupied or mentally distant. The same is true for targets of other things—like terrorism: alert people are less likely targets and well-secured buildings are less likely targets. Softer target examples would be daydreaming people who are open invitations for those seeking easy targets. Just don't make yourself an easy target.

## WEAPONS NOT PERMITTED ON-SITE

Certainly in government buildings, airports, and even in some schools, the security checkpoints that are designed to prevent weapons from coming into the buildings are understood to mean "no guns" here. In the last decade, more states have passed laws regarding a private property owner or a place of business posting prohibitions about guns and weapons not being permitted on their property. Even event venues such as convention centers and stadiums are now found with "no weapons" postings. What is your company policy about weapons at work? Does the policy cover guns, knives, archery equipment, electronic and chemical weapons?

## HAZARDOUS MATERIALS

Some jobs require daily handling of hazardous materials. Federal guidelines require training; special equipment and clothing; specific signage on containers, trucks, and areas; and special decontamination processes that govern business operations. From a law enforcement perspective, a general citizen's day may put you in contact with the following hazardous materials: gasoline, natural gas (most homes are heated by natural gas), some cleaning products, pesticides, and lawn and garden chemicals.

The key is to recognize when there is a problem and to know that calling 911 is legitimate.

## INTERNET SAFETY AT WORK

Workplace productivity has been impaired by the Internet and time spent on-line that is not related to work accomplishment. Although time spent on-line can seem harmless or be described as a "way to take a break without leaving my desk," actual harm and crime can occur. For example, the trading of pornographic pictures can be a crime, and it does happen on company-owned computers. Also consider these crimes that can be committed on-line: hacking, information theft, imitating children in order to lure them to meet an adult, embezzlement, and fraud. Next consider the use of on-line profiles, information sharing, hiring practices that can include misrepresentations, over-statements, and outright lies about who someone is and what someone is really about, because the Internet provides a false sense of protection to those who choose to lie and deceive others. Learn what your company policies about Internet use are, and share these policies with your employees. Every day someone in your company may be using on-line tools to commit crimes or at the very least to steal company time by pursuing nonwork activities. Many police departments now have detectives who specialize in on-line crimes. To learn more about the crimes that can be committed or are being committed on your company computers, contact your local police or sheriff's department and ask about their available services.

## COMMUNICATION SYSTEMS

At work, when traveling for work, or when at an off-site meeting, knowing what your communication options are is a critical part of being safe. Just because you have a cell phone doesn't mean that it will work in your office or in the concrete meeting room or that you'll be allowed to use it in a hospital room. Learn what your telephone options are when you are working. Also identify who the primary safety contacts are in your workplace. There may be a safety officer who is responsible for worksite safety, as well as a floor captain who is responsible when medical or other emergency situations arise.

Police use a clear chain-of-command approach to communicating in emergency situations. Since 9/11, an Incident Command System (ICS) for emergency response has been developed for all emergency responders. This system along with Critical Incident Management (CIM) training has been delivered to all emergency workers in the country. The importance of a single coordinated response to critical incidents has been realized by emergency response administrators. In response to this need, training on ICS and CIM has been made mandatory by many state and local emergency response agencies across the nation.

Using a command-and-control approach to decision making is critical when handling emergencies. Executing a safety or emergency evacuation plan requires on-the-spot problem solving and direction giving. In Jana's book *Moving Out of the Box,*[2] she suggests in Chapter 9 that there are times when schools, workplaces, and public gathering places all are in fact dependent on a command-and-control decision structure that leads to immediate action for safety rather than taking time for a come-to-consensus decision that may not be reached before danger has consumed a situation. Identifying who the people making command decisions are in the event of workplace emergencies is a part of safety planning. Some organizations identify floor captains, department or unit checkpoint people, or floor sweepers who are responsible for implementing safety plans in the event of danger.

## WORKPLACE SAFETY—ELECTRIC COMPANY VALUES SAFETY

Safety tips come from a variety of sources, and as the police say, "Check your source; if it is reliable, then take appropriate action." While driving, Jana noticed that a utility truck for Idaho Power had a decal saying "Safety Is a Value." Upon further research at the website for the corporation, safety discussions occur under the topic of water, trees and electric lines, energy emergencies, and electricity. The following is from Idaho Power's website page about electricity outages:

> For example, if rotational outages are necessary, there are things customers can do to help avoid delays in getting power restored. Turn off all appliances, machinery, and equipment in use when the power goes out, except for one light. When this light comes on, power has been restored. Turning off everything else will help protect your appliances against voltage fluctuations that may occur as a result of a circuit overload when power is restored. Once power has been restored, wait a few minutes and begin restoring appliances and lighting in 10-minute intervals. Keep a telephone that does not depend on electricity. Turn off electric ranges or space heaters (in winter) during a power outage; doing so will prevent the possibility of a fire if you are away from the office when power is restored.

These turn-off equipment precautions will help prevent injuries that could occur if machinery and equipment were to suddenly restart and will help to prevent circuits from being overloaded when power is restored.

Idaho Power also suggests that in an emergency you need to know how to protect your health and workplace if electricity is suddenly unavailable and from their company education materials: "Common sense and careful preparation will help you avoid problems and inconveniences. It's a good idea to put together an emergency kit including: matches, candles, a battery operated flashlight, a first-aid kit, extra blankets, a battery-powered radio, batteries, bottled water, canned and dried foods if people are not able to get home, a manual can opener, a wind-up clock or battery-powered clock, and a telephone that does not depend on electricity. Check with the gas, water, and electric utilities in your area to see how they recommend preparing for emergencies."

## WASHINGTON GROUP INTERNATIONAL—SAFETY IS EMPHASIZED

While working on her book *Building Community in Buildings*,[3] Jana discovered that safety is of such great importance to Washington Group International that site visitors as well as employees are included in their safety planning. In fact,

Washington Group International has "Safety Tips for Our Visitors" guide sheets (which are localized to each site) at their lobby reception desks. The guide-sheet information includes a request that you check in and out of the building and register your vehicle. The hours of the building are listed. The safety commitment is stated along with phone numbers for safety assistance or for reporting safety hazards. Steps for providing accident assistance and calling for 911 help are listed. A printed reminder that no alcohol, drugs, or firearms are permitted on the "premises, including parking lots" is included. "Smoking is prohibited inside of Washing Group International facilities and vehicles." Tips on using the telephone system are included. A phone number is listed for assistance in moving furniture or heavy items and for lighting or HVAC concerns. Fire emergency procedures are detailed and end with a reminder not to use the elevators in such an instance. As a visitor to the building, Jana felt safe knowing that the corporation had thought through these details and communicated them clearly upon her entry to the facility.

Additionally, at the Washington Group, there are designated employees who serve as emergency/fire wardens. There are at least two wardens per floor. They all receive first aid, CPR, and AED (automated electronic defibrillator) training. Each warden also serves on the safety committee to be the go-to person for employees regarding health, safety, and ergonomic issues and facilitates employee exit procedures during emergency drills and actual emergency events including checking the floor to assure that everyone has exited and made it out safely, including any visitors to the building. Safety is so important at the company that at any meeting with five or more people, a safety message is the first item on the agenda. This reinforces the commitment to safety for the visitors and employees and keeps them focused on daily safety.

## RECOGNIZING DRUG USE AT WORK

The Drug Free Workplace Act of 1988 set into motion compelling reasons for employers to ensure drug-free work places. Intoxicated workers present safety hazards on the job, not to mention marked reduction in the ability to do their jobs. It is useful for supervisors and fellow employees to be able to recognize the signs and symptoms of drug usage on the job.

Since the early 1990s law enforcement has used Drug Recognition Experts (DRE) to determine if a person is under the influence of a controlled substance. This program has proven useful in reducing the number of drugged drivers on our highways. A DRE using a series of physiological, physical, and cognitive examinations can predict with nearly 80% accuracy what drug or combination of drugs a person suspected to be under the influence may be using.

The DRE program has made its way out of the squad car and into the classroom. A shortened version of the DRE has been developed for educators; this program has been effective for teachers and counselors to spot and intervene with students using drugs. Many law enforcement agencies are willing to share this information with private industry. Useful drug recognition training can be supplied to private sector personnel in a matter of a few hours that will help them in spotting the drugged worker. Contact your local or state law enforcement agency for information on this program.

Some industries such as trucking and aviation require quarterly tests. Policies dealing with employees found to be using drugs range from immediate dismissal (being fired and not being eligible for rehire) to an unpaid day off or to company-paid addiction recovery programs. Drug use is happening in your workplace, whether it is using illegal drugs, which is a crime, or legally prescribed drugs being used inappropriately or being taken without due consideration to their effects. For instance, there have been driving-under-the-influence (DUI or DWI in some states) arrests made for people taking legally prescribed drugs who didn't realize how impaired the drug was making them. Again, drug use is happening every day in your workplace.

To recognize the signals of drug use, start looking for diminished coordination, excessive drowsiness, irritability, perspiring when it doesn't seem natural, bloodshot eyes, unusual smells emitting from a person, and even really excited and talkative behavior. Another way to recognize there's a problem is when you notice a dramatic change in a person's behavior or work performance. While this alone may not indicate drug use, it does provide a large clue to a change in the person's life for which he may need and even want help in dealing. For further information, seek out local or state police agencies, which in various states are now offering educational programs.

## DOMESTIC VIOLENCE HAPPENS AT WORK

By the name "domestic violence," it appears to be a non-workplace issue. However, work is the one known place someone wanting to commit violence toward a spouse, former spouse, or boyfriend/girlfriend can go to find the victim. As a result, your workplace is not free from concern about domestic violence. While working in Minnesota during the early 1990s, Jana remembers hearing a radio announcement about an industrial park that had been evacuated because a domestic violence situation had "come to work" in the form of an angry former spouse who came to find his "wife" at her manufacturing job, found her, and held her hostage. Make sure that your company has an emergency plan in place for just such a situation (again, the police department can help). Just because the domestic violence doesn't "show up in person" at your office as happened in the Minnesota case, that doesn't mean your workplace is free from its effects. Here's why. The Center for Disease Control estimates that the annual cost of lost productivity due to domestic violence equals $727.8 million, and more than 7.9 million paid workdays are lost each year. When someone is missing from work, do you really know why? Consider what may need to be done to help the missing employee. You may literally be saving a life.

## WORKPLACE ATTACK DANGER ZONES

Restrooms, parking areas, elevators, and hallways can all be places where potential attacks, robberies, muggings, or rapes can occur. In large-city, multistory office buildings, many restrooms now require a key for entry just because of the potential dangers that can occur when everyone is allowed access to restrooms. Sad, but true. Parking areas that are remote, not well lit, and not monitored by security guards can leave you open to attack as well. Carry your cell phone with you, and if you are really concerned about your safety, have the phone already dialed to 911 so that all you have to press is "send" in the event that you need help. Elevators, like restrooms, are enclosed spaces that allow someone to corner you and attack you. Never get onto an elevator with only one other person if you don't know the person. You are safer on an elevator alone, or with a group of people. Hallways are similar to parking areas because they too can be remote, poorly lit, or unmonitored by the security team. Become aware of all areas in your building and workplace that are and are not monitored by security cameras. Choose your pathways carefully and remain diligent to the task at hand: getting to and into your car. It is easy to become preoccupied with thoughts of the day and forget about your surroundings.

## WORKPLACE SAFETY INTERVIEW 2—LIGHTING LESSONS AND DRIVING SAFETY

Dan Allers, founder and owner of Idaho Theatrical Lighting and Idaho Cinematic Equipment, has worked with the Secret Service to light five U.S. presidents, has worked with Billy Graham's personal security team, on U.S. military bases, and with a variety of confidential corporate meeting events to ensure that both well-lit and safe environments exist for the speakers and for participants. Here are some of the things Allers has learned as a civilian during his twenty years of working to light corporate and public events. Allers's interview covers a variety of workplace safety topics and suggestions.

KEMP:   You've lit a number of events with very high levels of security. What can you share with us about lighting a public space that demands safety for the speakers and participants?

ALLERS:  The events I've lit have been for both live and television audiences; as a result, the audience and the speakers have all been equally lit. A high level of light equates to greater safety. The lighting plans are thought out and rehearsed in advance. Sometimes approval of the plans has to be given by an advance security team a day or so in advance of the event. Some groups I've worked with have what they call "circles of control" in which only certain people are allowed at the podium before, during, and after the event, followed by a color-coded badge set of circles of approved people who can be onstage and backstage, and then the people allowed into the room for the event have to pass through a metal security detection system and bag check before they can enter the room. Of course, everyone working an event like this has to pass a background check.

KEMP:   What is it like working with the Secret Service as a civilian contract worker?

ALLERS:  The Secret Service's attention to detail is extremely high, which requires a great deal of patience as the details get worked through and handled. Understanding that they have a job to do and a protocol to follow is critical and can take working several events before you get the feel for their systems.

KEMP: When have you seen plans change during rehearsals? And during an event?

ALLERS: First it is critical to have a plan and do things right from the start. Make sure the plan is safe. Be able to speed up the implementation of the plan when the situation calls for change. And when the last minute timing of things changes, be flexible and roll with the changes while still making everyone look professional.

KEMP: As a part of your work, you have a class "A" commercial driver's license and drive trucks varying in size from small moving trucks to forty-ton semi-trucks. What driving safety tips can you offer for all drivers?

ALLERS: Look ahead of you and around you at all times to be aware of what is happening or about to happen on the road. Watch for brake lights as far as one-quarter of a mile in front of you so that you can make adjustments and stay safe. Leave room around all sides of your vehicle so that you can maneuver safely as conditions change. Watch for drivers that are moving in and out of traffic, changing lanes abruptly, or driving erratically and putting many people at risk. When you see a semi-truck changing lanes to the left, remember that the driver can see more than you can in a car, so don't pull into the right lane to pass. And, a note about weather conditions: people in cars seem to think that semi-trucks are just as agile as cars and lightweight trucks. Every vehicle has a different stopping distance dependent on its weight, the type of brakes that are installed, the type of tires, and the weather conditions. Remember that in all weather conditions, trucks take longer to get going and longer to come to a stop than cars do. And, allow extra time in your travel schedule—a flat tire may need to be changed, a 51-point safety check may be asked for at a port of entry, road construction may add hours to your itinerary, or a change of weather may foil your plans.

KEMP: You also fly from worksite to event site to concert site for your work. What travel tips have you picked up over the years?

ALLERS: Because of the equipment and tools I need to carry for my work, I am typically a target for the TSA [Transportation Security Administration]. I realize this and work to maintain an attitude of patience because as frustrating as the check-in process has become, the TSA people are just doing their jobs, too. I've also adjusted what I carry on and what I put into checked luggage, as all business travelers have. So, back to planning: give yourself more time than you think you need to get through security checks. Some of the events I work expose me and my equipment to pyrotechnics, which makes me even more of a search target for TSA and military site inspections. Some of my trips are one-way, paid with a company credit card and within a few days of travel, all of which trigger TSA to search me.

KEMP: Is there anything else you'd like to add about lighting and workplace safety?

ALLERS: Be prepared to do the plan, work the plan, and change the plan because everyone has an agenda for the meeting and the safety and security of the event. In some of the event situations, you don't have an opportunity to build a long-term relationship. You are doing a job for this singular event, which may never happen in the same way again.

## AT THE END OF THE WORKDAY

Business safety plans include your personal plan for safety during your workday and the company's plans and policies for safety of employees and property and handling emergency and crisis situations. If you are genuinely not aware of your organization's safety plans, start asking questions. Every workplace whether there are only two of you working together or 200,000 working for the organization needs a clear set of safety plans. Risk assessment professionals can help in the creation of the plan. Law enforcement entities can conduct some risk assessments as a part of creating or refining a plan. They can also provide tip sheets and guides such as the following from the Boise Police Department Crime Prevention Unit.

### A Safe Workplace Starts with You

- Do you help to make our workplace secure?
- Did you lock your car when you left it in the parking lot this morning?
- If you are the last to leave at night, do you lock the door to your office or notify security?
- Did you report that broken light in the stairwell?
- Do you insist on identification from repair persons who come to work in the office? Are you extra alert when they are there?
- Do you know the location of the fire exits in your building?
- Do you keep your purse with you or locked in a drawer or closet instead of on your desk or on a table?

- If something suspicious or frightening happened—a stranger loitering near the door, a burglary, a telephone bomb threat—do you know the telephone numbers for security and the police and fire departments?
- Do you keep track of the office keys in your possession, storing them in a secure place and not handing them out to unauthorized persons?
- Do you shred important papers before discarding them in the wastebasket?
- Do you avoid letting telephone callers know that your boss or fellow workers are out of town?
- If a coworker were the victim of crime, would you know how to help?

## Safety in Transit

- If you are working late or reporting in early, try to meet another employee to ride together and enter or leave together. If you're in a one-person office or store, check with neighboring businesses to see if any of their employees have similar schedules. Make certain you have the most up-to-date schedules if you take public transportation.
- Don't get into elevators with people who look out of place or behave in a strange or threatening way. Report such individuals to security or the police.
- Don't use the stairs alone. Stairwells can be traps as well as a way to save time or get some exercise. Never enter a stairwell to escape pursuers or potential attackers. Go to an office where there are other people.
- Be extra cautious when using restrooms that are in isolated locations, poorly lighted, or open to the public.
- If you bank for your business, vary your route and time of departure. Conceal the bank bag.

## Parking Lot Sense

- Park in well-lighted, heavily traveled areas if possible. If you know you are going to be staying late, check for lights when you park in the morning. If there are no spaces near the lights, move your car to a better location at noon or when other employees begin to leave for the day.
- If you are working late, ask the security guard or a coworker to escort you to the parking lot.
- Always lock your car and roll up the windows all the way. If you notice any strangers lurking in the parking lot, notify security or the police immediately.
- Don't leave any valuable items in plain view inside your car. Leave them at home or lock them in the trunk.

- When you approach your car, have your key ready and check the floor and backseat before you get it.

**Office Security**

- Keep your purse, wallet, or other valuable items with you at all times or locked in a drawer or closet. Don't leave a purse on a desk or a wallet in a jacket that's left on a chair or coat rack.
- Never leave your keys lying about.
- Never leave change or cash on the desk or in a top drawer. Instead, place any cash in an envelope and put it in the drawer that you can lock.
- Check the identification of any strangers who ask for confidential information or any delivery or repair persons who want to enter an area restricted to employees. Don't be afraid to call for verification.
- If you notice any suspicious persons or vehicles, notify security personnel or the police. Be especially alert in large office buildings and after normal working hours.
- Report any broken or flickering lights, dimly lit corridors, doors that don't lock properly, broken windows, or broken pay phones to maintenance and security.
- Be discreet. Don't advertise your social life or vacation plans and those of your coworkers to strangers visiting your place of work.
- Keep the emergency numbers for security and the police and fire departments posted near every phone. It's also a good idea to write the address of the building on or near the phone. People often forget addresses when reporting an emergency at work. Post a list of employees who are trained in CPR or emergency first aid along with their extension numbers.
- If you are responsible for office keys, don't leave them on your desk or in a top drawer where they could easily be taken and copied. Only give out keys to persons who have legitimate need and make sure they are returned.
- Never write down safe or vault combinations or computer passwords.
- Know your coworkers and look out for each other. Ask a friend to watch your desk while you're in another room or out for lunch, and volunteer to do the same. Find someone who leaves at the same time or takes the same bus or subway and walk together.
- If you're going to be away from your desk, ask someone to answer your phone or have the calls forwarded to another phone.
- Always let someone know where you'll be whether it's coming in early, working late, going to the computer room, or going out to lunch or to a

meeting. If you have an accident, they will have an idea where you are and eventually come looking for you.

- Make sure all equipment in your office—computers, printers, copying machines, calculators—have been engraved with an identification number.
- Make sure copiers are turned off after hours and critical files are secured.

Workplace safety is dependent on every employee, customer, and visitor to a worksite. When something doesn't look safe, tell someone who can take action to get the situation addressed. If something immediately dangerous or life-threatening is happening, call 911. Work with your company managers and owners to establish or refine the safety policies for your business, and most important of all, have in place your personal plan for workplace safety.

## WORKPLACE SAFETY PLAN

1. Know what all of the company/organization's safety plans and crisis management plans are.
2. Know who the designated floor captains are before emergencies occur.
3. Know how to get to the exits nearest your workstation, your company conference rooms, the company cafeteria, and the restrooms.
4. Know how to dial 911 from your company phones.
5. Check with the gas, water, and electric utilities in your area to see how they recommend preparing for emergencies.
6. Learn how to recognize signs of drug impairment in others you work with.
7. Be aware of domestic problems that are coming to work.
8. Recognize an employee who may be having difficulty handling stress.
9. Know your company sexual harassment and/or hostile work environment policies.
10. If you are not aware of workplace safety plans, talk with your supervisor about what the plans are. If you are the person in charge, get started and build your workplace safety plans. Call the police and fire departments and ask for their help in building your plan.

## NOTES

1. Jana M. Kemp and Ken Baker, *Building Community in Buildings: The Design and Culture of Dynamic Workplaces* (Westport, CT: Praeger/Greenwood, 2007), 138.

2. Jana M. Kemp, *Moving Out of the Box: Tools for Team Decision Making* (Westport, CT: Praeger/Greenwood, 2007).

3. Kemp and Baker, *Building Community in Buildings*, 142–43.

# Seven

# What about Weapons and Safety?

Guns kept in the home for self-protection are 43 times more likely to kill a family member or friend than to kill in self-defense.[1] Gun homicide is the fourth leading cause of death for young people 10–14 years of age and the second leading cause of death for young people 15–24.[2] With these alarming statistics at hand, a full discussion about weapons for self-defense must start with how you first arm yourself with something other than a weapon. In a nation where the notion "Might makes right" is deeply seated in the American psyche, lessons of knowledge, wisdom, and love and how they keep people safe often take a backseat to the stories of violence winning the day. Later in this chapter after looking at firearms as a weapon of defense and some other weapons that may be available to you, we will come back to the idea that the very best defensive weapon is to develop the skill to avoid conflict in the first place and when you appear to have no other choice, to have the ability to think through the problem and solve it.

## FIREARMS

It is estimated that between 90 and 147 million people in the United States own a firearm. Thirty-seven of the 50 states have "Right to Carry" (RTC) laws.[3] In fact, the Second Amendment of the United States Constitution guarantees the "Right to Bear Arms": "A well regulated militia being necessary to the security of a free State, the right of the People to keep and bear arms shall not be infringed." Even though it has more to do with each state's ability and right to protect itself from an enemy, it cannot be denied that the Second

Amendment does give an individual the right to own firearms. RTC laws give individuals the right to carry a concealed firearm when the individual meets the specific requirements of the state that issues the license. There are communities in the United States that have taken the Second Amendment a step further. Consider this headline in the *New York Times* on January 16, 2007: "*A Rifle in Every Pot,*" telling about the small town of Greenleaf, Idaho, about 35 miles southeast of Boise, the state capital. In 2006, Greenleaf passed a city ordinance that suggested that every head of household in their town own a firearm. Greenleaf is a town in which violent crime is nonexistent. In Greenleaf's case the ordinance was primarily symbolic and was in response to the lawlessness that occurred in New Orleans after Hurricane Katrina. The city was worried that refugees with very different values about right and wrong could end up in Greenleaf. They were taking their destiny into their own hands. The ordinance raised little concern in this small conservative community where some 80% of the residences are estimated to already own a weapon. Greenleaf was serving notice to those who may chose to prey on this peaceful place that they were capable of taking care of themselves. As seen by this story and the daily gun-related violence occurring in large cities, it is an understatement to say that we are a gun culture.

Michael A. Bellesiles in *Arming America: The Origins of a National Gun Culture*[4] does an excellent job of dispelling the myth that Americans have been fascinated with guns and shooting from the very time the *Mayflower* landed at Plymouth Rock. America's fascination with guns extends back into the days of the Wild West. It was not until this time that it was typical for the common man to own a firearm. Often we read and are told that firearms are part of our coming of age as a nation. We are told tales of how the early colonial settlers hunted for subsistence and defended themselves with their muskets. According to Bellesiles, only the very rich, upper class owned guns. The early settlers were commoners and farmers, and they traded what they grew with the Native Americans for meat. The guns that were owned originally in this country were from Europe and often were in a state of disrepair. When they did work the majority of the settlers did not know how to use them.

This became a problem during the Revolutionary War; state militias in training for battle with the British had very few guns of their own and depended on the government to supply them. What weapons were supplied were poorly maintained because very few gunsmiths lived on this continent. This is not a popular view; we hold our past as sacred and were taught as little children that Davy Crockett could shoot the eyelash off a gnat at 100 yards with his flintlock rifle. Mostly myth with a little fact has created our view of the early settler and his prowess with a gun. Even up through the Civil War it was uncommon for regular folks to have firearms in their homes and to own a gun for self-protection. It was not until much later in our history that we see guns in the hands of the everyday citizen, and to own a gun for protection of one's self and family was just unheard of.

In Doug's three decades of law enforcement, he cannot recall an incident of an individual who owned a gun for self-protection or home defense discharging a firearm in self-defense against an attacker. He can however cite numerous occasions of accidental discharges of firearms, where someone was seriously injured or killed or more tragically where a child used the family gun to commit suicide. Deciding to own a firearm for self-defense is a very personal decision. In the gun culture we live in firearms are readily available, and if you are not a felon, are not mentally incapacitated, and have about $500 to pay for a weapon, you can be armed. It is a decision that many people have already made. If you have made the decision to own, then you should have also made the decision to understand how to properly store and handle your weapon.

Common sense comes into play here. Here's a reminder: if you own a gun, that gun is 43 times more likely to kill a family member or a friend than to kill an intruder or an attacker in self-defense. This most certainly does not have to be the case. You can take this number to nearly zero by following the basic rules of gun safety. It is imperative that you first learn how to handle your firearm. You must be intimately familiar with all of the working parts, how to load and unload it safely, where the gun safety is, and how it engages and disengages. Never point the weapon at anything you do not intend to kill. It is that simple, you are holding in your hand the power of taking a life. It is worth repeating again: Never point the weapon at anything you do not intend to kill. Take your weapon to a professional range so you can practice loading, unloading, and shooting it. If you are a novice gun owner, the operators of the range can arrange to give you some basic instruction on using your weapons. The National Rifle Association and other organizations also offer gun safety training. Now that you understand how to use your gun safely, the next most important part is how to safely store it. The most fool-proof way to store a gun is in a gun safe or gun locker. This is especially true if you have children in your house. Being an officer, Doug has a gun in his home. Normally he keeps it where he can access it if needed quickly. The gun is kept concealed and unloaded with the ammunition concealed in a separate location. This has not always been the case. When his kids were younger and living at home, Doug kept his handguns locked up because for him it was more important to eliminate the hazard to his family from an accidental discharge than to address the possibility of an unwanted intruder. When Doug's children were small and now when the grandkids come for a visit, his guns are locked in the trunk of the car.

The challenge of owning a gun is how to keep family members safe and at the same time how to have a gun readily available when you need it. Our suggestion is that you put your guns in a gun locker or safe. There are a variety of sizes and shapes of lockers and safes that can be purchased for a variety of prices. If you choose not to lock up your weapon so that you have better access to it, then at the very least you should store the ammunition separately from the weapon. Everyone living in the house needs to know where the gun is and why it is there. They all should also be trained in how to use it and when to use it. Realize that by having a gun unlocked in your home you have created a deadly situation. The only way to mitigate this risk is to be thoroughly trained in using it.

The next reality-check question that must be asked about owning a gun is "Are you mentally prepared to use it?" In other words, if you have purchased a gun to protect yourself and your family when the time comes and you determine that it is time to pull the trigger, can you do it? For a variety of reasons, this is something that should not be taken lightly. The first is that if you are not able to take the life of another human being with your firearm, you run the risk of that human being taking the gun from you and using it against you. Some may argue, "I will just use it to scare the attacker off." This might work; however, the would-be attacker you face may be a hardened criminal who will not be phased by the presence of a gun. It may give him something to consider for a moment, but as soon as he senses that you are hesitating to use the weapon, he knows you are not going to and will move in on you and take it away. Hesitation can be deadly. If you are going to have a weapon merely to scare off an attacker, then you are well advised to not have any bullets for it. Leave it empty or better yet disable it so it will not shoot. By doing this at least you will not become a victim of your own gun. Most people do not buy a gun for self-protection and then disable it. When they buy a gun for themselves, they have every intention of using it if the need arises.

The problem, as stated above is that most people have not thought through the ramifications of killing another person. Law enforcement officers are taught that when you sight the muzzle of your weapon on another human being, you better have justification to kill him. If not, the gun should not be out of your holster. Another thing that officers are trained to do is to consider the question of killing another person very seriously. Every officer has made the decision that if the need arises, they would be able to kill another person to protect themselves or others. If they have not fully made this decision, then they have become a liability to themselves, their departments, and the community.

As an armed citizen you will need to have a similar conversation with yourself. Are you mentally prepared to take another life? This is a serious reflection. We know people who choose not to own a weapon for this very reason. This does not mean that they are weak or less prepared; it just means that they have made the decision that is the best for them. The psychological price paid for using deadly force when not mentally prepared will be great. Our suggestion is that you have this discussion not only with yourself but with your entire family. If you have decided to own a gun for protection, then the entire family has to understand what that decision means. Take the time to make it absolutely clear that the weapon is off-limits to the children: ensure that they do not have the ability to access the weapon or ammunition. Once that lesson is firmly established in each person's mind, then they should be familiar with how the weapon works. It is a good idea for every family member that is old enough to have handled and shot the weapon on an approved range. By doing this you are teaching respect for the weapon as well as preparing those who could use it, to do so if the need arises.

The authors believe strongly that deadly force for the purpose of law enforcement needs to remain primarily in the hands of professionally trained officers. Lt. Col. Dave Grossman,[5] in his book *On Combat: The Psychology and Physiology of Deadly Conflict in War and in Peace,* speaks of three types of people in this world: wolves, sheep, and sheepdogs. The wolves are those who have a propensity toward violence and no empathy for others. They would try to harm us or our property in some way. The sheepdogs are those who have a capacity for violence and a deep love for fellow citizen. It is their job to keep the wolves away from the sheep. Finally, the sheep are those law-abiding individuals who make up the vast majority of our society. When sheep feel fear they move closer together, depending upon each other for some degree of protection. As they move together it becomes easier for the sheepdog to do his job. The sheepdog generally knows how the sheep will respond and goes about the job of keeping them safe. If some of the sheep decide to take on their own protection and leave the flock, it may make it more difficult for the sheepdog to do the job. However, if the wolf has been in their midst time and time again, they may feel the need to be proactive and take necessary precautions. Since September 11, 2001, the sheep, or general citizenry, have taken a little more responsibility for their own safety, and at the same time they have also become more tolerant of sheepdogs or the individuals and organizations working to keep them safe.

## FIGHTING BACK

Over the years, data has been tracked about those who fight back during a crime of violence. According to the 2003 Criminal Victimization in the United States study[6] conducted by the U.S. Department of Justice, there were 3,716,800 crimes of violence committed in which some form of self-protective measure was employed by the victim. Of this number 62.6% reported that the protective measures helped, 10.2% reported that self-protective measures hurt, and the remainder reported that protective measures neither hurt nor helped or are not sure what effect they may have had. Of those who felt their protective measures were helpful, 44% reported that they avoided injury or greater injury by fighting back, 17.4% escaped their attacker, 16.9% scared the offender off, 10.1% believed the self-protective measures they used helped in some other way, 6.9% protected other people, and 4.2% protected their property. The self-protective measures reported in the survey were as follows: attacked offender with weapon, attacked offender without weapon, threatened offender with weapon, threatened offender without weapon, resisted or captured offender, scared or warned offender, persuaded or appeased offender, ran away or hid, got help or gave alarm, screamed from pain or fear, and took other measures.

The study indicated that the offender was attacked with a weapon in only 0.8% of all cases. In contrast 21.8% of victims resisted or captured their attacker. In cases of robbery 20.5% of victims resisted their attacker, resulting in 32.7% being injured and 11.0% escaping injury. Compare this with the 14.8% who ran from their attacker: 11% were injured and 17.7% escaped without injury. The message appears to be clear, if you have the opportunity to run, do it: run as fast and as far as you can. Run toward activity of any kind; go to where there are people. The bad guy is not likely to follow you into a place where there is a chance of being identified or caught.

## LESS LETHAL APPROACHES TO SELF-DEFENSE

If you have determined that killing someone in self-defense is not for you, you might consider one of several "less lethal" alternatives to owning firearms. A variety of weapons sold as "less than lethal," meaning they are not intended to kill someone, are available to citizens. The authors do not advocate any of the following devices, but merely list them for informational purposes. Note that the manufacturers of these products will often market them as "less-than-lethal" force, giving the impression that they are not deadly force. However, you should be aware that the use of any of these products can result in great bodily harm and has even at times resulted in death. In many states the requirements for owning and using these weapons are the same or similar to owning and carrying a firearm; in some states they are banned. Less-than-lethal weapons include TASERs, stun guns, pepper spray, and your presence of mind. Before purchasing and carrying one of these alternatives to a firearm make sure to learn what the requirements for your state and community are.

## TASER

The TASER or Thomas A. Swifts Electronic Rifle, named after the cartoon inventor and adventurer Tom Swift, are now available for personal and home use. The TASER, which was invented in 1969, uses small darts attached to wires to deliver a neuromuscular interruption (NMI) "stun" to an individual. A TASER has an effective range of 25 feet. Used by law enforcement for several years this device has been an effective tool in subduing people who are threatening harm to themselves or others. Models of the device are now available for purchase by the general public for as little as $350. Time will tell if TASERs prove to be a viable alternative for personal protection.

Laws on the use of TASERs vary from jurisdiction to jurisdiction. Often they are very similar to the firearm laws of the place where you live. Be sure to become intimately familiar with the regulations of carrying and using a TASER in your community before choosing this device for personal protection. Once you are familiar with the regulations to carry, it is very important to become familiar with the use of the weapon. Most TASER-like devices will have a cartridge that attaches to the triggering mechanism. It is the cartridge that contains the business end of the TASER. You need to know how to quickly and safely change or reload the cartridge of the device you have purchased. Law enforcement officers are required to regularly certify or qualify with a TASER just as they are required to qualify with their firearm on a regular basis. It is just as important for you to understand how to handle, care for, and maintain your TASER as it is when you own a firearm.

## STUN GUNS

The stun gun was on the scene before the TASER. This device delivers an electric shock of from 100,000 to one million volts, which can effectively neutralize an attacker. These devices range in price from $100 to as little as $10.95. The major drawback of these devices is that you have to come in contact with the target. This small device can be concealed easily in a pocket or purse and has the greatest effect if it comes into direct contact with the skin. This is why the neck, shoulders, and side of the head are a good target for a stun gun. This means you have to be close enough for attackers to get their hands on you, which is not the preferred scenario when handling your personal protection. Distance is safety when dealing with an attacker. A stun gun can be a deterrent if you are proficient with the device. If not, at best it will be ineffective and at worst it will likely be used against you.

## PEPPER SPRAY

Another personal protection device for consideration is Oleoresin Capsicum (OC) spray, better know as pepper spray. It is made from the resins of plants in the chili family, hence the name "pepper spray." This weapon causes tearing, burning, and even temporary blindness. It has the effect of incapacitating those who have been exposed to it. It has an effective range of up to 18 feet. It has the advantage of being very compact in size and comes in a variety of configurations. You can get pepper spray in rings, lipsticks, and other common and concealable-container devices. It is relatively inexpensive. Like the stun gun there are drawbacks, one of which is in the administration of the product. You are as likely as the target to be affected by the effects of the spray, so you need to be ready to deal with the discomfort that application of this product may bring. Doug remembers one hot summer evening when dealing with an intoxicated subject who was trespassing at a residence. Doug and two other officers were in the front of the house; the suspect was standing on a porch slightly elevated from Doug's position. The suspect was being very aggressive and threatening, refusing to leave the residence; he was being what law enforcement refers to as a "No" person, and Doug made the decision to deploy OC. What Doug did not take into account was the difference in elevation between him and the bad guy, who was higher than he was, and the wind direction was not in Doug's favor. As Doug fired the spray up at the individual, his aim was low, and at the same time a gust of wind caught the majority of the stream and blew it directly back into his face. The fight was over for Doug even before it started. Luckily, there were two other backup officers who had better position and aim than he had and stepped in to control the suspect while Doug was trying desperately to get away from the fire in his face and maintain some sense of dignity.

One way to minimize getting OC'd by your own device is to use the "gel" or "foam" version. These products are sticky and when applied adhere to the target, thereby reducing the amount of drift that may occur. The last thing you want to do is to incapacitate yourself when dealing with a threatening individual. Regardless of the type of pepper spray or other "less lethal" weapon that you use, three things are important: (1) a thorough understanding of the proper use and effect of the weapon, (2) understanding of the limitations of the weapon, and (3) a thorough understanding of the laws concerning the carrying and use of weapons in the state and jurisdiction that you live in.

It is imperative that you learn how use your weapon of choice. If you merely purchase the product, bring it home, and place it on the shelf or in your purse, you are not being as prepared as you could be and are asking to have the weapon used against you. The savvy criminal knows when he has run into someone who knows what they are doing or whether this just another sheep who in desperation has obtained what she thinks is going to protect her. It is also important to know what effect your weapon is likely to have on an attacker. If you are using a TASER and you are expecting the device to completely incapacitate an attacker long enough for the police to arrive, you may be in for a surprise. A TASER generally will incapacitate a person briefly. However, the effect wears off rather rapidly, and if you do not have a way to subdue and confine the attacker, you may have to administer repeated shocks, or you may even lose control of the situation. This is true with any weapon; short of killing someone, weapons all have a limit as to how effective they will be. Pepper spray for instance will incapacitate most people for several minutes, with a severe burning and even temporary blindness. However, some people who are under the influence of drugs or with certain mental impairments do not seem to be adversely effected by pepper spray.

Finally again, you must do your homework on what your state laws and city ordinances are concerning the various weapons. In some jurisdictions like Washington, D.C., for instance, nearly all of the weapons that we have talked about are not legal to purchase, possess, or use. Other jurisdictions have laws that are similar to owning and carrying a firearm, and still others simply do not address less-than-lethal weapons.

## PERSONAL WEAPONS

We have talked about the traditional weapons that are generally pictured when discussing weapons for defense. Let's consider the more nontraditional yet much more readily available weapons. We often forget about our best defensive weapon: the one that sits on top of our shoulders. Using your head to keep yourself out of trouble will go a long way toward keeping you safe. For instance, police officers learn that their very presence sends a signal to the people they are dealing with. This is why it is important for them to look and act professional in uniform. Using presence and body language, officers can send such messages as "I'm here to help," "I now have control of this situation," or "This situation is unacceptable and needs to change—now." Conversely, they can send these messages, too: "I am not comfortable in this situation, "I am angry about having to be here," "I have better things to do with my time," or "I am scared to death; how do I get out of here?" From a citizen's point of view in daily life situations, presence means: walking like no one should mess with you. This takes on the appearance of head up, scanning the area around you, walking with a confident stride, and exuding confidence about yourself and your space. Personal presence is a weapon: the way that you carry yourself and present yourself to the world around you is your first line of defense. The proper poise can keep you from being selected as a target from the very beginning of a meeting or an interaction. Other weapons were mentioned in Chapter 2, such as proper lighting at your residence. Lighting can be an extremely effective weapon because it can prevent an attack from ever taking place. The best kind of weapon you can have is the one that keeps you from having to come face-to-face with a wolf, predator, or opportunistic attacker.

Prevention of danger and safety planning go hand in hand. On the planning front, have you ever walked through your house and made note of the items that can be used as a weapon? This is an interesting exercise to try. You will be surprised at what you find. For instance, Doug has a fireplace in his living room that has a heavy set of brass fireplace tools, any of which would make an excellent striking weapon if needed. Continuing on in your house, you may find a vase, statue, or lamp that has weight to it that can be use to strike. In the kitchen you have a variety of weapons. Obvious are knives and skillets; less so are teapots or perhaps an iron. In your garage and shop are a number of effective weapons: axes, hatchets, hammers, rakes, and tool handles of various sizes and weights. Tables and chairs can be used to throw at or block the progress of an attacker. You will be surprised at what you find as you do this exercise.

More important than the quality of the weapon that you have when you need one is the fact that you have thought about it and can rapidly move into a defensive position and effectively defend yourself. The only way you can do this is to think about it. You must do your homework and your mental rehearsals. To be able to think rapidly and arm yourself with whatever is available is a skill that you have to practice mentally. A good example of a group of citizens who used what was available for a defense attack are the passengers of United

Flight 93 on September 11, 2001. These passengers found what was available to use to defend themselves: they used serving carts, coffee urns, and hot water and attacked the terrorists that were in control of the plane. In their case, their defense turned into an offense out of necessity: they knew their fate and decided the only thing that made any sense was to fight back. They all lost their lives, but they prevented additional lives from being lost because they were able to think about what could be a weapon and turned everyday items into such effective offensive weapons that they changed the intended results into a less deadly outcome.

Many of you have boarded one or more airplanes since September 11, 2001, and have likely sat on a plane, looked around, and thought about what you would use if placed in a similar situation. You have mentally rehearsed and thought about these scenarios. We believe this is why since United Flight 93 there have been several incidents of passengers successfully overcoming people who posed a threat aboard airliners. Because many people now mentally rehearse the airline scenario, it has become much more difficult for would-be terrorists or other attackers to accomplish their intentions. We now hear stories of passengers overcoming threatening behavior by physically overcoming the threat and effectively neutralizing it until the plane is safely back on the ground, where the authorities can take control. These acts of heroism by every-day people are accomplished by those who have mentally prepared themselves for the scenario. Each of you has the same capability. It is a matter of preparing yourself. Everything about personal safety, family safety, and safety at home, work, and play starts with planning.

Whether you make the choice to keep a formal weapon such as a gun, pepper spray, or TASER for defense or chose to depend on the more informal type of defensive weapon, such as common household goods, or simply preparing your mind to problem solve when faced with a dangerous or threatening situation, owning a weapon is your choice to make. The important thing is to make a plan, think it though, and rehearse it. A plan is virtually free, does not take much time to establish, and may save your life or the life of a loved one.

## WEAPONS SAFETY PLAN

1. Develop your own skills for avoiding conflict and confrontations.
2. Determine why you want to own a weapon of any kind.
3. Learn how to use whatever weapon(s) you decide to purchase.
4. Be sure that every member of your family knows what the rules of weapons safety are.

5. Monthly, walk through your house and identify what you can use as a weapon.
6. Know the rules and regulations concerning weapons in your community.
7. Properly store and lock all firearms.
8. Mentally prepare yourself for possible use of deadly force.
9. When resisting an attacker you are less likely to be injured if you resist by running than by physically fighting back.
10. Less-than-lethal does not mean that someone will not be seriously injured or killed if one of these weapons is used.

## NOTES

1. A. Kellerman and D. Reay, "Protection or Peril? An Analysis of Firearm Related Deaths in the Home," *The New England Journal of Medicine* 314(24) (June 1986), 1557–60.

2. Linda Pickle, Michael Mangiole, Gretchen Jones, and Andrew White, Atlas of United States Mortality, Centers for Disease Control and Prevention, National Center for Health Statistics, Hyattsville, MD; Hyattsville, MD; 1997. DHHS Pub. No. 97–1015.

3. Rick Bartlett Investigations, Defensive Firearms Training, CCW Concealed Weapons Permit, http://www.azccw.com/ (accessed July 29, 2007).

4. Michael A. Bellesiles, *Arming America: The Origins of a National Gun Culture* (New York, NY: Alfred A. Knopf, 2000).

5. David C. Grossman and Loren W. Christensen, *On Combat: The Psychology and Physiology of Deadly Conflict in War and in Peace* (United States PPCT Research Publications, Belleville, IL. 2004).

6. Catalano, Shannon, *Criminal Victimization in the United States*, 2003 National Crime Victimization Survey, Bureau of Justice Statistics, Office of Justice Programs, U.S. Department of Justice, NCJ doc. no. 205455.

# Eight

# What to Know about Disasters

Disasters do happen, and when they do, law enforcement is called on for a variety of tasks: traffic direction and control, emergency communications, evacuation procedures, and protecting business and residences from looting and other criminal problems that stem from communities in chaos. You can recognize that a natural disaster is in the making by learning to identify how the weather changes leading up to a tornado or hurricane. You can also learn to recognize the indicators leading up to mudslides (dry season followed by lots of rain) and wildfires (dry season followed by lightning or a human-created ignition spark). You can actively monitor weather stations to learn in advance what weather conditions may create damaging or disastrous effects in your area. Another approach is to buy a weather-service radio so that you can listen to the continuously broadcast weather news. Learning to recognize when a man-made disaster is about to strike is less predictable. Man-made disasters typically occur when the failure of character and decision making on a criminal's part puts you in harm's way or when a human-built structure fails without warning. Regardless of the type of disaster, by having a plan of action in place and in mind you can better, more quickly, and more safely respond to whatever comes your way.

Also, regardless of which type of disaster is in the making in your community, your local news channels on television and radio will be likely to cover what is happening so that you can avoid the disaster area, prepare for the disaster that is about to strike your area, or redirect family members out of harm's way. Keeping current with what is happening in the natural and built environment of your community in order to stay safe includes knowing where road construction is occurring, knowing which waterways are flowing at capacity or over their banks and near flood stage, and knowing the status of wildfire in your area and if evacuation warnings or orders have been given.

Community responses to disasters typically include individuals from all walks of life coming together to immediately address the problems that have occurred or are unfolding. During the disaster, everyone's focus is on "what needs to be done now." After a disaster, a whole new team of professionals are involved in putting the pieces back together again. For instance, the American Red Cross often coordinates with law enforcement responding to disasters. The organization also provides hundreds of preparedness and emergency planning tips in booklet form and at their website: http://www.redcross.org. A variety of service organizations also work with law enforcement in response to disasters. For instance, in Istanbul, Turkey, a QuakePark teaching space opened as a result of a Rotary Foundation grant that built the facility, earthquake simulators, and teaching space in order to demonstrate what happens during an earthquake and to teach people how to survive an earthquake as safely as possible.

## NATURAL DISASTERS

*Time* magazine, on August 28, 2006, ran the headline, "Floods, Tornadoes, Hurricanes, Wildfires, Earthquakes? ... Why We Don't Prepare." The piece was written by Amanda Ripley and depicted the number of times each natural disaster occurred over a 20- to 100-year period. A major part of the article focused on the "national culture of unpreparedness" that prevails in the United States. A year later, when the Minneapolis Interstate Bridge 35W collapsed for no clear reason, the lack of infrastructure maintenance and disaster preparedness, along with news of New Orleans' deteriorating water treatment facility, again prompted questions about failures of being prepared. As we've mentioned, it is important that you make a plan and rehearse or practice it, therefore being better prepared for just about anything that happens to you. Historically we have more information than at any other time in history when it comes to natural disaster response. Natural disasters happen. Although they can not be prevented, their effects can be minimized when you are prepared. Law enforcement agencies work hand in hand with emergency response personnel to respond to natural disasters. Here are the overarching guidelines for responding to natural disasters.

First, know which of the following natural weather and potential disasters are most likely to occur in your area. Hurricanes occur in coastal areas and result from strong winds and storms at sea blowing inland. Tornados, microbursts, and high winds can occur nearly everywhere. In snow country and in high elevations, avalanches can occur in both the form of snow and of rocks and soil. Snowstorms and blizzards happen seasonally in areas where snow falls and when high winds blow falling snow. In many areas rain and hail can also fall. Although rain alone is rarely damaging, it can create dangerous driving conditions. Hail on the other hand not only creates dangerous driving conditions, it can also damage cars and houses, as well as knock people out if they get hit by a hailstone. Volcano eruptions happen periodically around the world in such western U.S. terrains as Hawaii, Oregon, and Washington. Also, a more regional phenomenon is the earthquake. Then there are floods. The United Nations reports that 500 million people around the world are affected every year by flooding. Floods can occur along a waterway, canals, or road and can make their way into areas even good distances from the actual water source. Flash floods are the result of a rainstorm that creates so much water flow that normal waterways can't carry all of the water.

## WILDFIRES

In drier climates, wildfires can be sparked in fields, forests, and deserts. Wildfires consume both animal and human habitats, so having a fire-management plan for a home in wildfire territory is important. In our country, living just about anyplace outside of major population areas is an area prone to wildfires, but as we have seen in California in recent years, even some high-population areas can still be devastated by a wildfire. Wildfires come in two major categories: forest fires and rangeland fires. Forest fires occur when timberlands burn uncontrolled. They will consume large areas of timber, burning trees and shrubs to various degrees, depending on the intensity and location of the blaze as well as the weather at the time of the fire. Forest fires can be fairly predictable; weather, topography, and resources available to control them give fire managers a good idea what the fire will do. However, forest fires can turn deadly without warning and quickly trap people who are trying to control the blaze as well as those who may be living or recreating in the path of the fire. The other type of wildfire is the rangeland fire. This type occurs when range grasses and sagebrush are ignited. Generally, they are fast moving and burn everything in their path. If you live in an area prone to either forest or rangeland fires, there are several things you should have already done to be prepared and divert a possible disaster.

Preparing your defense against a wildfire begins when you choose a location to build that is the best for defending against wildfires. Build using fire-resistant materials, especially roof, siding, and windows. Look at your property: do you have a defendable space completely around your house? A defendable space means a cleared area that reduces or negates the possibility of fire burning to your house.

The amount of space that you need depends on the topography around your house; if you live on a hill, you will need a much larger space on the downhill side than if the property is flat. Fire travels very rapidly uphill. In the defendable space you should remove as much vegetation as possible; trees remaining should be thinned so that there is a minimum of 15 feet between the crowns. This will reduce the likelihood of fire traveling through the crowns of the trees. Sprinklers installed on the perimeter of your defendable space will help retard fire moving toward you house. The website http://www.fema.gov gives a very detailed list of things that you can do to prepare your property to survive a wildfire.

If a fire comes, evacuate as quickly as possible. Don't wait; fires can move rapidly and cut off your escape route. Leave lights on in every room of the house so it can be seen in heavy smoke. Turn the gas off, and move any combustibles near the house away. Close but do not lock all doors and windows that firefighters may need to gain entry. The area will be under an evacuation order, which mean law enforcement will be watching the area.

If caught in your vehicle during a firestorm, turn on your lights, roll up the windows, close all vents, and drive slowly. You can survive a fire in your vehicle. If smoke becomes so heavy or fire cuts off your route, find a place with the least amount of trees and brush near it. Pull to the side of the road, and turn your engine off, but leave your lights on. Get on the floor of the vehicle and cover yourself with jackets, blankets, or whatever you have available. It will get hot and smoky, and your vehicle may even be rocked by the winds being created by the fire. Stay in your car: it will not burn up. You are safer in it than out of it. The fire will quickly pass and then you can continue your evacuation.

If caught in the open during a firestorm, locate an area with as little fuel as possible. Avoid very steep hillsides and rock chimneys or canyons. Try to find a small depression in the ground. Clear any burnable debris away from you. Lie face down and cover yourself with whatever clothing, blanket, or sleeping bag that you may have available. Stay put and let the fire pass. The tendency will be to stand and run when the fire gets close. Resist the urge; you cannot outrun the fire, and on your feet you will be much more susceptible to being overcome by smoke.

As with any natural disaster, preparing, planning, and keeping calm are keys to surviving a wildfire.

## SNOWSTORMS

Other natural disasters that can occur in many places in the country are snowstorms and blizzards. Being caught in a snow or ice storm while driving can present a hazardous situation. Wintertime driving requires a vehicle with good tires that is supplied with emergency equipment to survive if you should get stuck. Most important is having adequate warm clothing and/or a sleeping bag to keep warm. Your body will need calories to fight the cold; having some high calorie snacks and water will help you stay warm. If you become stuck in your vehicle, do not leave it. Working in northern Idaho, Doug has investigated, on several occasions, vehicles that have become stuck in the snow. The drivers who got out to walk often were found only several hundred feet from the vehicle frozen to death. It is difficult to judge distance and the effort it takes to walk in below-freezing weather in deep and blowing snow. Stay with your vehicle, conserve energy, and wait for the snowplow to find you.

Major snowstorms can bring major cities to a halt. Many still recall the blizzard of January 1996, which was responsible for more than 100 deaths and brought much of the eastern United States to a complete standstill. Schools and businesses shut down for several days, and many roads were impassable. Power outages often accompany these storms. In fact, there are many weather disturbances that can cause power outages: hurricanes, tornadoes, and flooding can all trigger power to fail. Most power outages are brief and do not interrupt our lives much. However, there are times in very severe weather, such as Hurricane Katrina, that power may be lost for long periods of time.

Knowing that outages will occur from time to time is reason enough to have an emergency kit in your house. See Appendix 3 for a list of what your home emergency kit should contain. Being prepared for these times will allow you to survive even a several-day outage without too much discomfort.

As a result of some natural disasters, contagious illnesses can circulate. These can occur anywhere, to anyone at any time. The key is to listen to and watch for media reports about diseases and viruses that may be at work in your community.

Second, once you are aware of the potential natural disasters that can befall your area, make a plan for responding to those emergencies. Once you've identified the potential disasters that can occur in your community or travel areas, you can build a plan that matches up with what you are most likely to face.

Third, prepare and stock an emergency kit. Tips have been given throughout the book and are also found in the appendixes for building a kit that meets your potential needs. Finally, stay informed. Preparing once is not enough. Update your plan as family circumstances change. Inspect your emergency response kit twice a year to make sure that food is fresh, that water is still drinkable, and that batteries are still charged. Each day, be aware of the changing weather and environmental conditions that may require a response from you and your family members.

In an effort to aid community response to disasters, a variety of corporations have committed their resources to providing information and education about them and inventorying items needed in response to natural disasters. For example, Wal-Mart has enough data now about what people buy in response to a hurricane, a blizzard, or a tornado so that inventory of the most-purchased items can be directed to the stores closest to disaster sites, making the most-needed supplies more readily available. Target teamed up with the American Red Cross to create a communication campaign that informed adults and children about how to make a plan of action for responding to disasters. Target also teamed with the American Red Cross to support National Preparedness Month (September of each year), a national program sponsored by the Department of Homeland Security. The goal of the program is to increase public awareness about the importance of preparing for emergencies and to encourage individuals to take action and to build their own safety plans and emergency response kits.

## MAN-MADE DISASTERS

Unlike natural disasters, or as insurance companies like to say "acts of God," man-made disasters happen when a human being intentionally creates harm for many people or when a human-built structure falls apart causing harm to many people.

## DAMS BREAKING

Man's desire to control the environment, to create energy, and to manage agricultural lands has lead to the building of dams across a number of waterways. Once a waterway's flow is contained and controlled in a new way, other potentially negative effects come into play. When a dam breaks, your ability to get out of harm's way is entirely dependent on your proximity to the dam and to the natural immediate flow of the now-released water. To avoid being swept away in a man-made flood, live outside of flood zones, which are identified by Federal Emergency Management Agency (FEMA); work outside flood zones; and travel with a knowledge of where dams are located and what pathways released water would likely take. Have an idea of an evacuation route; this usually means going to high ground. Beware, however, that if you must travel through a low-lying area prior to going up, you may put yourself at greater risk. When planning, consider more than one way to escape a flooding area; roadways may become congested with traffic and hinder an escape.

When a dam breaks, law enforcement gets involved by calling for, enforcing, and aiding in evacuation to safer ground. They will protect the evacuated area as much as possible from looters and other criminal elements while the evacuation is in effect.

## BRIDGES FALLING

Over the years, railroad bridges have collapsed, river bridges have gone down, and bridgeways have crumbled in earthquakes. By the very act of building a bridge over a natural feature or over other man-made structures, human beings have introduced a new scale of potential disaster into everyday living. On August 1, 2007, the Minneapolis Interstate Bridge 35W collapsed without warning. An Associated Press headline on August 4th read "Miracle in Minneapolis: Rescue Crews' Quick Response and the Design of the Bridge May Have Saved Many Lives." The aftermath stories from those in cars, trucks, and the one bus indicate that somehow most everyone kept their wits about them and responded to the situation rather than panicking. That is perhaps the greatest miracle and the best part of the story. From the woman who said she saw something happening, slammed her foot onto her brake pedal, and pulled up her emergency brake, thereby saving her from a tumble off the bridge, to the woman who refused to stay trapped where she was because a truck had fallen onto her car, individuals took action. Consider the bus full of children and young adults. They all got out because one young man had the sense to kick out the back door of the bus and start getting kids out. Other people then came to help. Individuals came together to take action in response to a single event that none of them had likely ever imagined happening. Each person acted on a survival instinct; they didn't freeze, and they didn't whine while waiting for help. Perhaps some of them had been in harm's way before and knew that action was imperative. Perhaps some of them actually had rehearsed "what if" scenarios and knew that action was required, and perhaps still others got lucky because the people around them were taking action to help. It will likely take a year or more before the real cause of this disaster is determined. Yet, the immediate and permanent story remains that it is a "miracle" that so many people survived. The key is that being prepared, rehearsing "what if" scenarios, and maintaining your sense of calm can in fact save your life.

## IDENTITY THEFT

Identity theft is a man-made disaster because when other people steal information that creates a financial disaster in your life, it can take years to recover from a single theft of your identity. Identity theft occurs when someone takes enough of your personal information to take on your identity and transact commerce in your name through your bank account and credit card companies. Stolen checks can be forged and then used to empty your bank account. Stolen credit cards or credit card numbers can be used by nearly anyone to make purchases in your name. A stolen birth date, social security number, and driver's license number can let someone else apply for credit in your name. Fraudulent checks can be used to make payments at garage sales, places of business, and restaurants. Some estimates place the annual cost of identity theft in the United States at $50 billion a year.

Here are some tips for avoiding identity theft. First, don't carry your social security card with you. Keep it in a safe place and carry a copy if you must. When the original card is requested for employment or other legitimate purposes, then you can make arrangements to bring the original card with you to a next meeting. Second, don't give away your information freely. Remember the tip from Chapter 4 that giving your telephone number at a cash register is not a good idea. Simply decline to give a number. Third, don't respond to unsolicited e-mails, mailings, phone calls, or requests for information. If you didn't initiate the inquiry, then someone else is trying to get information to use against you or to use for fraudulent and illegal purposes. Fourth, every month review your credit card statements for accuracy. Be sure that there are only charges that you have made on the statement. If you don't recognize a charge, call the credit card company to get details and to confirm whether or not it is really a charge that you made. Fifth, protect your mail. Do not pay bills from your own unsecured mailbox. Instead, make payments only at post office mailboxes. Another reason to protect your mail is that hundreds of details about your personal and financial life arrive via the mail: credit card statements, mortgage statements, investment reports, insurance information, utility bills, phone bills, and even gifts that arrive in the form of checks. Where you can, use a post office box for all of your mail rather than a physical street address. By using the post office box, you are protecting the privacy of your mailed information, and you are additionally protecting the physical address of your home. Sixth, protect your computer from viruses, spyware, cookies, and pop-up ads. Do not respond to ads you did not request to see. Buy computer software that protects your system from viruses. Hire a computer professional to debug and remove spyware and cookies from your system. Data mining can happen from anywhere at anytime when you are connected to the Internet. So, protect your data, your information, and yourself. Finally, review your credit report at least once a year. Doing so allows you to confirm that no one has opened a credit card in your name and to confirm that only your data is showing up on your credit report. Having your identity stolen in any way can cost you hundreds to tens of thousands of dollars, can consume dozens if not hundreds of hours to undo any damage done to your name and credit standing, and can destroy your peace of mind. So, do everything you can to protect your identity, your personal information, and your financial records, and as the debate continues over instituting a national identification card for every person to carry, determine how you want your private data to be accessed and then make a stand for your position.

## PROTESTS AND RIOTS

Protests and riots are man-made disasters because they result when anger or even celebrations spin out of control and harm people and property. From Detroit's Super Bowl riots in 1967 that killed 43 people, destroyed over one thousand buildings, and led to more than seven thousand arrests, to Kent State's 1970 protest turned riot over the war, man-made disasters include human beings coming together en masse in such a way that disaster ensues. Think, too, of the 1991 Rodney King beating event in Los Angeles that lead to rioting and looting throughout the area. The World Trade Organization meetings in Seattle, Washington, in 1999 and the recent immigration rally turned riot at MacArthur Park in Los Angeles on May 1, 2007, both caused extensive damage and numerous injuries. A series of poor decisions typically leads people from peaceful gatherings into a series of violence-oriented events. Sometimes the riot started when police moved in to confront an assembly that they saw as having the potential to get out of hand. Already raw emotions are sparked and a riot erupts. For law enforcement it is a fine line keeping control of a peaceful assembly and avoiding an evolution into violence.

To keep yourself safe, pay attention to large gatherings of people to determine whether peace is prevailing or whether a turn toward violence is afoot. Call 911 for help if you sense that danger is ahead. Follow directions being given by law enforcement. Sometimes they do seem heavy-handed and seem to be making matters worse. However, you can be assured that they have a plan to keep control of the situation. If need be, their plan may contain pepper spray, water cannons, and barricades. Follow directions, and you will be more likely to get out unharmed.

## BOMBS AND ACTS OF TERRORISM

The reality of our world is that terrorist attacks are likely to occur again on our soil. Responding to these disasters will be the same as other disasters. As a citizen your responsibility is to be vigilant. If you see suspicious activities, report them. Every state now has a Department of Homeland Security that is busy planning for prevention and response to another attack. You can help by providing information. More than one terrorist attack has been thwarted by a citizen seeing people video-recording or photographing public places that didn't seem right to them. Further investigation into some of these has uncovered plots by terrorist cells to do harm to a mall, stadium, or other place people gather in large numbers. It is incumbent on each of us to be vigilant in these challenging times in which we live.

## RESOURCES

When immediate action is required, dial 911. Then work with all uniformed services to determine what immediate actions are needed to prevent further harm and to begin recovering from any damages. After the disastrous event has occurred, continue to work with law enforcement to protect valuables and property, with hospitals on medical recovery, and begin working with agencies such as FEMA and the Small Business Administration to plan for major property recovery efforts. Work with your insurance agent now to determine what kinds of coverage you have and what you need in order to financially handle the aftereffects of a disaster.

As stated early in this chapter, disaster may strike so suddenly that you do not have an opportunity to get out of harm's way. The point is to have a plan of action that you and every family member are aware of and are able to implement in the event of a disaster. What follows is an emergency and disaster plan worksheet for you and your family to complete. Having this plan in hand and rehearsing or practicing with it two to four times a year will make responding to a real emergency more successful.

## EMERGENCY AND DISASTER PLAN WORKSHEET

1. Where will you meet your family members?

   (a) When you are at home?
   (b) When not everyone is at home?

2. How will you communicate with each other? List cell phone and contact numbers for:

   (a) Mom
   (b) Dad
   (c) Child

(d) Child

(e) Child

(f) Doctor(s)

(g) Emergency contact if parents aren't reachable:

  (1) Grandparents, aunts, and uncles

  (2) Other

3. What is each family member responsible for bringing to the meeting place?

4. Who is responsible for a monthly or quarterly rehearsal of "what to do if . . ." plans?

5. Who is responsible for making sure food, water, and charged batteries are in the designated meeting spot?

6. In the event of a tornado, my family members know to:

7. In the event of an earthquake, my family members know to:

8. In the event of a blizzard, my family members know to:

9. In the event of a hurricane, my family members know to:

10. In the event of a _____, my family members know to:

11. If someone breaks into our house, family members know to:

12. If someone gets separated from the rest of us, the plan is to:

13. If you get separated from your family, what will you do?

14. If you are not at work or school when a disaster strikes, what will you do?

In addition to having personal, family, and business plans for disaster response and recovery, work to ensure that neighborhood preparedness plans are also in place. The way one neighborhood responds to a flood may in fact create new flooding in a neighborhood downstream, so coordinating within a neighborhood and among neighborhoods is important. An act of terrorism can shut down one building, one block, or an entire city. Participate in building a response plan that reaches out to all potentially affected individuals and groups.

Disasters happen. Being prepared in advance is the prevention piece of this chapter. The more thoroughly you have prepared the quicker you and your family will recover, and the sooner you can lend a hand to help others in need.

## DISASTER SAFETY PLAN

1. Have a personal and business plan for responding to disasters. Communicate the plan to all concerned.

2. Know how to reach law enforcement and local, state, and federal agencies that can help respond to the disaster. Start with 911.
3. Keep emergency supplies at home, in your car, and at your office.
4. Keep backups and copies of important information stored off-site.
5. Know what you have in the event you loose it. In other words, keep an accurate inventory of what you own at home and at work in an off-site location.
6. Meet with your insurance agent regarding disaster and crime insurances.
7. Monitor your credit rating for unusual happenings.
8. Buy a shredder and use it to shred personal information that you do not want in the hands of others.
9. Cooperate with evacuation orders.
10. Report unusual or suspicious activity near major infrastructures such as dams and petroleum tank farms.

Nine

# What You Need to Know about Bad Guys

Throughout children's literature the villains in the stories are often wolves. There are many kinds of wolves. There are those who are charming, quiet, polite, unassuming, complacent, and sweet and who pursue young women at home and in the streets. Unfortunately, it is these gentle wolves who are the most dangerous ones of all. Then there are those who are vicious and attack with a total disregard for their victim.

Who are the people that you need to beware of? How do you know who the wolves are that may come knocking on your door? Why do you even care? Let's start with the last question. In order to mount an adequate defense against the would-be thief or assailant, it is important to first understand him. Modus operandi or MO is a Latin term for how a particular criminal operates. It describes the style of work or characteristic patterns and is how the law enforcement community categorizes crimes and criminals. The MO is the criminal's pattern of operation or method of preparing for a crime. The MO is the criminal's signature or preferred method of operating. With an understanding of criminal MOs, you can begin to get a picture of the criminal or the wolf that may come knocking on your door, so to speak.

The first thing to understand is that in, cases of property crime, the thief is after your property not you. To borrow a line from *The Godfather,* "it's not personal, it's business." Whether she is a burglar or armed robber, she does not necessarily want to hurt you; she just wants what you have. Earlier in the book we talked about how to make yourself less vulnerable to attack. Your goal is to make yourself and your property too difficult to get to or to increase the risk of apprehension beyond reasonable limits. Make her choose another target. It's not good news for your neighbors, but we are talking about "personal" protection. Share what you know about hardening targets with your neighbors and harden the whole neighborhood, forcing the criminal to ply her trade someplace else. Here's a look at the garden-variety criminals on the street so you know what you are up against.

## WHO IS A BURGLAR?

Generally the burglar comes in a couple different varieties, which vary primarily with their experience. First, most criminals ply their trade within one mile of where they live. We know that the more inexperienced burglar tends to pick his target as he travels about his neighborhood, usually on foot. Often these are teenagers traveling in groups, bored, looking for some excitement. Their crime generally starts as an afterthought; when Doug interviewed kids suspected of breaking into homes and committing theft as well as vandalism, he was often told that "we were bored, just hanging out with nothing to do. We saw that there was no one home, so we decided to go in and look around." This group of burglars can be referred to as the smash-and-grab type. Impulse is the hallmark of their crime. They decide on a whim to break into a house, or they may have heard from a friend who heard from a friend that the homeowner had a rare coin collection that would be worth a lot of cash. Once the decision is made, they act.

They will find a door or window, usually out of sight from the street and other neighbors, and kick it in or smash it out. Because they did not really plan their crime, they did not think to bring any tools to make their entrance easier. A more industrious smash-and-grab crook may search the area around the house for some kind of tool to assist in entry. Often they will find what they need in a garden shed that is unlocked. Once entry is gained the smash-and-grab thief will move randomly through the house looking for valuables. Often they raid the liquor cabinet. Vandalism is a companion crime to many juvenile burglaries. The thrill of breaking into someone's house, especially as a group, often results in a kind of frenzied behavior that results in thousands of dollars of property being destroyed. Generally, the monetary damage done gaining entry and the vandalism to the interior of the home far outweighs the value of property taken.

The burglar who makes a living at his trade is more methodical than the inexperienced or juvenile burglar. He will often case a target for quite some time, making sure that his risk of being caught by either the homeowner or the police is as low as it can possibly be. He, too, normally picks a target near to where he lives. Feeling comfortable in the area is important to the burglar. He knows the movement of traffic and when people are at work or home. He knows the movement of police patrols and depends on them being routine and predictable in their behavior. He knows when the police department shift change occurs, knowing that there is a lower level of staffing on the street during a shift change. In other words, the professional burglar does his homework. Once inside the house, the experienced burglar goes to where he knows most people keep their valuables, the master bedroom or the living room. He does not bother with the rest of the house; experience has told him it is a waste of time for very little reward, and he wants to minimize his exposure.

Richard Wright and Scott Decker[1] in their ground-breaking study of active burglars interviewed them about how they pick their target. Inevitably, the majority said it was a measure of how much could be gotten in the quickest amount of time with the lowest risk of detection. Quite often they had some idea of what they were going after. They learned about their targets from personal observation or tips from acquaintances or from being employed by a service agency that provided access to homes. Now you know: Anytime you allow someone into your home, you run the risk that they may be casing it to steal from you or to sell the information about your house, property, and habits to a burglar.

Here are some precautions to take when allowing service workers into your home. First, when hiring people for housekeeping, yard maintenance, or home repair, be sure that you do a thorough background check on them. Always get references; reputable agencies that do this kind of work will have references and can show that their employees have been background-checked. Next, if at all possible, be home when service people are at your home. It is quite common for the home owner to not be around when the housekeepers are working or to leave a door unlocked for the lawn person to come in and get water and use the bathroom. When service people have free run of your home, they are free to go through your things and to make a detailed list for use in coming back to steal it on their own or to sell it to someone who will. It is natural to be friendly and strike up conversations with people who are working in your home. Be cautious not to reveal personal information such as work hours and days off or when your next vacation is. You may be inviting someone to come into your home and have the leisure of knowing that they have free run of your home for several hours or even days.

How can you tell a burglar when you see one? The short answer is you really can't. They depend on blending in to go unnoticed. Generally, be aware of who is in your neighborhood. Wright and Decker describe the average burglar as being in his mid-20s to 30s. Some were in their 40s, but they were by far the minority. Seventeen percent of those involved in their study were female. They were normally unemployed or worked only sporadically. Quite often they had drug habits, which kept them committing crimes to stay high and keep the party going. Here we get to the crux of the matter: Those who commit property crimes are most often angry, desperate, and defiant individuals who are poor.[2]

They have a preferred lifestyle of living on the streets. They are poorly educated and because of their drug and alcohol problems usually have a problem keeping a good job even if they can find one. Like most people, they too have the desire to possess the things that they see everyone around them has. The pressure to have these things as well as the preference for the life of parties and excitement often culminates in the commission of a burglary to obtain the necessary cash to keep the lifestyle going. They tend to be rather prolific in their crime, committing from one to fifty crimes per month, with the average being six to ten.

## WHO IS AN ARMED ROBBER?

The armed robber looks much like the burglar. He tends to be as much or more hooked into the life on the street. He is drawn to what he sees as the good life: parties, drinking, and drugs. He is looking for fast cash. Burglaries do not equate to hard cold cash fast enough. He is not into converting property into cash. When he needs money, he needs it now; he does not have time to fence property. The armed robber is much like a shark in that he is constantly cruising for prey. In his everyday movement through his environment he is constantly aware of who may be a victim in his world. There are times that he specifically goes out to hunt: these are the times when he has identified specific needs, such as the rent is due or there is no food in the house, and goes out to find a way to fulfill them. Other times he will be involved in a completely different activity, and when a very lucrative target shows up that he cannot resist, he reverts to hunter mode and makes a "kill." In this the case the "kill" is a robbery.

## WHAT DOES AN ARMED ROBBER LOOK LIKE?

As with burglars, you will not spot armed robbers before they attack. They usually hunt alone or sometimes in pairs. They stay in the shadows, hoping to find one of the sheep who strays from the flock. They attack rapidly and depend on fear and surprise to complete their crime. They will demand your cash and valuables. By far, the majority of armed robbers do not want to injure you. They know that if they do, they are upping the ante on the crime. Police will put more resources into catching an armed robber who is causing bodily harm to victims. Armed robbers also know that the use of a firearm in the commission of a robbery will bring them an enhanced sentenced if caught. Although this is not enough for them to not do the crime, it does seem to curtail them in actually using the weapon to murder or wound a victim.

The armed robber is a creature of the streets. He will most likely be unemployed and involved in drugs and alcohol abuse. Wright and Decker's study describes the average robber as being in his early to mid-20s, with the youngest being 15 and the oldest 51 years old. Some of the participants in their study report committing their first offense by the time they were 12 years old. Sixteen percent of the study was female. On average, armed robbers committed two to three robberies per month.

## WHO IS A HOME INVADER?

The home invader is an armed robber who has developed a different MO. He prefers to hunt where you live. He has decided the risk is less to commit a crime face-to-face in the protection of your own home. Once inside your home, the risk of detection by others is significantly reduced. For the home invader there is a certain thrill in violating your home and personal space and then controlling you and your family. The home invader knows that he has the upper hand, and that is one of the things he likes about the crime.

Home invaders look like your neighbor: you will not be able to tell them from other members of your community. As with the burglar and armed robber above, the home invader is a creature of the streets. He or she will most likely be unemployed or only occasionally employed and yet have a drug habit or lifestyle that requires large amounts of cash flow. Invading homes is seen as the only option to get what they want.

## WHO IS A RAPIST?

Generally speaking, the face of the rapist is one that the victim knows. The majority of rapes that occur are perpetrated by someone that the victim has some kind of relationship with. There is debate over why men rape. Many believe that it is just the natural sex drive out of control. Others will tell you that rape is a crime less about sex and more about power and control.

Regardless of the view, rape is a violent act, one that degrades and humiliates its victims.

Rapists have been described in several ways. Hazelwood, the well-known Federal Bureau of Investigation (FBI) profiler who is now retired, describes them generally as being either unselfish or selfish rapists. The unselfish type will exhibit some care or concern for his victim; he may ask if she is cold or if she is comfortable. He seems to recognize her humanity and wants to have a relationship at some level.[3]

The selfish rapist wants nothing to do with his victim other than use her as a sex object. He will often use profanity with her and will seek to injure or humiliate her.

In *Men Who Rape,* Groth[4] uses a more traditional description of these predators. There are several varieties of rapists: most common is the Power Assertive Rapist. This offender will threaten to do violence but does so to gain compliance from his victim. He will humiliate his victim both sexually and verbally. He selects victims his own age and often will drive them to a remote location to commit his crime. Once there, he will rip and tear her clothing off. The Power Assertive Rapist will appear to have a very high opinion of himself or a lot of ego. Exhibiting power over her sexually is his means of psychologically reaffirming his own "macho" image of himself.

The next most common rapist is known as the Anger Retaliation Rapist. He genuinely dislikes women, and a big part of his crime is about punishing them. He receives gratification by intimidating, controlling, and injuring his victim. He does not premeditate his attack and uses a "blitz" style. He often chooses women who are older than he is and who represent someone who has wronged him in the past.

The Power Reassurance Rapist appears to be the unselfish type. He often will stalk a victim for a period of time before committing the crime. In his mind this stalking behavior is a kind of dating, and often he sees himself as having a relationship with his victim. He will conduct a "blitz" style attack on a woman his own age. Once his victim is subdued, he may appear gentle in his actions and speech. It is not uncommon for this type of rapist to try to recontact his victim either in person or by phone.

The most dangerous rapist and fortunately the least common is the Anger Excitation Rapist, more generally referred to as the Sadistic type. He truly desires to inflict pain and hurt women. It is not uncommon for him to kill his victim. His attack will be well thought out, and he will take his victim to a pre-planned destination. Once at the destination, he will feel safe to torture and abuse his victim over a long period of time. He will often chose a victim who is older and a different race than he is, which helps to support his belief that his victim is bad and needs to be punished by him. He will have no regard for his victim whatsoever. In fact, a victim who complains of fear or pain is giving him exactly what he wants. One who attempts to dissuade him from his actions will likely receive additional punishment for trying to change his well-scripted plan.

The final very common type of rapist and the one who often goes unreported is the Opportunist Rapist. This offender is truly raping for sexual pleasure. He uses opportunity as his weapon. He will take advantage of a woman if a good opportunity should present itself. This is the date or gang rapist. He often is known by his victim or at the very least might run in very similar social circles. He will often take advantage of a woman by giving her alcohol or other drugs, or he may actually spike her drink or food when she is not looking. He may work in concert with two or three other rapists to find a target and set up the sexual encounter. The reason these crimes go unreported is that the victim often feels at fault for allowing herself to get into this situation, especially if she is acquainted with them in some manner. She may feel embarrassed or not be willing to put herself under scrutiny from law enforcement or the public.

As mentioned earlier, the majority of rape victims know their attacker. He may be a boyfriend, acquaintance, relative, or even a spouse. Depending on his typology, he may appear to be a charming, pleasant "Ted Bundy" type, or he may be a withdrawn loner who lurks in the shadows waiting for a victim to come within range.

## WHO IS A CHILD MOLESTER?

When we think of child molesters, we often think of the guy lurking at the playground wearing a long raincoat. Although this description may fit one type of molester, there are many other types. They come in all sizes, shapes, and colors and from all socioeconomic fabrics of our society. They generally come in two categories. The first is the Preferential Molester or what is known as the Fixated Pedophile. This individual has an abnormal sexual attraction toward children or "pedophilia." He has sexual fantasies about children and will have highly predictable sexual behavior. He hunts for a child who has a particular look: it may be blue eyes and blond hair or particular age and sex, for example, an 8-year-old male. All of his victims will meet his criteria very closely. In fact, when a child grows too old or somehow changes and no longer meets his criteria, the Fixated Pedophile will find a new victim who looks right.

When the Fixated Pedophile no longer shows an interest in the child, many children disclose their abuse. They are no longer getting attention from the molester, and they become jealous.[5] Although this may seem shocking to many adults who wonder how an abused child could become jealous, it is important to remember that many child molesters often care for kids and are sometimes, in fact, nice to them. The Fixated Pedophile does not see himself as a threat to children, but rather as someone who genuinely understands kids and, in his mind, treats them very well. Because he does treat them well, his victims often become very attached to him. When they are discarded, they become angry and will tell someone what has been happening.[6] The Preferential Molester will seek opportunities to interact with children. This may be as a Girl Scout or Boy Scout leader, church youth leader, or day care provider. There have been some cases in which a Fixated Pedophile will marry a single mother with children to gain access to them. This type of offender will start offending as a teenager. He will engage in window peeping and self-exposure, which will eventually lead to contact with his preferred target, children. Left unchecked, one Fixated Pedophile may have hundreds of victims.

Preferential Molesters come in three varieties: Seduction, Introverted, and Sadistic. First, the Seduction molester relates to children; he will spend a great deal of time in "grooming" his victim, often through what appears to be a "courtship" process. His fantasy is that he has a legitimate relationship with the child. He will make an effort to get to know the child's likes and dislikes. He will buy gifts and take the child places to gain his trust. The Seduction molester will make and attempt to get to know the child's parents, often targeting neglected children, knowing that they will be less wary because of their need for adult contact. As much as the Seduction molester looks to be a kind, caring friend to the child, he can also be vicious. It is not uncommon for him to use threats and violence to prevent the child from disclosing the abuse. He will tell the child that if anyone finds out about what they do, parents, siblings, or pets will be harmed or killed. He will also threaten them that they will be in trouble along with him if they are found out.

The next type of Preferential Molester is the Introverted molester. This is the stereotypical child molester. He is the guy we all imagine when we think of child abusers. We visualize him wearing a long raincoat and hanging around the edges of the playground waiting to lure a kid into his trap. This is a fairly accurate depiction of this type of pedophile. The Introverted molester will have minimal communication with his victims; he does not have the skill to "groom" them as the Seduction molester does. He may expose himself or make an obscene phone call to a child in an attempt to gain access. The Introverted type of molester is the type who will molest strangers and very young children because they are the easiest target, one that he can simply grab.

The final type of Preferential molester is the Sadistic molester.[7] The most dangerous and the least common of the fixated pedophiles, the Sadistic molester must inflict pain and suffering to attain the sexual gratification that he needs. The Sadistic molester will often use lures to attract children to him. The classic example of this would be the ice cream truck driver who uses his wares to entice children into his truck. The Sadistic molester will most commonly abduct his victims and take them to a predetermined place to molest them and quite often to kill them. Some of the Sadistic-type molesters kill as part of the sexual experience; others kill simply to keep from having any witnesses to the event.

All three of the Preferential Molesters will most likely collect child pornography and child erotica. They are likely to keep journals of their interactions with children. They will make entries of each of their conquests with a child. Often it will be very detailed and specific, and other times it is more of a code that rates the child and the satisfaction gained from the molestation. They will often take a souvenir of the attack that will remind them of the event, things like an article of clothing, a toy, or a piece of artwork that they did with the child. Pornography, diaries, and souvenirs are all kept in an effort to relive the molestation. A Fixated Pedophile's very existence is consumed with the desire to have sex with children.

The Internet has brought many of these pedophiles to the surface. Never before has it been as easy to access children as it is today on-line. Places like Internet service provider chat rooms, Internet Relay Chat, and MySpace, which are places where kids gather in community, are prime hunting grounds for Fixated Pedophiles. They can stay in near-anonymity and seduce children into meeting them in the real world. They also have ready access to child pornography from any given number of sources off of the Internet. The behavior of Fixated Pedophiles is need-driven, that is, they can't help themselves: they have to do what they do. This is one reason you see respectable businessmen and professionals putting themselves at risk trying to meet up with young girls whom they have met on-line. The NBC program *To Catch a Predator* has done a very dramatic job of illustrating this. Week after week they continue to set up men looking to have sex with minors. As you watch this pathetic behavior, the burning question is "why do they keep doing it?" They keep doing it because they have to. It is need-driven; the impulse is so strong they cannot control it.

The second general classification of child molester is the Situational Offender. They by far are the most common type of abuser. They are more commonly known as incest offenders. These are men who molest their own children. Often they are other family members: brothers, uncles, grandfathers, or stepfathers. They prefer age-appropriate sexual partners, but because of some stressor or family dysfunction, they turn to abusing one of their own children or another family member. Often there will be drug and alcohol involved in these situations, which serves to lower the inhibitions of the perpetrator. There are a variety of reasons why these men will abuse a child of their own family. Sometimes it is that the Situational Offender would prefer an age-appropriate partner but simply lacks the social skill to get one. They turn to a child to have their needs met. Because they are usually older, they will use coercion to gain compliance from the child victim. Other it is simply a lack of restraint on the abuser's part. They will take advantage of a child because they can and they want to. This kind of abuser may use force to get what he wants. Still another kind of Situational Offender is the type who sees having sex with a child as something "new and different"; it becomes a new thrill for him. He simply is bored with age-appropriate partners. A final kind of situational offender is the social misfit. This is where you will often see another family member such as brother or uncle molesting the child. Their primary criteria in selecting a victim is, are they non-threatening? They often gain compliance from their victim by their size.

The child abuser can come from any demographic of society. He knows no socioeconomic boundary. He is as likely to be wearing a three-piece suit as jeans and a t-shirt. He will appear to be very normal. Often he is a successful businessman and other times a friendly bachelor neighbor who lets all the neighborhood kids play in his yard and garage. So, how do you tell if the neighbor is a molester? Arm yourself with as much information as possible. Nearly every state or local community maintains a sexual offender registry that is available to the public. Offender regristries can be found on the Internet. You can enter your address and find where every convicted sex offender in your neighborhood lives. Know where your children spend their time and what they are doing. Your involvement with your children is their best protection from becoming a victim of a child molester. Retired FBI agent Ken Lanning makes a very valid point when he says "parents should beware of anyone who wants to spend more time with their children than they do."[8] Be wary of people who have an abnormal desire to seek out and hang out with children. If your child suddenly becomes secretive and shows up with gifts that seem elaborate and does not have a reasonable explanation of how she came by them, the adage applies: if it seems too good to be true, it probably is. Parents have a sixth sense when it comes to suspecting someone with an inordinate interest in their child. If that alarm goes off, "something just doesn't seem right here," trust that feeling. Double-check the adult who has taken interest in your child or niece or nephew. The pedophile will always have a way to access children, for example, as a scout leader, teacher, camp counselor, or day care worker. They must be around children and find ways to accomplish having access to children.

## WHO IS A MURDERER?

Since 1990, the FBI reports that the rate of murders and violent crimes per 100,000 people has gone from 10 in 1990 to just under 6 in 2005; however, media time in most cities seems consumed by reports of weekend homicides or murders. If you become a victim of homicide, the chances are very good that you will have known your killer. It is the exception when someone is killed by a stranger. Murder is most often a crime of passion; an argument occurs (often over what seems to be the silliest or smallest of issues); tempers flare; and someone ends up dead. Lives are ended, and lives are ruined because of three seconds of anger and lack of control.

Still there are those who kill strangers with unsettling frequency. Generally, we class these individuals as sociopaths or psychopaths, people lacking a conscience. Sociopaths are self-absorbed individuals who care only for themselves. They have little or no feeling for others. Their killing is usually attached to some sadistic sexual urge that they follow through on. These monsters kill because it meets some unmet need that they have and because they lack the normal social restraint to control their behavior. True sociopaths can control their actions; they simply chose not to.

Serial killers are most often sociopaths. The FBI estimates that there are from 20 to 50 serial killers operating in the United States at any given time. These highly ritualistic killers generally prey on people who exhibit high-risk behaviors, such as prostitutes, street people, and vagabonds, people who when missing are often not reported. If a serial killer is killing in your area and law enforcement is aware of him, they will release information about the crimes. Pay careful attention to these bulletins. Generally, information about the type of victim and location of the crime and how the suspect operates if known will be released. This will give you information of certain locations to avoid at particular times of the day or night. Single women are the most common target for a serial killer. If one is operating in your community avoid traveling alone if you can help it. At night be sure your doors and windows are locked. Beware of individuals who approach you for information, help, or just idle chat: remember the sociopath can appear very polite and charming. The infamous serial killer Ted Bundy was known for his charm, and this is how he seduced many of his victims. He would lure them into his vehicle and later would sexually assault and murder them.

The bottom line is, to avoid being a victim of a serial killer, practice all of the safety tips that we have been repeating over and over. Be aware of your surroundings, avoid high-risk behaviors, trust your instincts, and have a plan if attacked. There are no guarantees that you will not become a victim of a serial killer or any random killer for that matter; however, with a little planning and preparation you can reduce the risk to such a small percentage that you will not have to fear becoming a statistic yourself.

Other killers that are even less frequent than the sociopath are the mentally deranged killers, those individuals who are acting from a distorted perception of reality. In 2007 in three western states, residents saw three young men murdered at the hands of one of their former classmates. One of the young men murdered had been in elementary school with the murderer. Another was murdered in a parking lot when he was leaving work late at night, and the third was a college classmate who had supposedly said things hurtful to the murderer. Such acts are powerful reminders that strange things can happen any time and very unexpectedly, and it is a reminder that when you have a plan for your personal safety, you can take action even in the midst of a surprise attack or in a potentially harmful situation.

## DEALING WITH BAD GUYS WHEN THEY SHOW UP IN YOUR OWN FAMILY

Jana has heard kindergarten teachers say, sadly, that by the time a child leaves kindergarten his or her teacher can tell you whether they will have behavioral problems in future classrooms and can predict with fairly high accuracy which children will be in trouble with the law at some point in their young lives. As a result, if you have children, Jana and Doug urge you to watch for "bad guys growing in your midst." Consider the young men of Columbine High School who created the April 1999 massacre. They were growing up in the midst of what neighbors said were normal, nice families, yet in retrospect, there were dozens of clues that something was not right. Criminals come from all walks of life and from all family backgrounds and can be any age. Consider the Florida preteen charged with murder as an adult because he beat a younger girl to death. Consider the Idaho 14-year-old boys charged as adults for raping a young girl classmate.

Criminals can come from anywhere. Recognize whether your child is moving toward a path of crime. Look for changes in behavior, a drop in grades, or a loss of interest in things that they once loved to do. Observe whether you child has changed friends recently or if he is becoming more secretive about who he's with and what he is doing. Doug has raised four teenagers, and as all parents do, he recognizes that there is a point when they change from being children and begin moving to adulthood. This is the job of a teenager. They begin to separate from their parents, and there is a certain amount of rebellion that comes with the territory. This is not what we are talking about here. If you are being honest with yourself and watching what your child is doing, you will know the difference between normal adolescent rebellion and truly defiant behavior that could lead to a lifetime of sorrow, wrong-doing, and crime.

Also, recognize whether your adult child is on the path of criminal behavior or has already become a criminal (for example, see Doug's story in Chapter 2 about the daughter who reported to friends that her father had lots of prescription drugs in the house). Denial is not safe. We repeat denial is *not* safe. Look at the reality you are in with your children. Being naïve, forgiving, charitable, or even defensive and overprotective of the child when you sense or even already know that your child has been investigated by law enforcement or even detained or arrested by law enforcement is only adding fuel to the fire already alive in your child to associate with criminals or to become one him- or herself. Family after family can tell stories about "things we should have paid attention to along the way." Don't let your family become another statistic on a crime-tracking database.

There is no doubt about it: there are bad guys out there. More often than not they look just like you and people you know; the difference is that they are people who think differently from the rest of us. When asked "What do you see as the difference between someone who stays out of jail and someone who ends up in jail?" Ada County Sheriff Gary Raney states, "short-term thinking. Criminals generally do not think of the longer-term consequence of their actions in the same way that you and I do. Whether it be drug experimentation, taking a swing at someone because they've made you mad, or pulling a gun and shooting, a 'criminal mentality' more often acts upon immediate thoughts rather than having a thought process that can accurately consider the totality of the circumstance and consider consequences." Raney continues with what he wishes everyone would use—"the three-second rule. If everyone would stop for just three seconds and think about it before they commit a crime, my jail would be almost empty."

Criminals make thinking errors. This is why they get caught. One thing that they are usually right about, however, is that prey is easy for them to find. They can depend on the fact that the majority of people don't spend much time thinking about how to prepare against the wolf. They depend on people's naivety and good nature. They can exploit both. Remember we are not trying to increase paranoia with the information that we are presenting: the goal is to increase your knowledge and therefore your preparation to avoid or get out of danger. If you can understand, even at a very basic level how a criminal thinks and works, then it is relatively easy for you to stay two steps ahead and keep yourself out of harm's way.

## A PLAN FOR RECOGNIZING THE BAD GUYS IN MY NEIGHBORHOOD

1. Do people you see in your neighborhood seem to belong there?
2. Do you often see the same people watching your house from the street? Or see cars that don't belong in the neighborhood frequenting neighbors' houses?
3. Get to know the juveniles in your neighborhood.
4. Get to know the parents of the juveniles in your neighborhood.
5. When traveling away from your home into unfamiliar areas, drive around the block one time and check for individuals who seem to be watching the street.
6. Single females going to clubs alone: buy your own drinks or accept them only from people you know and trust.
7. When walking to your car in a parking garage or parking lot, keep your key in your hand and be ready to open your door.
8. Check the backseat of your car before entering.
9. Research the sex offender registry for your area; identify those living close to you. Make sure your children are aware of how to avoid these people and their houses.
10. Intervene early when any antisocial or criminal behavior happens in your own family or with your own children.

## NOTES

1. Richard T. Wright and Scott H. Decker, *Burglars on the Job: Streetlife and Residential Break-ins* (Boston: Northeastern University Press, 1994).

2. Ibid.

3. R. Hazelwood, *Practical Aspects of Rape Investigation* (Boca Raton: CRC Press, 1995).

4. Nicholas A.Groth and H. Jean Birnbaum, *Men Who Rape: The Psychology of the Offender* (New York: Plenum Press, 1979).

5. Office of Juvenile Justice Delinquency Prevention, *Child Sexual Exploitation: Child Abuse and Exploitation Investigative Techniques* (2nd printing). U.S. Department of Justice, Office of Justice Programs, Washington, DC, April 1995).

6. K. V. Lanning, *Child Molesters: A Behavioral Analysis*, 4th ed. (Alexandria, VA: National Center for Missing and Exploited Children, 1986).

7. Ibid.

8. Ibid.

# Ten

# Being Vigilant without Being Paranoid: Keeping Your Resolve to Stay Safe

The predator wolf in the story of the three little pigs was outsmarted by the third pig that had built a secure home, had good problem-solving skills, and clearly took action on the spot when his plans appeared not to be working. In our daily lives, conversations about safety don't typically include the warning "I'll huff and I'll puff and I'll blow your house down." Today's criminal predators typically sound just as threatening as the wolf but more like "give me all your money" or "get out of your car" or "give me your keys" or "give me your tennis shoes." Now by this point in *Prepared Not Paranoid*, when reading these sentences you likely moved immediately into your practiced response and plan of action for safety. In a time when the media bombard us with safety-related stories, when U.S. national identity cards are hotly debated, and when passports are more in demand for travel, the recommended level of being alert seems at a constant high, making paranoia and distress more real. In a time when the desire for privacy and security is fed by fears of personal harm befalling you or your loved ones, it seems easy for paranoia to creep into daily life. However, armed with all the new information and knowledge from previous chapters, you can now decide what you'll do to stay out of harm's way and to be more prepared for any situation. If you've ever been a victim, you know the fear that follows. Now you can choose to live your life from a prepared point of view and with a mindset and body language that communicate "I am not a victim." How well have you built your house for safety, and how often do you practice your problem-solving skills? Finally, how often do you overcome the threats and fears in your life to go about "living happily ever after?"

If you've never been a victim, terrific! Keep making wise choices about what you do, where you go, and whom you befriend. The first result is that the better the decisions you make and the more confidently you move through life, the safer you will be. Doug Tangen, whom we heard from earlier, says, "[Be aware that] the most common behavior we see in victims is that they acted like a victim. Instead, be aware of your surroundings, make eye contact, walk erect with your head up, and look confident. Look self-assured on the outside, even if you don't feel that way on the inside. Predators look for the weak, unaware, and timid people." The second result is that the more you guide your children to make best-possible decisions and to walk with confidence, the safer they will be. When you and your children know what to do to be safe, you are preventing yourselves from being timid and slow to react. The old joke says it another way: Two people were walking along in the forest talking about outrunning a grizzly bear should it appear, when one says, "I only have to outrun you." That rings true here in the discussion of crime because as presented in several chapters, you want to harden your target and not leave yourself or your property worth the effort of a criminal's attention. This chapter provides further ways for staying vigilant, being involved in your safety and well-being, and learning where in law enforcement to turn for help.

## FEEL-SAFE FORMULA

In Chapter 1, you learned whether your Feel-Safe Quotient was Always at Risk, Aware but Not Feeling Safe, Oblivious/Unaware, Safe but Wanting More Confidence, or Safe and Constantly Learning. As Sheriff Deputy Curt Egge says, "There is no substitute for embracing the truth of human behavior and adjusting to it. We must be actively engaged in our environments on all levels and enjoy all of life, the pleasant and the not-so-pleasant realities of the human heart." Being prepared for danger is about staying safe so that you can enjoy all of life while at the same time being ready to respond to any of the "not-so-pleasant realities" that you may also be facing at any given moment. Now, discover what the elements of the Feel-Safe Formula are and how you can increase your Feel-Safe Quotient by working with the formula to be ever more prepared and not paranoid. Discover how to be prepared and feel safe, rather than fearful and paranoid or over-concerned and paranoid.

The elements of the Feel-Safe Formula are as follows: (1) have a safety plan, (2) be ready to problem solve at any moment, (3) get enough sleep, and (4) be as physically fit as you can be. These four elements add up to keeping you as safe as possible each day. The mental preparations of having created a safety plan and of having strong problem-solving skills that you can implement at any moment help keep you safe. The physical actions of getting enough sleep and being physically fit also help protect your safety. For example, by getting enough sleep, you can be alert enough to effectively problem solve should the need arise, and by being physically fit, you can fight for your life if you have to. Throughout the book we've said that a safety plan is your place to start, and it includes a kit or collection of items (see the appendixes for more checklists) that you keep in your car, in your travel gear, and at home.

More on the importance of sleep: For nearly a decade, researchers who study sleep and its effect on human health have told us that overnight shift work places additional stress on people. Mayo Clinic doctors have also pointed out that not getting enough sleep (typically 7–9 hours for adults) causes diminished thinking abilities, safety concerns, and increased chances for health problems. Without the right amount of sleep, reaction times are slowed, problem-solving skills are lowered, and being quick-to-anger becomes a normal state; in order to keep yourself as safe as possible, figure out how much sleep you need to get every night and then protect and get the hours that you need. When you are well rested, you can take better care of yourself in all situations, and when you are well rested, in the event that you witness a crime you can be a better witness. Although in the mid-1900s Sir Winston Churchill became known for his afternoon naps (which he said led to greater productivity), it was not until 2005 and after that some employers began attending to employees' needs for sleep by providing time for power naps. During the early 2000s, some sleep-focused companies were finding success offering power-sleeping modules in such places as airports and train stations.

We also heard from Gulf War veteran Rebecca Evans, who says, "Get enough rest. We had to be alert and on time in the military. Being late simply is not an option for our Forces, so rest is critical. Most of us took sleeping seriously. I felt this rule was set in motion because of the dire concern over our safety, and about being alert, especially when we worked twelve-hour shifts and the work was stressful and intense. With rest, we could respond to emergencies with clarity and a keen sense of proper reactions based on all of our training. So, get a good night's rest so you can be fresh, alert, and fully able to honor your responsibilities."

The need for sleep that rejuvenates mind and body is undeniable. In fact, police officers are trained that "sleep deprivation could cost you your life." Why? Because police officers are dependent on instantaneous decision making, fine motor skill control and manual dexterity, and rapid response times. Having enough sleep can make the difference between staying safe, getting hurt, or dying. The problem for officers is that many times they have to stay awake during the periods of the day that humans are meant to be sleeping. Working various shifts has proven to be as big a challenge for officer safety as learning to use cover and concealment when in a shoot-out. Today many officers are working ten- and twelve-hour shifts. Working these long hours in the early hours of the morning takes a toll on both an officer's mental and physical health. It is very important that they understand what the dangers of not getting proper rest can present.

## A RETURN TO THE FEEL-SAFE SURVEY QUESTIONS

Revisiting the thirty survey questions from Chapter 1 is in order before the book ends because they are really thirty potentially dangerous behaviors that you can overcome to make yourself safer as you move about your day. Each survey statement is listed and followed by a description indicating why it is potentially dangerous, how you can overcome the dangerous aspects in order to gain more confidence about your safety, and the actions that can be taken every day to be safe without becoming paranoid.

1. People tell me I'm naïve. Although being naïve carries a sweet and even romantic image, being naïve puts you in danger because you remain unaware of the harm that can befall you in certain situations and environments. Being overly naïve makes it easy for other people to take advantage of you. To overcome this potential danger, become more aware of the mean, sad, bad things that human beings do to each other so that these same things don't happen to you.

2. People tell me to make better decisions. When people are suggesting that you make better decisions, they are telling you that they see you making decisions that hurt you, hurt your work, or hurt others. They are also telling you that they care about you and want you to put yourself in better situations by making better decisions. To overcome this potentially dangerous habit of making poor decisions, learn to discern when negative or dangerous consequences may follow your decisions. Remember that high-risk behaviors are often connected to bad decision making.

3. I do things by the same routine every day. Although routines make life easy to manage for you, they also make you easy to track for people who want to cause you harm. Routines can also give you a sense of

false security because you have been doing it the same way for so long it just feels right. This is a kind of denial thinking. To overcome this potentially dangerous habit and to expand your problem solving skills, take a different route to work, change up the time you work out, and explore new routes for getting everywhere you go.

4. I exercise or engage in most activities alone. You may find that pursuing activities alone is relaxing for you. However, be aware that doing almost anything alone puts you more at risk of being attacked, mugged, or raped. To overcome this potential danger, find friends who enjoy the same activities you do and make an outing out of the activity. Use the buddy system that you likely learned as a kid and travel in pairs.

5. I constantly worry about my safety. This point of view or mindset is dangerous because worry can reduce your ability to plan and act. Refocus your worry energies into making a personal safety plan and into taking classes that give you skills for protecting yourself. To overcome this dangerous mindset, keep reading this book, sign up for a self-defense class, work with the police department to do a survey of your house and its safety factors, and walk with confidence.

6. I consistently worry about the safety of my family. This point of view or mindset is also dangerous because worry can reduce your own ability to plan and act and prevent your family members from learning how to protect themselves because you are so busy running safety interference to protect them. Refocus your worry energies into making a personal and family safety plan and into taking classes that give you skills for protecting your family members. Then sign up your family for classes, too. To overcome this dangerous mindset, keep reading this book and create a family safety plan.

7. I'm unaware of my surroundings most places I go. Being unaware leaves you open for surprise attacks, for tripping over something all on your own, and putting yourself at risk. To overcome this potential danger, become more aware of your surroundings. Watch for dark parking places, for isolated situations, and for moments that your instinct tells you that you are in danger. When traveling in unfamiliar surroundings, it is advantageous to conduct a "recon" of the area before getting out and exploring on foot. Conducting a recon means that you drive the area first in a vehicle; if you are on public transportation, ride through the area one time and note potential problem spots that you will want to avoid. Be alert for groups of people congregating for no apparent

reason. Observe graffiti that is present and if it is recent. If it is during normal business hours, notice if there are business people moving about doing business. What does your sixth sense tell you about the area you are in? Does it "feel" safe?

8. I don't know any of my neighbors by name. Because of the hectic schedules of your week and weekend, you may feel like you don't have time to get to know your neighbors. When you don't know who your neighbors are, you also don't know who really should and should not be in the neighborhood. This is true in secured housing situations as well as in open-access neighborhoods. To overcome this potential danger, get started. Go meet all of the neighbors who live on your floor. Go meet the neighbors that live within fifteen houses of yours. Find out whether each household has kids and at what ages, pets and of what demeanors (a pit bull is a different risk factor than a cat), and any health concerns that require special attention or help in an emergency.

9. My house/residence is not well lit. Poorly lit homes invite criminals because they can hide in darkness while breaking into your home or waiting for you to come home so they can attack you. To overcome this potential danger, get better lighting around your house, especially the entry doors to your home. Ask for a lighting or safety assessment from the police department or a security company.

10. I am the victim of crimes. If you have already been a victim of crime, what do you already do differently to keep yourself safe? Reading this book is a good start or continuation in your striving not to be victimized again. It's about making healthy choices for where you live, what activities you pursue, and where you work. It's also about moving about your life with so much confidence that criminals stop seeing you as a victim.

11. I leave my house unlocked. You are inviting people to rob you. If you regularly leave your house unlocked, your kids know this, their friends learn this, and suddenly many people you don't know end up knowing that your house is an easy target. To overcome this potential danger, lock your house. Limit the number of people with a key or key-code to get into your house.

12. My family does not have a safety plan. After reading this book, you will. By not having a clear safety plan when a disaster strikes, you are adding stress to an already stressful situation. By not having a safety plan for action, your children are not learning how to respond to dangerous situations when they are away from you.

13. I leave my car unlocked. Just like leaving your house unlocked, you are inviting people to steal from you. Most car robbery and contents stealing happens to vehicles in which the car doors were left unlocked. Overcoming this potential danger is simple: lock the doors.

14. When I get in my car, I just get in and go. Most people do this. However, the danger is that someone could be in the backseat or in the rear of your vehicle. You may think this borders on being paranoid; however, crimes do happen to people in cars because someone was already in the car before the owner got into the car. To overcome this potential danger, be more aware. Glance around and into your vehicle before getting in. If someone is there, keep walking and dial 911, or get into a place where lots of people are and ask to use a phone to dial 911.

15. I carry my wallet/purse in a way that makes it easy to steal. This includes leaving your purse visible on a seat in your car. Wallets carried in back pockets are easy to steal. Purses carried in your hand rather than over your shoulder are easy to steal. To overcome this potential danger, use a purse shoulder strap. Travelers are often coached to use wallet carriers that go around their necks and inside shirts or blouses.

16. I carry my keys in such a way that I can lose them easily. This means that if you throw your keys into a shopping cart, you can loose them easily or someone else can walk away with them. So many cars have automatic unlock and alarm key-fobs that once a potential criminal has your keys, it is easy to find your car and leave. Another way to lose your keys is to leave them lying out on a store or bathroom counter. To overcome this potential danger, carry your keys in a front pocket of your clothing, attached to a belt loop, or in your purse. Before you head out to your car, get your keys ready so that you are not fumbling for them at the car door, because this leaves you open to being an easy target for a criminal.

17. I don't have any self-defense skills. Being aware of your surroundings is a form of self-defense, as are martial arts and carrying a weapon. However, the key idea here is that preparing a plan, being more aware, and deciding in advance how you'll act if threatened is the best way to avoid having to defend yourself in a hand-to-hand situation.

18. I am not physically fit and don't think I could get away from an attacker. If this is how you feel, your body language is communicating the same message to potential attackers. To overcome this potential danger, start gaining confidence about your ability to protect yourself.

Consider working to improve your physical fitness. Take classes to learn how to be safe, how to make safety-oriented decisions, and how to physically defend yourself.

19. I don't know where all the emergency exits are at work. People get stuck in burning buildings because of not knowing where the exits are. Earthquakes, tornadoes, fires, floods, power outages, hurricanes, and explosions create situations in which you need to leave the building via the stairs and emergency exits. To overcome this potential danger, find out where the nearest staircases and exits are in your workspace. Then, once a month walk the path and take the stairs to see what it takes to get out of your building in an emergency.

20. When shopping, I forget how to get to my vehicle or transportation safely. Wandering around in a parking lot is not safe. Anyone noticing you will see that you are an easy target for an attack or a purse stealing. To overcome this potential danger, pay attention to where you park. Make note of the letters, numbers, animals, or names placed to make it easy to remember where you parked. If using public transportation, memorize the route or bus or train number you need to get on to get home or back to the office.

21. When traveling, I never take the time to find the stairway in the hotel. In the event of a fire or a power outage, you need to use the staircase, which means you need to know where it is. To overcome this potential danger, always find the staircase. Physically walk from your room to the stairwell door so that you could get there in the event of an emergency.

22. When traveling by plane, I don't read the safety card so I wouldn't know how to get out of the plane. The chances are that you will not need this information. However, by failing to learn what your exit options are, you are leaving yourself in an at-risk position. To overcome this potential danger, listen to the preflight and during-the-flight instructions. Also, read the safety card. Planes have different exit-door procedures and different exit door locations depending on the size of the plane. As the preflight instructions tell you, "In the event of an emergency, the nearest exit door may be behind you." Know what your options are.

23. When commuting by train or bus, I realize that I don't know how to stop the train or bus and how to get out. Accidents happen. Strange, unexpected, and threatening things happen. Medical emergencies happen. Sometimes the vehicle needs to be stopped so that problems can

be addressed. To overcome this potential danger, look for instructions on how to stop the transportation or ask someone who works for the transportation system. Learn what to do. Don't solely rely on someone else's knowledge.

24. When I meet new people, I quickly invite them to my home. If you are an outgoing person who makes friends easily, that's great. However, inviting someone you don't know well into your home puts you, your family, and your property at a potential risk. To overcome this danger, meet new people in neutral locations like restaurants. Find out where the person works and get to know them in a work setting and in a social setting before inviting them to your house. Really get to know the person before inviting him or her to your residence.

25. I don't spend time to meet the parents of my children's friends. (If you don't have kids, what would you do if you did?) Your children are more vulnerable than you are. Said another way, your children are more at risk in a new person's house than you are, so why let your kids go somewhere that has no adult supervision or adults whom you don't know and whom you may or may not trust with your kids? To overcome this potential danger, take the time to "meet the parents" and find out what their house rules are. Do the rules match your house rules? For instance, do your kids know that they can only sleep over at a friend's when both sets of parents have given permission and when at least one parent will be at home at all times? What other rules do you have about visiting and playing?

26. I don't know how to conduct checks of the sexual predators living in my neighborhood. Nearly every neighborhood and workplace, no matter how expensive the homes or how secured the area, is subject to having one or more sexual predators living within walking distance. Being aware of where someone lives is a good way to protect yourself and your kids. Remember, sexual predators can be male or female and can have attacked an adult or a child. To overcome this potential danger go to your state police website and look at their sexual offender list or visit a site such as www.familywatchdog.com and find out who is living close to you.

27. I don't participate in neighborhood activities. Not participating in neighborhood activities means you probably don't know your neighbors (also see number 8 above). To overcome this potential danger of the neighborhood not knowing who you are and therefore being less likely to look out for your safety, start attending neighborhood events.

28. People say I say "yes" too often. When someone says this to you, listen carefully. The message is that you are giving yourself away and leaving yourself at the risk of being taken advantage of once or worse yet on a regular basis. To overcome this potential danger, learn to say no, learn to set limits and stick to them, and learn to set boundaries that no one can cross with you.

29. People tell me to "snap out of your victim mindset." This message is telling you to change your outlook, your attitude, your "poor me" complex, and your "take advantage of me" body language because people are either tired of being around you or are genuinely concerned about your safety. To overcome this potentially dangerous mindset that you hold yourself in, keep learning and build personal and family safety plans for action.

30. People tell me I'm too nice for my own good. This is another message of concern about your safety and well-being. Any time someone says you are being too nice, take heed. If your friends see this, so do people who don't know you very well and who may want to pursue you as a victim of their desires. To overcome this potential danger, choose any of the above items to work on and learn to discern when saying "no" is your best course of action for your safety. Even if you choose only half of the above items to focus on improving, you'll be making yourself safer as you move about each day's activities.

Whether you choose to focus your, your children's, or your friend's efforts on one or all of the preceding thirty behaviors, you have consciously chosen to live life more safely. In addition to better protecting yourself, there are things you can do to access help effectively and to be a good witness in the event that you see a crime committed against someone else or against someone else's property.

## HOW TO BE A GOOD WITNESS

Most crimes have a witness to at least a portion of the criminal event. When you find yourself witnessing a crime, here's what to do. First, be sure you are in a safe place and then call 911. Next, if you are still safe, describe everything you see to the 911 dispatcher. Notice what people are doing, what they are wearing, whether they have any noticeable tattoos or scars. Notice whether the person is thin, medium, or heavy-set. Pay attention to the shirt, pants, and shoes the person is wearing. Notice how people are talking—what their voices sound like and what words they are using. Make note of the vehicle(s) that appear to be driven by the criminals. Better yet, if you can write down a license plate number, even a partial one, this is a helpful detail. Finally, pay attention to details. Teach your kids to pay attention to details. Even by glancing at a person or situation you can pick up details. If you become a witness to a crime, make sure you stay just that. Be sure not to become part of the crime. Stay concealed out of harm's way. If you can't do that, and simply observe, then let it go. Being a witness is not more important than your managing your own safety. When it is safe to do so, stay around to tell the police what you did see.

When law enforcement officials arrive, stay on the scene and provide your information. Be as specific as you can. Don't be surprised if you are talked to more than one time by a variety of officers. The first officers on the scene may want to know who you are and what you saw. Then detectives may ask you for the same information, and finally depending on the nature of the crime, someone from the prosecutor's office may ask you what you saw as well. Remember all these people are after just one thing: The facts! They most likely will not ask you for your opinion or what you think might have been happening. They just want to know what you observed, so keep your comments to just that.

## TIPS FOR SURVIVING A CRITICAL INCIDENT—WHAT POLICE LEARN

Officers are taught from the first day they walk into the academy to survive. Not only are they taught survival techniques of the body but also of the mind. They are taught that they must be in top physical condition to overcome an assailant. They are taught that they must be proficient at empty-hand self-defense. Most importantly they are taught over and over that no matter what, they cannot give up. They are taught to survive. Survival begins with a reason to survive. It might be their wife and kids or it might be a special event in their future. Whatever it is, it has to be personal and it has to be motivating. Each of us should have a reason to live.

What is it that makes you want to get out of bed every day? The things that you have a passion for and the things that excite you into action are reasons for living: your reason for surviving. This is what needs to be imprinted into your survival tape. If and when that time comes when your life is in real danger and survival is on the line, your reasons-to-survive tape will run. When you have a reason to survive the encounter, your body will do everything in its power to follow your mind through to victory. Fight hard, and hold nothing back. Remember that someone committing a crime against you is not being nice to you, so you are under no obligation to be nice or submissive to them. However, always remember that your survival often means giving the attacker what he wants: for instance, in armed robberies and other property crimes, most people who comply with the requests of the attacker survive. You will have to evaluate the incident and make a determination about what kind of attacker you are dealing with at the time of attack. This is where the information in Chapter 9 will again be helpful to you. Once you have survived, it is time to heal. Many have found this to be as painful or more so than the actual victimizing event.

When the critical event happens, the event itself is only the beginning of the trauma. During the event you may experience a distortion of senses. Things may appear to go into slow motion. This is one of your mind's ways of protecting you in order to give you an extra advantage by slowing down the event. There have been reports of officers involved in shootings of actually being able to see the bullets in flight. Another distortion may be sound. The loud report of a large handgun or rifle may sound like a tiny pop. These distortions are all part of the protective mechanisms the body uses to survive the incident. The body is equipped with what is known as the reticular-activating system. It contains both the sympathetic and parasympathetic activating systems. The sympathetic system is that part of us that gets us ready to fight or run. When we are confronted with a threat, our heart rate increases, our blood pressure goes up, and our respirations increase. This is our body attempting to get us ready for what is to come. It is accomplished by chemicals that our body produces being delivered into our blood stream. Blood from the extremities will be shunted to core organs in case we spring a leak. This shunting of blood has a secondary effect; we begin to lose digital dexterity. It has been noted during critical incidents that officers may have difficulty completing routine tasks such as reloading their weapons because of decreased blood flow to their fingers.

Once the threat is past, our bodies want to come back to a state of homeostasis or equilibrium. This is where the parasympathetic comes into play; this system uses another bunch of chemicals to bring our breathing, pulse, and blood pressure back to normal limits. For the officer who quite routinely goes from one critical incident to the next this sympathetic–parasympathetic cycle takes a toll on their physical bodies. This is something that they must manage if they expect to stay in the business for a long time. For the citizen this is not an issue. Along with the physical effects, officers also have to discover ways of dealing with the cumulative effect of dealing with pain and suffering on a daily basis. Police officers, firefighters, paramedics, and other emergency services workers are known to suffer from the effects of post-traumatic stress disorder (PTSD).

PTSD can also become a problem for the victim of a critical incident. Many of those who survived the 2001 World Trade Center attack continue to be victimized by this disorder. PTSD seems to present itself several weeks to months after the critical incident. The disorder may present itself as a profound sadness or depression that was not there before. Victims may have persistent nightmares and thoughts about the attack. In severe cases something may trigger the event to play over in the victim's mind while going about normal daily activity. All of the above can be disorienting and unsettling. Often counseling will be necessary to overcome PTSD. If you have been or become a victim and begin to experience these kinds of symptoms, do not hesitate to seek professional help. Just as your body needs a doctor and time to heal after you break a bone, so, too, does your mind need a doctor and some time to get back to 100%. Find a reason to fight for your life—it will help you stay alive.

Officer Curt Egge's spouse and author of *Bullets in My Bed,* Jan Egge[1] says at the conclusion of her "critical incidents" chapter that for someone who has been involved in a critical incident, it is important to "realize that a traumatic thing has happened. Understand that how you feel is okay. Give yourself time to deal with the incident. Contact help. Start talking it out or start a journal. Be totally open and honest with yourself and others. Allow others to help you get through this. Know that there are many people supporting you. And, find a healthy outlet for your emotions."

## WAYS TO LEARN MORE

Citizen Police Academies are one mechanism for learning more about police work. For nearly two decades, police departments across the country have been offering opportunities to citizens to learn about the work done by police officers and departments. The three- to eleven-week courses are called Citizen Police Academies and provide an overview of what happens in the various lines of work that comprise a law enforcement agency.

Law enforcement spouse and Citizen Police Academy Alumni Association president of four years Jan Egge lists these resources as great ways to keep learning: "Citizen Police Academies, Neighborhood Watch, personal safety classes, community emergency response team (CERT) training, and rape aggressive defense systems (RADS) training." Whatever ongoing education you choose to pursue, keep building your skills and your confidence so that paranoia does not set in.

In addition to adult education programs, many states and municipalities have programs for teens to learn about law enforcement careers. Contact your local police or sheriff's organization, call your state police agency, or conduct your own Internet research to locate the program right for you and your teen. Yet another way to learn what life on the street as an officer of law enforcement is like is to contact an agency and ask about participating in a "ride-along." A ride-along allows a citizen to ride along with a police officer for a shift to learn what police work is really like. Going on a ride-along allows you to also learn more about the challenges and crimes facing your community.

## WHOM DO YOU CALL FOR HELP?

You will find that law enforcement agencies can be somewhat mysterious in organization and even a little difficult to navigate to get to the person whom you really need to talk to. Understanding how police departments are organized and where to go if you need help or are ready to learn more about ways to be and stay safe will help you if and when the time comes that you must call on the police. In order to help you better understand the divisions of labor in law enforcement, the following overviews are provided so that you can determine where you want to turn to keep learning and to serve your community. Also know that law enforcement, fire departments, and medical team members interact as partners on a daily basis to bring all return-to-safety elements together when needed. Today, high-technology computer and telecommunication systems in and between law enforcement agencies are making crimes easier to investigate and to solve because criminals often work in multiple jurisdictions. Some agencies produce hardcopy newsletters once a year and send them to citizens or include them as newspaper inserts. Many agencies now post helpful and current information on their websites so you can conduct further area-specific research online. Watch for these helpful resources in your community. Ultimately, remember that if an immediate danger is facing you, call 911.

Law enforcement services include the following. We introduce them here briefly so that you can be more familiar with where to turn for continued education, surveys, assessments, and of course for immediate help.

Police stations are operated by a city to serve city residents. Traffic violations and all of the crimes discussed in this book are handled by police departments. Some police stations include jails.

Fire departments are called for fires, some medical calls, and for car accidents. Although fire departments are not involved in law enforcement per se they are involved in solving arson crimes. Closely connected to fire departments are emergency medical team and ambulance services. Again, while not involved in law enforcement directly, the medical reports filed by first responders and medics can sometimes be used in criminal investigations and cases.

Sheriff's offices are headed by an elected official, the sheriff. The offices are operated by a county and handle all of the same tasks that police departments handle, just in a different jurisdiction. Sheriff's offices also operate jails.

Substations house officers who can help with urgent problems and work on a regular basis with a smaller area of the jurisdiction in which they are employed.

State Police departments are operated by state government and vary greatly from state to state. Generally they are responsible for statewide law enforcement activities, patrol of the state highway system, and operation of crime labs. State governments also operate prisons. The difference between a prison and a jail is that jails normally house misdemeanor prisoners, those serving sentences less than one year, and state prisons house felons who are normally serving multiple-year sentences.

Fish and Game Department officers can be state or federal employees. They enforce laws in state and federal parks, forests, and land areas. Crimes handled by these officers range from traffic violations to poaching.

The Federal Bureau of Investigation (FBI) is operated by the U.S. government and is responsible for enforcing federal statutes. Today the FBI's focus is on antiterrorism.

The Bureau of Alcohol Tobacco and Firearms (ATF) is operated by the U.S. government and is responsible for federal regulation of alcohol and tobacco products. Their main emphasis is on regulation, manufacture, and sale of firearms. They also have expertise in explosives.

Homeland Security is a U.S. government agency and was created after the 2001 World Trade Center terrorist destruction. It is comprised of parts of fourteen agencies, all of whom focus on various aspects of keeping the country safe from terrorism, border threats, and natural disasters. Most cities and states have a contact person for the Office of Homeland Security.

The Central Intelligence Agency (CIA) is operated by the U.S. government and is responsible for conducting foreign intelligence operations.

Bureau of Prisons (BOP) is operated by the U.S. government and is responsible for housing federal prisoners serving multiple-year sentences.

The Secret Service is operated by the U.S. government and has the main function of protecting the president and a variety of other public officials. They also are responsible for investigation of counterfeiting.

INTERPOL is an international police force whose primary responsibility is to foster cooperation between the 186 member nations in combating international crime.

Within police and sheriff departments there are hundreds of responsibilities assigned to local levels of law enforcement. Most commonly, citizen interaction with law enforcement is at the local level. In addition to the duties and responsibilities described in what follows, the operation of jail facilities happens at local levels. The role of jails in law enforcement is that when many laws are broken there is a specific jail-time penalty that must be served.

Dispatch services are most commonly known as "911." The responsibilities of the dispatcher are to take 911 calls and determine which agency or agencies need to be dispatched to the scene.

Reverse 911 programs allow a municipality or law enforcement agency to call or e-mail citizens (who've asked to be on the notification list) to warn them of community disasters, missing people, or other potential dangers. Call your local sheriff or police department to see whether this is in place in your community.

Neighborhood service teams and contact officers are assigned to specific geographies to serve the community, to handle current problems, and to investigate crimes. Some are also tasked with providing neighborhood education about crime prevention. Learn whether your local agencies have designated neighborhood service teams or contact officers.

Patrol operations are the backbone of the local police department. In today's community-oriented policing environment, the patrol function of the police is much more than officers driving around in radio cars responding to calls for service. Today the patrol officer is much more connected with the community. In many departments a patrol officer will be assigned to a particular geographical area of a community and will work with citizens from the assigned area to solve problems as they arise. It is common for an officer to attend a neighborhood meeting to discuss parking problems, speeding motorists, or other traffic issues in the neighborhood. One officer may join with a task force of citizens to deal with graffiti that is appearing in the neighborhood. Another officer may join a particular neighborhood group to discuss and investigate a developing gang problem. Of course in the case of an emergency you can still call 911 and get an officer to respond to deal with any criminal problem that may arise.

Traffic enforcement is a focus in many growing communities today that struggle with traffic problems. Many agencies today have STEP teams (special traffic enforcement program) to deal with traffic in communities. The officers assigned to the STEP team have received special training in traffic enforcement as well as in crash investigation. Often these officers are crash scene reconstructionists, highly trained professionals who have special abilities in analyzing a crash scene. Motorcycle officers are often a division of the STEP team. Motorcycle officers are ideal for traffic work because of their ability to easily navigate congested traffic areas.

Canine units are specialized patrol units made up of an officer and a trained dog. They are used primarily to search for felons who are running from officers and to detect narcotics in a patrol environment. Canine teams are becoming more and more common in police departments across the country. Not all canine teams utilize "bite" dogs. Today many narcotic and bomb detection dogs are rescued from the pound and put through detection training along with their handlers and provide a vital function to officers working on the roadways and in airports and other public places.

Horse patrol is one of the oldest of units in the patrol division and is often called the mounted unit. Many larger jurisdictions use horses to patrol parks and other places that a police cruiser will not easily go. As well, they often work special events like parades and celebrations where crowd control is needed.

Depending on the size of the agency the Crime Scene Investigators (CSI) may be a separate division connected to the crime lab or simply specially trained patrol officers who are called on to gather evidence at major crime scenes.

In the post-9/11 environment, more and more law enforcement agencies are developing criminal intelligence units. These units will often work as part of federal task forces sharing information on terror and organized crime in their jurisdictions.

Crime labs are primarily operated by either the state police or federal law enforcement organizations. Some larger local agencies have the resources to operate independent crime labs; however, the majority are federal- and state-operated. The crime lab provides all the forensic services necessary to the criminal investigator. Today a well-equipped crime lab is capable of performing DNA analysis, firearm ballistics, fingerprint identification, questioned-document examination, and drug identification plus much more.

Detectives units handle the investigative function of most police agencies. Within many detective units you find specialized units dealing with specific crimes. One of those is the crimes against persons unit, which investigates cases that occur against people. These crimes include homicide, rape, and robbery. Depending on the size of the agency, each of the previous listed crimes may have its own detail to work them. Another unit, property crimes, is devoted to the investigation of those crimes against our property. This is where burglaries, theft, and fraud are investigated. One of the fastest growing criminal activities in our culture today that will be handled in this unit is identity theft. Identity theft is becoming a major problem in large and small jurisdictions alike. Also, there is the vice and narcotics unit, which is responsible for investigating what are sometimes referred to as "victimless crimes" because only the person involved is being harmed. Officers and communities fight daily battles in the "war against drugs." Some days it appears that the community is losing; other days the battle turns in our favor and major strides are made in eradicating the devastating effects of drugs on victims who did not choose to be part of the war.

There are additional units within a detective division. Domestic violence, which is a growing problem in many communities across our country, is getting more and more attention, primarily because a great number of homicides are domestic violence-related. In an attempt to save the lives of women in abusive relationships, many agencies have established special units to address the issue. The juvenile unit is the group of detectives who have been tasked with solving crimes committed by and against children under 18 years of age. Gang intelligence units are common in many departments. They are similar to the criminal intelligence unit, yet the gang unit focuses on the gang problems in a community. The unit spends time documenting gang members and activities as well as working cases that are believed to be gang-related. The gang intelligence unit is responsible for education efforts. They let the community know the extent of the problem and how to respond to observed gang problems, and to existing and potential gang members they give information on the hazards of gang affiliation and strategies for staying out of gangs. School resource officers (SROs) are often a part of juvenile units. The SROs are usually housed right at the school and handle any crime that occurs on the campus as well as dealing with juvenile issues within the community in which the school is located. An SRO also often responds to crimes against a child who attends their assigned school, even though the crime may have occurred off-campus.

Special weapons and tactics (SWAT) teams are also known as crisis intervention teams (CIRT) or in the case of the FBI, hostage rescue teams (HRT). Regardless of what they are called, they all serve a similar function, responding to critical incidents in which people are armed or barricaded or both with hostages. These highly trained officers are called on to provide some of the most difficult of all services to their communities. They confront armed assailants and more often than not resolve very volatile situations without the loss of life.

Victim and witness programs are increasingly a part of law enforcement work because more and more emphasis is put on helping the victims of crimes. Victim and witness units are a part of police departments and prosecuting attorney's offices. These units concentrate on the needs of the victims of crime. The mission is to keep victims informed to the status of their cases and to help them navigate their way through the criminal justice system. The victim-witness officer or coordinator will also help victims of crime to secure services that will assist them in recovering from the crime(s) they have been subjected to.

Community outreach programs are those in which officers volunteer in the community. Police assistance leagues (PAL) bring awareness of the amount of commitment many law enforcement officers have to improve the quality of life in their community. Officers volunteer their own time to work with at-risk community kids to participate in sports and other worthwhile activities. Another aspect of police volunteerism is citizens who give their time and talents to law enforcement agencies for special projects and assignments.

As was said in the Introduction, in a world in which children and adults alike live in a daily fear for their safety, it is time to reclaim our individual ability to be as alert and as safe as possible without living in paranoia and fear. A variety of famous police television shows have said over the years, "Hey, be careful out there." This saying applies to you as much as it does to that team of officers getting ready to start a shift on the streets. What the "be careful out there" message is saying to those officers is this: remember to stop and think before taking every call for service. Remember your training and be prepared for anything that comes your way. Don't get complacent, and don't get hurt.

## THERE IS ALWAYS A CHOICE

One of the outstanding things from Jana's police academy experience that she repeats and sometimes even acts out when giving workshops and conference presentations is the week three Friday afternoon lesson: "There is always a choice, always an option, but will you be prepared to pursue it?" Here is Jana's version of the story.

> Week three of the academy was intense. During the first part of the week we were in classes about child abuse, domestic violence, and responding to suicide calls. I literally began the week with my hands over my eyes because I couldn't bear to look at the images: I'm not at all good with blood (which partially influenced my decision not to become a sworn officer). Eventually I pried my own hand away from my eyes and saw what officers sometimes see when responding to calls. After three intense days viewing just how horrible human beings can be to children and adults, we were in a two-day class called weapon retention. The object was to keep possession of your gun, and never to let the bad guy(s) get it. After hours of exercises and bruises on nearly every class member's arms, we hit Friday afternoon and the following exercise to keep yourself alive.

"Let's say the bad guy gets your gun and gets you down on your knees. You still have options," said the instructor, full of conviction that we learn what our options could be. "Never put your hands above your ears, stay alert to the situation; watch for an opening, say when the bad guy has the gun up against the back of your head, and then seize the moment. Take ahold of that gun barrel, and with all you've got, grab hold and pull yourself with a twist and a turn to a standing position while stripping your gun (or a gun) out of the bad guy's hands."

I was in awe. I was exhausted. I got the concept. Intellectually, I had a revelation: I understood that even in a worst-possible situation there are still options. In other words, a new plan became part of my potential for action. During the practice of this exercise, I genuinely struggled with the coordination, balance, and speed of motion that would be required to implement this action plan. Without intense practice, I can five years later confidently say that while I know this is an option, because of my failure to continually practice this maneuver, I have no confidence that I could perform the action today."

The vivid point is that we each, every day, have choices we can make that help to keep us safe or that put us in harm's way. Throughout the book we have used children's nursery rhymes and fables, and real stories from the street to illustrate important points. What we have conveyed are often simple truths that you really already know because you have heard them from your youth or heard the scary stories from your neighbors and friends. *Prepared Not Paranoid* is reinforcing your years of learning and giving you ways to put stay-safe practices into action. Transforming learning into action requires a conscious choice on your part. Just as Jana points out in the previous story, we always have a choice. Make the conscious choice today to not be a victim. Make the choice to plan on how you will respond should you find yourself face to face with the big bad wolf or in an emergency. Planning gives you freedom, the freedom to not live in paranoia but to live in the strength of knowing that you are prepared. It is the most that you can do, and it is enough.

## KEEP YOUR RESOLVE TO STAY SAFE

1. Have a plan and work your plan.
2. Keep your mental edge: keep your mind prepared and your mental target hardened. Ready yourself for good decision making and action.
3. Attitude matters. Carry yourself with confidence that says "I am not a victim," and be willing to act in the event that you are attacked.

4. Use the Feel-Safe Formula, because (1) having a safety plan and (2) being ready to problem solve at any moment in combination with (3) getting enough sleep and (4) being as physically fit as you can be adds up to improved daily safety.

5. Get enough sleep. Again, this is critical to your success in responding and reacting to whatever comes up in your environment and to whatever happens to you.

6. Pay attention to details. Teach your kids to pay attention to details. Be a good witness.

7. Know that the criminal's weakness is that he plans on the element of surprise. When you are prepared and can throw a criminal off his plan-of-attack, you can often foil his plan.

8. Don't live in denial about your safety.

9. Don't be in denial about someone in your family being a criminal or potential criminal.

10. Keep learning so that your plans get ever better: sign up for a self-defense class; register for a course about safety; or participate in a citizen police academy. Just keep learning.

11. Survey your residence. Replace weak locks with strong ones, and put in adequate exterior lighting.

12. If you own a firearm, know how to use it and keep it secure!

13. Avoid a high-risk life style and behaviors such as excessive partying.

14. When traveling, plan all aspects of your trip. Leave nothing to chance, and let selected others know your itinerary.

15. Practice hotel safety. Know the locks on the door and know where the emergency stairwell exits are.

16. Have a reason to "stay alive."

17. Share what you've learned about being safe with your family, friends, and coworkers.

18. Practice preparedness not paranoia.

19. Go back to Chapter 1 and take the Feel-Safe Survey again to see where you score now.

20. A Chinese proverb says "Preparedness prevents peril," and that has been the point of this book.

## NOTE

1. Jan Egge, *Bullets in My Bed* (Boise, Idaho: Legendary Publishing Company, 2006).

# Checklists for Your Car and Home

One of the things Jana discovered while attending the police academy is that every instructor had great suggestions about what to include in the police vehicle, so she kept a running list, some of which follows. The whole list is not included, of course, because many items pertain only to outfitting a law enforcement vehicle.

## SAFETY ITEMS FOR YOUR CAR

- You! You are the first item on your safety checklist. You need to know how to drive safely, how to change a flat tire, and how to safely get help if the car breaks down. Consider purchasing some kind of emergency roadside service. For example, this is the business that AAA is in, and at a reasonable rate you always have a number to call if you should break down. When you buy a car or insurance policy, emergency roadside service is often an option that you can purchase separately. If you don't have roadside service, you can always call 911 and ask for a tow truck or an officer to be sent to your location. Make good decisions about stopping to help someone else. In most places the current recommendation is to call 911; give them the location and what you observed, and keep driving. Keep your fuel tank filled to one-half or more at all times. Several seasoned law enforcers recommend this.
- A first-aid kit, including Band-Aids, gauze, and triangle bandages; Ace compression wraps; CPR mask; wire or SAM splint; cling wrap; aspirin,

Advil, or Tylenol; instant ice and heat packs; scissors; sunblock; first aid cream; and aloe lotion for burns.

- Tools for changing a tire, a spare tire that is inflated and serviceable, and tools for fixing the car.

Car emergency kits are sold in auto and other retail stores. They typically include flares, jumper cables, flashlights, emergency blankets, Fix-A-Flat®, and assorted items. Websites abound offering prepackaged kits and suggestions on how to build your own. Here is a list of recommended items:

- 12-foot jumper cables
- Four 15-minute roadside flares
- Two quarts of oil
- Gallon of antifreeze
- First aid kit (including an assortment of bandages, gauze, adhesive tape, antiseptic cream, instant ice and heat compresses, scissors, and aspirin; see above)
- Blanket or sleeping bag
- Extra fuses
- Flashlight and extra batteries
- Candles, which can be used for light and for heat
- Flat head screwdrivers
- Phillips head screwdrivers
- Pliers
- Vise grips
- Adjustable wrench
- Tire inflator (such as a Fix-A-Flat®)
- Tire pressure gauge
- Rags
- Roll of paper towels
- Toilet paper
- Roll of duct tape
- Spray bottle with washer fluid
- Pocketknife
- Ice scraper
- Pencil, pen, marker, and paper
- Help sign
- Granola or energy bars
- Bottled water
- And a heavy-duty nylon bag or dedicated box to carry it all.

## SAFETY ITEMS FOR YOUR HOME

- A first-aid kit, including Band-Aids, 4×4 gauze, and triangle bandages; Ace compression wraps; CPR mask; wire or SAM splint; cling wrap; aspirin, Advil, or Tylenol; instant ice and heat packs; scissors and tweezers; sunblock; iodine swabs, first aid cream, and aloe lotion for burns; bug repellent, and cortisone or other lotion for bug bites.
- Fire extinguishers. In fact, rental properties in most states are required to have these.
- Smoke detectors, battery operated. Kitchen, hallways, near garage, and in each bedroom.
- Flashlights, battery operated, and extra batteries.
- Locks: deadbolt locks on exterior solid doors; a lock and a bar or barricade on sliding glass doors; on garage door people entrance; on garage door vehicle entrance; and on pet doors (see also Chapter 2).
- Family emergency plan—for fire.
- Family emergency plan—for other dangers from people.
- Family emergency plan—for natural disasters.

Note: For actual plans, research "Family Emergency Plans" on the Internet. You'll discover plans from the government, from the American Red Cross, from weather watchers, from FEMA, and from many other education-providing entities. Choose the one that works best for your family.

Speaking of FEMA and the federal government, both are recommending that everyone have a "disaster preparedness" kit on hand. FEMA, the American Red Cross, and others include the following items on their lists:

- A three-day water supply. Figure one gallon of water per person per day.
- Food that won't spoil and that will last for at least three days for all people who would be with you to eat.
- A manual can opener.
- One change of clothing and footwear per person.
- One blanket or sleeping bag per person.
- A first-aid kit that includes prescription medicines needed by all individuals dependent on the kit.
- Special items needed by infants and elderly, medicine-dependent, or disabled members of the family.
- An extra set of car keys.
- A credit card and some cash.

- Battery-operated flashlight and extra batteries.
- Emergency communication tools: a portable radio that is battery operated (and extra batteries), a battery-powered National Oceanic and Atmospheric Administration Weather Radio, and battery-operated cell phones, walkie-talkies, or other two-way portable radios.

# Workplace and Travel Safety Checklists

Nearly all of us work or visit workplaces. We all travel, whether it is while in a vehicle running errands, bicycling to work, vacation traveling, or commuting to work on public transportation. As a result of leaving our homes and heading in a variety of directions, there are a number of things to look for and to have on hand as a part of your personal safety plan at work and when traveling.

## AT WORK

- You! You are the first item on your personal safety checklist. Your mindset, demeanor, and confidence make you a target and potential victim or establish that you are not to be messed with and that it is better for would-be criminals to leave you alone.

Next, to be as safe as possible each day, you need to know the following:

- Know where the first-aid kit is and how to use it.
- Know who is trained in first aid, CPR, and emergency procedures.
- Know where the stairs and emergency exits are located. Walk to them once a month. Take the stairs once a month to remind yourself what it would take to get out of your building in an emergency.
- Know how to dial 911 in your building. Is it 9-1-1? Or is it 9-9-1-1 to get an outside line and then reach 911?
- Know where the fire-alarm pulls are located in case you have to pull one.

- Know who the floor captain for emergency situations is. If your company doesn't have an emergency plan, encourage them to build one. (Again, guidance for building one can be found on a variety of websites.)
- Know where the emergency rallying point is and who you report to once you arrive.
- Practice emergency evacuation drills at least once a year.
- Practice emergency lockdown drills at least once a year.

## TRAVELING

- You, Again! You are the first item on your personal safety checklist. Your mindset, demeanor, and confidence make you a target and potential victim or establish that you are not to be messed with and that it is better for would-be criminals to leave you alone.

### Airports and Planes

- Limit your number of carry-on luggage items. Doing so allows you to pay more attention to what is happening around you.
- Carry money in a secure easy-to-reach location.
- Store travel documents in a secure location.
- Do not agree to carry anything on a flight for anybody.
- Do not agree to watch other people's property.
- Report suspicious packages, luggage, and behavior.
- Listen to safety announcements given in the airport and on the plane by the flight crew.
- Visualize how you would exit the aircraft in an emergency.
- Check with TSA (on-line: www.tsa.gov) for current travel recommendations.

### Personal Vehicles

- Cars and trucks: see Appendix 1.
- Motorcycle: wear a helmet and protective clothing. Many states require helmets.

### Wilderness Travel

- Notify others of destination routes and alternative routes during and to and from travel locations.
- Maps of the area

- Compass and/or GPS
- First-aid kit, including sunscreen and bug repellent (see Appendix 1)
- Pocket knife
- Waterproof emergency matches
- Three-season tent or shelter
- Water filter
- Gas stove
- Rain parka
- Adequate footwear

## Out-of-Country Travel

- Passport
- Copy of passport
- Travel documents, securely stored
- Cash, securely stored and easily accessible
- Credit cards, securely stored and easily accessible
- Copies of credit cards in your luggage
- Emergency phone numbers including the American Consulate offices in your country of travel
- International Emergency Evacuation and Medical Insurance

## Staying in a Hotel

- Know where the stairs are. Count the rooms between your room and the exit stairs. Walk to them and open the door so that you know how heavy it is to open.
- Know the name and location of the hotel you are staying in; cab drivers need this information to get you to and from your hotel.
- Upon check-in ask how family members can best reach you and then communicate the directions to your family.
- Check that your room door closes properly.
- Don't prop the door open while getting ice or snacks or bringing in luggage.
- Lock the door behind you, and check all locks to make sure they function properly.
- Avoid booking sleeping rooms on ground floors because they are more easily broken into.

# Creating Your Personal Safe Space

The 2002 movie *Panic Room* starring Jodie Foster remade the image of bomb shelters prevalent in the 1950s. Even the 1939 movie *The Wizard of Oz* depicted the cellar as the safe space to go in the midst of the tornado. In tornado country, people know to go to the cellar or the basement. In earthquake country, people know to get outside away from overhead lines and power poles, and in hurricane territory, people know to stay away from windows, go to the interior of the house, or better yet if time allows evacuate.

Every half-century or so it seems the idea of a personal safe space that is specially constructed for keeping individuals, families, and friends safe arises as a potential must-have on your property. People want to keep loved ones safe, and people want to keep some key possessions safe, too. Thus far in recorded history, the best option has been to "get to safety" when natural disasters are afoot. So what about the daily toils that take a toll on personal well-being and even on safety? They can be addressed by the creation of a personal safe haven or safe space that provides rest, comfort, safety, and personal/family rejuvenation.

What is it that a personal safe space promises? It promises a place that is meant to keep you physically safe from outside threats, whether they are natural disasters in the making or man-made menaces. A daily-use safe space promises to be usable every day and to bring rest to the weary, rejuvenation to the broken-hearted, and joy to the hungering spirit.

A safe space runs the gamut from specially built spaces for use in emergencies to daily-use spaces that individuals and family members feel good about being in. For instance, creating an environment where everyone in the family can talk about and ask questions about anything, as long as it is done with respect, can be a part of daily-use spaces that are safe, or it can mean a private space where nothing gets disturbed or rearranged because only you enter to enjoy a good read or to pursue a favorite hobby or craft. A safe space may be one that that no one but you enters, or it may be a shared space that has certain ground rules for interaction and use. Some families establish one night a week as family game night: no movies, only family members, and fun to be had together.

In police work, daily-use safe spaces are interview rooms where interviews can be conducted and squad rooms for completing reports and other paperwork. Your space certainly doesn't need to be as Spartan as that, so what might you include in your feel-safe spaces at home? Begin by recalling the Recognizing Safety and Defining Danger discussions from Chapter 1. What smells, sounds, textures, visuals, and tastes make you feel most safe? The idea lists from Chapter 1 provide a starting place for creating your personal daily-use safe space.

## DAILY USE SAFE SPACE

Things you may want in your daily-use safe space include the following:

- A comfortable chair or seating arrangement
- The ability to control sounds and noise
- Access to reading material, craft supplies, and music
- Natural light
- Colors and textures that you like
- Plants
- No one else but you or people who respect you and your dreams or those who will listen to anything you have to say without judging it or telling you that you are wrong

For more information and ideas, research family rooms, home libraries, sewing rooms, hobby rooms, playrooms, bonus rooms, or another description that you feel depicts your approach to creating daily-use safe space.

## DANGER SAFE SPACE

The following are things you will want in your use-when-in-danger safe space:

- Food, for 5 days
- Water, 1 gal per day per person
- Wool blankets

- A first-aid kit, including Band-Aids, 4×4 gauze, and triangle bandages; Ace compression wraps; CPR mask; wire or SAM splint; cling wrap; aspirin, Advil, or Tylenol; instant ice and heat packs; scissors; sunblock; first-aid cream; and aloe lotion for burns (see Appendix 1, Safety Items for Your Home, for a more complete list).
- Sleeping bags
- Oxygen/ventilation
- Battery-operated radio and clock
- Cell phone, fully charged
- Prescription medications
- Food and water for pets

For more information, conduct your own Internet research on "Panic Room" or "Safe Room," as well as government sites such as http://www.fema.gov and http://www.redcross.org.

Appendix 4
# Additional Resources

Safety is a widely presented topic. In order to build your best personal plan for safety, you may choose to pursue additional resources, tools, and educational programs. The following list includes websites and resources that Jana and Doug suggest. This list is followed by a series of topics you can conduct Internet research on to gather current information.

## RECOMMENDED WEBSITES AND RESOURCES

http://www.redcross.org/ American Red Cross: Emergency planning and response.

http://www.usanonwatch.org/ USA on Watch: neighborhood watches.

http://www.nnwi.org/ National Neighborhood Watch Institute: signs and crime-fighting materials.

http://www.ncpc.org/ National Crime Prevention Council: neighborhood watches, and McGruff® the crime-fighting dog.

http://www.USA.gov/ Travel safety tips and links to Homeland Security and Emergency Services by state.

http://www.tsa.gov/ Transportation Security Administrations site: get travel information for air, highways, maritime, mass transit, and railroads.

http://www.travel.state.gov/ The U.S. Department of State's travel tips and guidelines.

http://www.dhs.gov/ The Department of Homeland Security, USA: information on all fronts.

http://www.nokep.org/ Next of Kin Education Project.

http://www.worldtravelcenter.com/ Evacuation insurance.

http://www.globalrescue.com/ Global rescue insurance.

http://www.internationsos.com/ Medical and Security Solutions: professional evacuation assistance when traveling abroad.

http://www.AAA.com/ American Automobile Association: safety tips.

http://www.bbb.org/ Better Business Bureau: business and consumer protection tips.

http://www.channing-bete.com/ Channing Bete Company publishes a variety of educational booklets ranging from gang topics to first aid basics.

http://www.ready.gov/america/makeaplan/ A federal government site full of safety and emergency planning information.

http://www.amberalert.gov/ Amber Alert program details: America's Missing: Broadcast Emergency Response.

http://www.ou.edu/oupd/psafe.htm/ The University of Oklahoma Police Department's tips for personal safety.

http://www.schoolsafety.us/ National School Safety Center, established in 1984 by presidential directive: school safety tips, materials, and programs.

http://www.nea.org/schoolsafety/ National Education Association's school safety tips.

http://www.nsc.org/ The National Safety Council provides information on all kinds of safety.

http://www.sawnet.org/ The International Foundation for Crime Prevention.

http://www.nationalnightout.org/ The National Night Out organization, which sponsors nights against crime and education programs.

http://www.nicb.org/ National Insurance Crime Bureau, a partnership of law enforcement and insurance companies working to prosecute insurance criminals.

http://www.xtr4.com/ Teen driving guides, simulations, and rules for getting an Idaho license from the Idaho Transportation Department. See what your state has available, too.

http://www.familywatchdog.us/ A site that allows you to enter an address and find out whether people convicted of sexual crimes live in your area. Check this out for your address, your kid's day care and school addresses, and addresses of your friends and children's friends.

http://www.projectsafechildhood.gov/ From their website: "Guided by the leadership of the Attorney General, Project Safe Childhood (PSC) aims to combat the proliferation of technology-facilitated sexual exploitation crimes against children. The threat of sexual predators soliciting children for physical sexual contact is well-known and serious; the danger of the production, distribution, and possession of child pornography is equally dramatic and disturbing."

http://www.isafe.org/ Founded in 1998, this organization provides Internet safety training and curriculum for keeping kids and family members safe.

http://www.crimestoppers-uk.org/ Crime Stoppers programs and education in the United Kingdom.

http://www.crime-stoppers.us/ Crime Stoppers programs and education in the United States.

http://www.missingkids.com/ National Center for Missing and Exploited Children's website.

http://www.weather.com/safeside/emergencyplan.html/ Emergency plan preparation information and guides from the weather perspective.

http://www.fema.gov/plan/prepare/plan.shtm/ Emergency plan preparation information and guides.

http://www.cmu.edu/oldhome/emergency/FamilyPlan.pdf/ Emergency plan preparation information and guides.

## RECOMMENDED READING

de Becker, Gavin. *The Gift of Fear: Survival Signals That Protect Us from Violence*. New York: Dell Publishing, 1997.

———. *Protecting the Gift: Keeping Children and Teenagers Safe (and Parents Sane)*. New York: Dell Publishing, 2000.

———. *Fear Less: Real Truth about Risk, Safety, and Security in a Time of Terrorism*. Little, Brown, and Company, 2002.

Dyer, Gerri M., ed. *Safe, Smart and Self-Reliant: Personal Safety for Women and Children*. Foundation for Crime Prevention Education (Safety Press), 1996.

Egge, Jan. *Bullets in My Bed*. Boise, Idaho: Legendary Publishing Company, 2006.

Gilmarten, Kevin M. *Emotional Survival for Law Enforcement: A Guide for Officers and Their Families*. Tucson, AZ: E-S Press, 2004.

And self-defense book(s) that meet your needs for physical defense methods.

## TOPICS FOR FURTHER RESEARCH

Abuse
Amber Alert
Assault

Attorney general's office for your state: many are offering safety programs now.

Avoid becoming a victim

Boating safety

Car safety

Car seat safety

Center for the Study and Prevention of Violence

Child abuse prevention

Children safety

Community policing

Community safety programs: corporations, nonprofits, hospitals, and government agencies offer them

Corporate safety programs

Crime prevention

Crime statistics

Crime Stoppers

Crime Watch

Defensive driving

Disease safety

Drug education

Drug prevention

Drug tests, home drug tests, and teen drug tests

Emergency family plan

Emergency plan

Family advocates

Firearm safety

First aid training

Gang prevention

Gun safety

Hurricane safety

Keith Code Superbike School

Law enforcement

Lightning safety

Media violence

Mothers Against Drunk Drivers

Motorcycle safety

National Center for Missing and Exploited Children

National Preparedness Month

Panic room

Personal protection
Personal safety
Pet safety
Profiling criminals
Safe Place Church programs
Safe Places
Safe room
Safety
School safety
Seat Belt Coalition (Idaho)
Security
Security companies
Serial criminals
Serial murderers
Snow safety
Teen drivers
Tornado safety
Travel safety
Victim services
Victimology
Water safety
Weapons safety
Weather safety
Workplace safety

.

# Index

## About the Authors

**JANA M. KEMP** is the founder and owner of Meeting & Management Essentials. She is the author of *Moving Meetings, No! - How One Simple Word Can Transform Your Life*, and *Building Community in Buildings* (Praeger, 2006), as well as publisher of the quarterly online newsletter *Better Meetings for Everyone*. She has also served as a business columnist for the *Idaho Press Tribune* and *Idaho Business Review* newspapers.

**DOUG GRAVES** is Deputy Director (retired) of the Idaho Peace Officer Standards and Training (POST) Academy division of the Idaho State Police. He teaches ethics, leadership, and child abuse investigation at the Idaho POST academy and at the Western Regional Institute for Community Oriented Public Safety (WRICOPS), as well as at other public and private organizations. He is Adjunct Professor at Northwestern University School of Public Safety and serves on the executive board for the International Association of Directors of Law Enforcement Standards and Training (IADLEST).

DUNWOODY